FINDING
YOUR WAY
AFTER
LOSING
A LOVED
ONE

COVENANT COMMUNICATIONS

BOOKS AND AUDIOBOOKS

BY MARLENE BATEMAN

Light on Fire Island

Motive for Murder

A Death in the Family

Crooked House

For Sale by Owner

Searching for Irene

Finding Your Way after Losing a Loved One

OTHER BOOKS AND AUDIOBOOKS

BY MARLENE BATEMAN

Latter-day Saint Heroes and Heroines

And There Were Angels among Them

Visits from Beyond the Veil

By the Ministering of Angels

Brigham's Boys

Heroes of Faith

Gaze into Heaven:

Near-Death Experiences in Early Church History

The Magnificent World of Spirits:

Eyewitness Accounts of Where We Go When We Die

FINDING YOUR WAY AFTER LOSING A LOVED ONE

MARLENE BATEMAN
JOSHUA M. SULLIVAN, LCSW

Covenant Communications, Inc.

Published by Covenant Communications, Inc.
American Fork, Utah

Printed in the United States of America
First Printing: January 2022

28 27 26 25 24 23 22   10 9 8 7 6 5 4 3 2 1

ISBN:978-52442-089-5

DEDICATION

The authors dedicate this book to everyone who has lost a loved one and pray that you will be comforted and inspired by the materials presented herein. It is our sincere hope that you will be blessed and strengthened by your Heavenly Father, who loves you deeply and is aware of everything that goes on in your life.

ACKNOWLEDGMENTS

THE AUTHORS WOULD LIKE TO thank those who reviewed this manuscript: Jennie Stephens, Melanie Trottier, Kaylie Sullivan, LeaRose Gange, Monica Miles, and John Wells. A special thanks to our helpful editor at Covenant, Kami Hancock, and to Kathy Oveson for her advice and editing expertise. We give additional thanks to our exceptionally talented editor Stacey Turner.

TABLE OF CONTENTS

FOREWORD

THIS IS NOT AN OFFICIAL Church publication and does not represent the official doctrine or position of The Church of Jesus Christ of Latter-day Saints. The authors alone are responsible for the content and any limitations. The doctrine of the Church is declared only by the Lord's anointed prophets, seers, and revelators, whom we sustain wholeheartedly. We have done our best to make sure the ideas in this book are in harmony with the teachings of the scriptures, the leaders of the Church, and Church doctrine. If there are doctrinal defects, they are due to our own shortcomings. We hope and pray that as you read, you will be consoled and strengthened by your loving elder brother, Jesus Christ, and your Heavenly Father, who watches over you with all the care and concern of a tender parent.

A note from the authors: One challenge of coauthoring a book is how to refer to each of us when relating a personal experience. We decided to refer to ourselves by name prior to sharing a personal story.

INTRODUCTION

Truly my soul waiteth upon God:
from him cometh my salvation.
He only is my rock and my salvation;
he is my defence; I shall not be greatly moved. . . .
My soul, wait thou only upon God;
for my expectation is from him. . . .
In God is my salvation and my glory:
the rock of my strength, and my refuge, is in God.
Trust in him at all times; ye people,
pour out your heart before him: God is a refuge for us.[1]

FINDING COMFORT AFTER LOSING A Loved One is an inspirational book that will provide comfort, reassurance, and hope after someone you love passes away. Filled with scriptures, inspirational stories, and uplifting quotes from prophets and Church leaders, this book provides consolation for all who grieve and offers help on navigating the mourning process. We do not claim to know all the answers, but this book shares many practical and helpful gospel-centered ideas and topics that will help you manage your grief.

---

1 Psalm 62:1–2, 5, 7–8.

Death is universal and can cause great sorrow and anguish. Although losing those we love is part of the mortal testing we face on Earth, no one is ever left alone in their grief. Heavenly Father is ever mindful of His children and will bless us with the strength and courage needed to rise above our loss.

This book has been designed to address the needs of all who mourn, offering inspiration with encouraging and enlightening quotes and scriptures that will lighten your spirit, assist you to cope with your grief, give you peace, and provide hope for a better tomorrow.

All loss—whether it occurs suddenly and without warning or from long-term illness, injury, or old age—generates powerful feelings. Being deprived of your dear one's presence can be devastating, even though you know that one day you will be reunited. Grief is not a disease that needs to be cured; it is an experience that needs to be worked through. Every person's grief is unique, yet the goal of healing is the same for all, to manage your grief rather than letting it manage you.

After a loss, the best things you can do are apply your faith, seek the comfort of the Holy Ghost, and strive to be patient. If you will turn to Heavenly Father in humble prayer and diligently work to obtain His word and direction in your life, He will bend close and tenderly guide you to a personal, inspired course of action that will help you move forward with your life.

Although your life may never quite be the same, there remain things for you to accomplish while you inhabit this classroom called mortality. As you progress through the grieving process, you will find that life is still worth living and is a beautiful, precious thing. In time, you will discover that peace and happiness can be yours once more. Losing someone you love is hard, but in time, it will become less hard.

Managing your mourning and taking action to regain joy are things you have to do on your own, although it helps to have support from family and friends, counsel from a good therapist, and encouragement from a support group. However, true healing comes only from God. Pray for inspiration and personal revelation to guide you. Be patient, trust in God, and know that as you work to move forward, you will once again find joy in your life. Be gentle with yourself, and when the sun sets on another day, know that you are one step further along in the healing process.

Although there is no quick fix, this book contains many inspirational stories, techniques, and practical ideas to help you navigate the tidal wave of emotions that come after someone you love passes away. This book should not be considered a substitute for professional counseling but can provide encouragement, comfort, inspiration, and guidance as you process your grief. The ideas and topics contained in these pages will help you progress from a grief you can't handle to a loss you *can* handle.

As healing progresses, you'll find a little more joy in your life. Although most people never fully get over a loss, it is possible to get through it. In time, you will be able to hear the music, see the flowers, and be there to help others as they face their own loss. With the healing grace and mercy of your Heavenly Father, you will be empowered to take joy in each day. "This is the day which the Lord hath made; we will rejoice and be glad in it."[2]

Each of us is a child of God, and as our Father, He loves us to our very core. Heavenly Father can call each of us by name because He *knows* us. We are not strangers to Him. He will never forsake us:

> Fear not: for I have redeemed thee, I have called thee by thy name; thou art mine. When thou passest through the waters, I will be with thee; and through the rivers, they shall not overflow thee: when thou walkest through the fire, thou shalt not be burned; neither shall the flame kindle upon thee. . . . Thou wast precious in my sight, . . . and I have loved thee . . . Fear not: for I am with thee.[3]

---

2 Psalm 118:24.
3 Isaiah 43:1–2, 4–5.

During times of heartache, God walks with us, His comforting arm around our shoulder. Heavenly Father desires nothing other than our happiness and well-being, and His greatest desire is for each one of us to return to Him. As His children, we can rely on God's power and grace to help us navigate the difficulties of mortality. We can trust that He will always be there to help us. "The Lord is my strength and my shield; my heart trusted in him, and I am helped: therefore my heart greatly rejoiceth; and with my song will I praise him."4

---

4 Psalm 28:7.

CHAPTER 1
WHAT IS THIS THING CALLED DEATH?

What is this thing that men call death,
This quiet passing in the night?
'Tis not the end, but genesis
Of better worlds and greater light.

O God, touch Thou my aching heart,
And calm my troubled, haunting fears.
Let hope and faith, transcendent, pure,
Give strength and peace beyond my tears.

There is no death, but only change
With recompense for victory won;
The gift of Him who loved all men,
The Son of God, the Holy One.[5]

WHEN DEATH SEPARATES US FROM those we love, it is natural to experience an array of physical, emotional, and spiritual sensations known as *grief* in those left behind. Webster's dictionary

5 Gordon B. Hinckley, "The Empty Tomb Bore Testimony," *Ensign*, May 1988, 66. churchofjesuschrist.org/study/ensign/1988/05/the-empty-tomb-bore-testimony?lang=eng

defines *grief* as a "deep and poignant distress caused by or as if by bereavement; a cause of such suffering."[6]

When we lose someone we love, our lives can change drastically, making our world and life seem dark and miserable. Kahlil Gibran said, "Love knows not its own depth until the hour of separation."[7] Although the pain can be intense, human resilience in the face of loss is possible, and through the mercy and grace of God, we can learn how to cope. "Blessed are they that mourn: for they shall be comforted."[8]

While it is not easy when someone we love passes, we can be strengthened through the gospel of Jesus Christ. President Wilford Woodruff said:

> Without the gospel of Christ the separation by death is one of the most gloomy subjects it is possible to contemplate; but just as soon as we obtain the gospel and learn the principle of the resurrection the gloom, sorrow and suffering occasioned by death are, in a great measure, taken away.[9]

As disciples of the Lord Jesus Christ, we know that death is not the end and that we will see our departed loved ones again. Death merely causes the physical body to be laid aside for a time while the spirit leaves this mortal realm to dwell in the spirit world.

For anyone who has laid a child in a grave, cried over the casket of a spouse, or mourned the loss of a dearly loved one, the Resurrection is our source of hope. After the Resurrection, our spirits will never again be separated from our bodies, and it is only

---

6 "Grief." *Merriam-Webster.com Dictionary*, Merriam-Webster. merriam-webster.com/dictionary/grief. Accessed April 13, 2021.

7 Kahlil Gibran, *The Prophet*, Gurteen. gurteen.com/gurteen/gurteen.nsf/id/prophet-prologue. Accessed June 1, 2021.

8 Matthew 5:4.

9 *Teachings of Presidents of the Church: Wilford Woodruff* (Salt Lake City: The Church of Jesus Christ of Latter-day Saints, 2004, 2011), 82. churchofjesuschrist.org/study/manual/teachings-wilford-woodruff/chapter-8?lang=eng

then that we can "receive a fulness of joy."[10] The reality of the Resurrection overcomes our heartbreak and replaces it with hope and faith in the great Atonement of Jesus Christ, which brings about the Resurrection and redeems each of us from the chains of death.[11]

When our dear ones go to the spirit world—the glorious existence that is the next phase of eternal progression—they will be filled with gladness, serenity, and bliss. President Brigham Young said, "The earth and . . . all that pertains to this earth . . . is no comparison with the glory, joy and peace and happiness of the soul that departs in peace."[12]

Life Continues Beyond the Grave

There is purpose in life and there is purpose in death. Our Heavenly Father, who knows the beginning from the end, orchestrates the events of our earthly existence and encourages us to grow and learn during mortality so we can enjoy life and joy everlasting in the next step of our existence. In the next life, all of us will continue to learn and progress, with mortality having provided a necessary and useful foundation for further progression. Our bodies and spirits were created to exist eternally; death merely serves as a necessary transition point that allows us entrance into eternity. Death is part of life, and eternal life is not possible without it. It is good for us to learn more about death and dying, for it is only by doing so that we learn more about life and living. The Prophet Joseph Smith said:

> All men know that they must die. And it is important that we should understand the reasons and causes of our exposure to the vicissitudes of life and of death, and the designs and purposes of God in our coming into the world, our sufferings here, and our departure hence. What is the object of our coming into existence, then dying and falling

---

10 See D&C 93:33; 138:17.

11 See D&C 138:14–19.

12 John A. Widtsoe, ed., *Discourses of Brigham Young* (Salt Lake City: Deseret Book, 1941), 370. Used with permission.

away, to be here no more? It is but reasonable to suppose that God would reveal something in reference to the matter, and it is a subject we ought to study more than any other. We ought to study it day and night, for the world is ignorant in reference to their true condition and relation. If we have any claim on our Heavenly Father for anything, it is for knowledge on this important subject. . . . Could you gaze into heaven five minutes, you would know more than you would by reading all that ever was written on the subject.[13]

How comforting it is to know that loved ones who depart this life have not ceased to exist but have merely moved on to the next phase of their existence! Death fulfills "the merciful plan of the great Creator,"[14] or as Rumi, a Persian poet, put it, "Death is our wedding with eternity."[15]

One of the reasons we know life continues after death is because in 1820, Joseph Smith saw God the Father and His Son, Jesus Christ, in the Sacred Gove. When Jesus Christ showed Himself, His very presence testified to the reality of life beyond the grave. Elder Dieter F. Uchtdorf said:

The more we learn about the gospel of Jesus Christ, the more we realize that endings here in mortality are not endings at all. They are merely interruptions—temporary pauses that one day will seem small compared to the eternal joy awaiting the faithful. How grateful I am to my

13 Joseph Smith, in *History of the Church of Jesus Christ of Latter-day Saints* (Salt Lake City: Deseret Book Company, 1950), 6:50. Used with permission. byustudies.byu.edu/content/volume-6-chapter-2/
14 2 Nephi 9:6.
15 Mewlana Jalaluddin Rumi, "Our Death Is Our Wedding with Eternity," AllPoetry. allpoetry.com/poem/14327662-Our-Death-Is-Our -Wedding-With-Eternity-by-Mewlana-Jalaluddin-Rumi

Heavenly Father that in His plan there are no true endings, only everlasting beginnings.[16]

Knowing that death is not the end and that it plays an important part in our eternal progression helps us put death in its proper perspective. It is a great consolation to know Jesus Christ overcame death and that at some future point, our body and spirit will be reunited. Job testified of this, saying, "I know that my redeemer liveth, and that he shall stand at the latter day upon the earth: and . . . in my flesh shall I see God."[17]

Birth and Death

Every life begins and ends with two mysteries. The first, birth, is considered a miracle because it brings a new spirit into mortality. The second, death, is also a miracle, because we do not cease to exist—our spirit lives on even after our physical body is laid in the grave. Death only separates "the spirit and the body [which] are the soul of man."[18]

There is nothing more common to mortality than birth and death. Everyone who is on Earth was born on it, and everyone must die in order to progress to the spirit world. Life does not begin with birth any more than it ends with death. Prior to our birth, we lived as spirit children with our Father in Heaven, eagerly awaiting our time to come to Earth and obtain a physical body, knowing that "this life [was to become] a probationary state; a time to prepare to meet God."[19] The blessing of receiving a mortal body is the first step toward acquiring an immortal body; the last step will come after we die and are resurrected.

We are mortal beings because even when we are born, the seeds of death lie within us. We are also eternal beings because in us lie the seeds of immortality. We are dual beings, composed of

---

16 Dieter F. Uchtdorf, "Grateful in Any Circumstances," *Ensign*, April 2014, 77. churchofjesuschrist.org/study/ensign/2014/05/sunday -morning-session/grateful-in-any-circumstances?lang=eng
17 Job 19:25–26.
18 D&C 88:15.
19 Alma 12:24.

a spirit that provides us with life and intelligence, and a physical body that houses our spirit. When we are resurrected, our bodies and our spirits will be joined together, never again to be separated.

Birth and death are milestones on our journey to eternal life—blessed moments when mortality and heaven intersect. Both events are essential parts of Heavenly Father's plan. Jesus Christ assures us there is no reason to fear death and has told us, "And it shall come to pass that those that die in me shall not taste of death, for it shall be sweet unto them."[20]

The Purpose of Mortality

During moments of temporary farewell, we often ponder the purposes behind our life in mortality. The gospel of Jesus Christ teaches that we came to Earth for two specific reasons. One was to gain a physical body, which is paramount to God's divine plan. The second was to have experiences that enable us to grow and become more like our Heavenly Father. Both of these objectives are vital to our existence, and we elected of our own free will and choice to come to Earth to accomplish these purposes.[21] This life is a proving ground to see if we will be obedient to God and remain faithful even when experiencing great sorrow and anguish.

Even though we understand the gospel plan, there will still be moments of great pain, such as when a sweet daughter dies of cancer, leaving behind a loving husband and four young children. Or when a missionary son, serving in a distant land, contracts a virulent illness and passes away. While God could prevent these and other heartaches, He usually does not, either because it is the deceased person's appointed time or the death is in accordance with His will for purposes unknown to us or because it would be unwise to shield us from the pains, sorrows, and suffering that can lead to us learning vital lessons that move us further along the path of our development.

While many hardships can come close to breaking our heart, they serve to stretch our souls, draw us nearer to God, and

---

20 D&C 42:46.
21 See 2 Nephi 2:11–16.

strengthen our faith if we use them as learning experiences. Elder Orson F. Whitney assured us of this divine purpose when he said,

> No pain that we suffer, no trial that we experience is wasted. It ministers to our education, to the development of such qualities as patience, faith, fortitude and humility. All that we suffer and all that we endure, especially when we endure it patiently, builds up our characters, purifies our hearts, expands our souls, and makes us more tender and charitable, more worthy to be called the children of God . . . and it is through sorrow and suffering, toil and tribulation, that we gain the education that we come here to acquire and which will make us more like our Father and Mother in heaven.[22]

---

22 Orson F. Whitney, as quoted in Spencer W. Kimball, *Faith Precedes the Miracle* (Salt Lake City: Deseret Book, 1972), 98. Used with permission.

CHAPTER 2
SUDDEN LOSS

O Lord, my heart is exceedingly sorrowful;
wilt thou comfort my soul in Christ.
O Lord, wilt thou grant unto me that I may have strength,
that I may suffer with patience these afflictions which shall
come upon me. . . .
O Lord, wilt thou comfort my soul.[23]

SUDDEN DEATH CAN OCCUR BECAUSE of a car crash, an unforeseen medical episode, accidental poisoning, murder, a natural disaster, workplace tragedies, and other calamities. Because of the lack of any psychological preparation, the sudden death of someone we love can be especially difficult.

Few things in life are more unexpected than such a loss. Family members say goodbye on the morning of a seemingly normal day, fully expecting their dear ones to return, but instead a police officer, rescue worker, or medical responder calls or knocks on the door, bringing the worst news imaginable. Such an abrupt loss can leave survivors dazed and traumatized—unable to grasp the full implications of a death that seems unbelievable and overwhelming. Survivors may feel as the psalmist, who wrote, "My heart is sore

---

23 Alma 31:31–32.

pained within me: . . . Fearfulness and trembling are come upon me, and horror hath overwhelmed me. And I said, Oh that I had wings like a dove! for then would I fly away, and be at rest."[24]

Immediately following a sudden loss, survivors often experience shock, but when that feeling of numbness wears off, survivors must face that their lives have been forever changed. Authors Brook Noel and Pamela Blair ask, "Where does sudden loss take us? It takes us to places we never asked to visit. It takes us on uncharted, mysterious, unfamiliar journeys to the depths of our souls, where we clatter and crash about, slog through the molasses of grief and come out the other side."[25]

God Can Intervene but Usually Does Not

Although there may be times when God will intervene to prevent the loss of those we love, there will also be times when He does not. Even if we are living the gospel to the best of our ability and ask for protection and deliverance—such as praying for a safe journey, for chemotherapy to kill the cancer, or for an operation to be a success—we may face arduous trials and loss of life. At those times, we may wonder why God did not answer our fervent prayers. During general conference in 2017, Elder Donald L. Hallstrom spoke about divine intervention and related a tragic incident that had occurred a few months earlier:

> Two temple-recommend-holding married couples, with three full-time missionary children and five other children between them, took off in a small airplane for a short flight. I am confident they prayed for safety before the flight and prayed fervently when their aircraft encountered serious mechanical problems before crashing. None survived. What about them?

---

24 Psalm 55:4–6.

25 Brook Noel and Pamela D. Blair, *I Wasn't Ready to Say Goodbye: Surviving, Coping & Healing after the Sudden Death of a Loved One* (Milwaukee: Champion Press, 2000), 260.

Elder Hallstrom went on to explain that currently we have limited knowledge as to why we are sometimes blessed with divine intervention and other times are not. If we have difficulty with the "fairness" of this, Elder Hallstrom suggested we might want to consider where we stand on faith. He said, "A critical question to ponder is 'Where do we place our faith?' Is our faith focused on simply wanting to be relieved of pain and suffering, or is it firmly centered on God the Father and His holy plan and in Jesus the Christ and His Atonement?" He added, "Faith in the Father and the Son allows us to understand and accept Their will as we prepare for eternity."26

Sara Tonon

Sara Tonon had no premonition when her forty-four-year-old husband, Marco, left their home in Torino, Italy, for work one morning. Marco worked as a surveyor and that morning drove to a home that the court was repossessing. The homeowner, ninety-one-year-old Dario Cellino, knew Marco was coming to survey the property. When Marco knocked on the door, Dario shot him in the chest, killing him.

That night, Sara took her three young children—ages seven, five, and twenty-one months—to her mother's house. Unable to sleep, Sara paced the floor. In the early morning hours, Sara knelt and prayed. She did not ask to know why such a tragedy had occurred; she simply prayed that Heavenly Father would bless her with the strength to cope. As Sara prayed, the following words came to her mind: "With Marco's death, you didn't lose anything, because when you met and married him in 2008, you gained the chance to have eternal life together. You have posterity and you won't lose them. You won't lose the kids. You won't lose each other."

Sara said, "That thought gave me the strength I needed to stand the news and the future. I didn't lose anything by losing

26 Donald L. Hallstrom, "Has the Day of Miracles Ceased?" *Ensign,* November 2017, 90. churchofjesuschrist.org/study/ensign/2017/11 /sunday-morning-session/has-the-day-of-miracles-ceased?lang=eng

Marco for this time, for we have eternal life together." The following day, Sara's brother gave her a blessing. Sara relates:

> I was told that one day you will be grateful, not for what happened, but knowing why it happened. I considered this as a gift from God. If I were mad at that man who killed Marco, if I were anguished or vengeful, it would be so hard, but I am not at all. I did not choose to be this way, so calm. I think it is a gift so that I can educate my kids with peace in my heart. I couldn't help them grow if I had that anger.[27]

Sudden Loss Can Cause a Crisis of Faith

Sudden loss can cause agonizing pain when survivors are forced to live through the unimaginable: a mother who turns her back for a moment while camping and discovers her three-year-old daughter has slipped away and fallen into a swiftly running river. Parents who must deal with the news that their teenager suffered a cramp while swimming with friends at a lake and went under the water. Or a wife who learns that earthen walls unexpectedly caved in when her husband, a construction worker, was laying pipe in a deep trench.

Such losses can cause a crisis of faith because deep inside—without even thinking about it—most people have an instinctual belief that if they do their best to be a good person, obey the commandments, and devoutly follow God's teachings, they will be protected from severe trials.

A crisis of faith can also be caused because some people believe that everything that happens is God's will, and so they hold God responsible for tragedies. Harold Kushner explains this idea in his best-seller *When Bad Things Happen to Good People*. Believing that

---

27 Scot and Maurine Proctor, "How One Italian Sister Found Solace after her Husband's Murder," *Meridian Magazine*, March 14, 2019. latterdaysaintmag.com/how-one-italian-sister-found-solace-after-her-husbands-murder/

God could have or should have stepped in to prevent the death of a loved one often leaves people feeling angry. In a world that no longer seems just and fair, people can feel validated in blaming God for this perceived injustice and feel bitter that He did not prevent the tragedy. Sometimes the trauma of losing a loved one can push people to reject their faith. Gripped by grief, people may cry, "If God is good, how could He allow this to happen?"

If you feel angry with God about the loss of your loved one, talk with Him. It's all right to cry out to God in your pain and ask plainly, "Why did this happen?" As Earl Grollman said, "It's okay to scream at God. He can take it."[28] As you pray humbly for answers, open your mind and listen carefully to hear His still small voice impart inspiration, wisdom, knowledge, and comfort. Heavenly Father may answer your questions instantly, or His grace may come bit by bit over the coming days, weeks, and months as you study the scriptures, pray often, and do the spiritual work necessary to allow God to expand your understanding and offer answers to your innermost questions.

Marriner Merrill

Elder Marriner Merrill found it extremely difficult to accept his loss when his adult son, who was married and had young children, died suddenly. For quite some time, Elder Merrill was simply unable to reconcile the thought that the death of his much-loved son could possibly have been in keeping with God's will. Then he received a sacred manifestation and was allowed to see his son, who explained why he had died.

On one occasion soon after the death of his son, as he [Marriner] was returning to his home, he was in his carriage so deeply lost in thought about his son that he was quite oblivious to things about him. He suddenly came into a state of awareness when his horse stopped in the road. As he looked up, his son stood in the road beside him. His son spoke to him and said,

---

28 Earl Grollman, as quoted in Brook Noel & Pamela D. Blair, *I Wasn't Ready to Say Goodbye* (Naperville: Sourcebooks, Inc., 2008; originally published by Milwaukee: Champion Press, Ltd., 2000), 51.

Father, you are mourning my departure unduly! You are over concerned about my family (his son left a large family of small children) and their welfare. I have much work to do and your grieving gives me much concern. I am in a position to render effective service to my family. You should take comfort, for you know there is much work to be done here and it was necessary for me to be called. You know that the Lord doeth all things well.

So saying, the son departed.[29]

Accepting on Faith What We Do Not Understand

When we suffer the anguish of personal loss, we must strive to have faith and remember that Heavenly Father desires only what is best for us, even if we can't currently see the long-term picture. Right now, our mortal understanding is limited, but one day our knowledge will be expanded. One thing we do know now is that a big part of the reason we are on Earth is to grow and progress, and the hardships we face often accelerate our personal growth and development.

When the person we love leaves mortality, we are to become as a little child before our Eternal Father. God desires us to be submissive, meek, humble, and patient while submitting to all things He may allow earthly life to inflict upon us.[30] The Savior Himself learned through His mortal trials: "Though he were a Son, yet learned he obedience by the things which he suffered; and being made perfect, he became the author of eternal salvation unto all them that obey him."[31]

Although we may feel bewildered and even upset at God when tragedy strikes, we must pause and realize that such misfortunes are not God's will. Even when tragedy strikes in monumental forms, such as great loss of life in a bombing or a mass shooting, we can know of a surety that God is just as grief-stricken and outraged as we are. One great purpose of mortality is to learn to accept on faith those things we do not fully understand and still be able to say,

---

29 Bryant S. Hinckley, *The Faith of Our Pioneer Fathers* (Salt Lake City: Deseret Book Company, 1959), 182–83.

30 See Mosiah 3:19.

31 Hebrews 5:8–9.

"Thy will be done."[32] Once we give our will over to God, the Holy Ghost—that great Comforter—can enter into our heart and soul and give us blessed peace. President Spencer W. Kimball offered further insight about our life on Earth:

> If we looked at mortality as the whole of existence, then pain, sorrow, failure, and short life would be calamity. But if we look upon life as an eternal thing stretching far into the pre-Earth past and on into the eternal post-death future, then all happenings may be put into proper perspective. . . . The gospel teaches us there is no tragedy in death, but only in sin.[33]

In time, our mourning will be replaced with everlasting happiness. "Therefore, the redeemed of the Lord shall return, and come with singing unto Zion; and everlasting joy and holiness shall be upon their heads; and they shall obtain gladness and joy; sorrow and mourning shall flee away."[34]

Coping with Anger

Some people are forced to cope not only with sorrow but also with anger at a person who acted negligently, irresponsibly, or recklessly and caused the death of their loved one. Anger might be directed at a drunken driver who crashed into a spouse's car, at a child's friend for driving too fast on a winding canyon road, at a manager who allowed unsafe work practices at a spouse's workplace, or at an apartment maintenance person who left the gate to the swimming pool open.

However, unresolved anger acts like a poison to the soul and will eventually hurt us and those around us. This makes it necessary to guard ourselves against anger, even if we feel it is justified. Unless we actively work to overcome our anger, it can canker our soul and lead us down a path we should not follow. The longer we harbor anger and allow it to stay inside, the worse we feel.

---

32 Matthew 6:10.
33 *Teachings of Presidents of the Church: Spencer W. Kimball*, (Salt Lake City; Deseret Book, 1977), 15, 18. Used with permission.
34 2 Nephi 8:11.

Eighteen years ago, Robert Kirby, a humor columnist for *The Salt Lake Tribune*, heard the news that an unidentified West Jordan police officer had been killed. Instantly, he became alarmed because his brother, Chuck, worked for the West Jordan police. Then Robert, who was a former police officer himself, learned that the slain officer was thirty-nine-year-old Ron Wood. Robert's initial relief at knowing his brother was all right turned to grief and rage that someone had murdered a police officer. Robert wrestled with his feelings for months, then decided to visit Ron Wood's parents.

"Despite having far more reason to hate than I did," Robert said, "they focused on forgiveness."

Ron Wood's father, Blair, told Robert, "There's no point in hating anyone. It would only ruin more lives. Ron wouldn't want that. And we don't want that for our family."

After that visit, Robert said, "I came away with my own need to at least temper my feelings about what happened. Constantly revisiting the source of my pain wasn't going to help make it better. . . . Over time, I put things in a perspective that was more beneficial to myself and those around me."[35]

Robbie and Alissa Parker

Robbie and Alissa Parker's six-year-old daughter, Emilie, was killed, along with nineteen of her classmates and six adults, at Sandy Hook Elementary School in Newtown, Connecticut. After the December 2012 massacre, Alissa was devastated. In her anguish, she asked her husband, "It's all true, right? All the things we believe about death and God . . . it's all true?" Alissa wrote, "My ship of faith was rocking . . . and the dark sea of doubt began to rise."

Alissa had difficulty forgiving Adam Lanza, the shooter. "He was a monster to me. . . . I was angry and comfortable being in that state. . . . I wanted to remain angry because I thought I owed it to Emilie. . . . If I let that go, I was letting him [Lanza] off the hook." But Alissa discovered that she would not be able to heal completely until she forgave Lanza. It took time, effort, a spiritual prompting, and finally, a visit to Lanza's father before

---

35 Robert Kirby, "Forgiving Hearts of a Slain Cop's Parents Eased my Rage," *The Salt Lake Tribune*, May 6, 2018, B1, B3.

she slowly began to feel a measure of peace. As is often the case, forgiveness is not a onetime occurrence. Alissa said, "It's a choice I have to make again and again."

One thing that brought Alissa and her husband peace was a special spiritual manifestation, in which Robbie saw Emilie in a lifelike dream vision. Later, Alissa had her own spiritual manifestation. One Sunday, Alissa said, "An enveloping warmth of peace and comfort spread through my whole body. . . . And then I felt her. I felt Emilie. Nothing could be clearer or stronger. . . . I breathed in the blessed sense of her."[36]

Applying the Balm of Gilead

In biblical times, the balm of Gilead was an ointment made from the gum of a tree in the land of Gilead. This ointment was an important trade commodity because of its special healing properties, and over time, the balm of Gilead became symbolic for the power to soothe and heal.

In a talk titled "Balm of Gilead," President Boyd K. Packer related that one night, he picked up a friend, John, and drove him to a missionary reunion. John was a deeply spiritual man who had lived a life of service. During their trip, John told Elder Packer that he had grown up in a small community and married his sweetheart and that when his wife became pregnant, they both looked forward to having their first child. Life seemed bright and full of promise.

However, complications arose when labor began. John sent for the doctor, who was unable to come quickly because he was tending to a sick family. His wife's condition had become desperate by the time the doctor arrived, but the physician managed to safely deliver the baby. A few days later, the young mother became ill and died from the same illness the doctor had been treating at the home where he had been prior to arriving at John's home.

Elder Packer said, "John's world was shattered. . . . He had lost his wife. He had no way to tend both the baby and his work.

---

36 Peggy Fletcher Stack, "When ex-Utahns lost children at Sandy Hook and in an airport mugging, they faced the question: Do they really believe in resurrection?" *The Salt Lake Tribune*, April 16, 2017. local.sltrib.com/online/sw/easter/

As the weeks wore on, his grief festered. 'That doctor should not be allowed to practice,' he would say. 'He brought that infection to my wife. If he had been careful, she would be alive today.'"

One day, John's stake president asked to talk with the struggling young father who had become so bitter. His advice was simple: "John, leave it alone. Nothing you do about it will bring her back. Anything you do will make it worse. John, leave it alone."

As John related his story to Elder Packer, the widower said he didn't feel at the time as though he *could* leave it alone because the doctor had made a horrible mistake and needed to pay for it. John then said:

> It was not until I was an old man that I could finally see a poor country doctor—overworked, underpaid, run ragged from patient to patient, with little medicine, no hospital, few instruments, struggling to save lives, and succeeding for the most part. He had come in a moment of crisis, when two lives hung in the balance, and had acted without delay.

Elder Packer said he wanted to offer the same counsel to us that his friend John had received:

> If you have a festering grudge, if you are involved in an acrimonious dispute . . . I say therefore, "John, leave it alone. Mary, leave it alone." If you need a transfusion of spiritual strength, then just ask for it. We call that prayer. Prayer is powerful spiritual medicine. . . . Forgiveness is powerful spiritual medicine. To extend forgiveness, that soothing balm, to those who have offended you is to heal. . . . I repeat, "John, leave it alone. Mary, leave it alone."[37]

37 Boyd K. Packer, "Balm of Gilead," *Ensign*, November 1987, 17–18. churchofjesuschrist.org/study/ensign/1987/11/balm-of-gilead?lang=eng

Forgiving Yourself

There may be times when you have to forgive yourself, such as if you believe you could have done something to prevent the death. Perhaps your loved one told you about some unusual symptoms they were experiencing and you insisted (wrongly) that he or she was fine and there was no need to see a doctor. You might feel anguish if you did not insist your son get some sleep before a long drive, if you failed to make sure your wife was taking her prescribed medication, or if you did not call or visit your friend when you knew he or she was depressed. Parents might castigate themselves for letting their teen go to a party without checking to make sure it would be properly chaperoned with no drugs or drinking.

However, the only thing these thoughts will accomplish is to make you miserable. Resist the urge to braid them into a whip of remorse that you use to flog yourself. You were not responsible for what happened. Resist the urge to be critical and brood about what you *should* have done. People make mistakes and fall short of acting perfectly, but we can pray and ask for forgiveness.

Perhaps you feel anguish over allowing relationship problems to linger for years. Then, when death occurs, it hurts to realize it is now too late to work things out. All that is left are regrets at not having acted sooner. Short-term issues can also cause pain, such as if your last words to the departed were angry ones. Marlene shares the following experience:

Years ago, a friend of mine, Laura, [names have been changed] had an argument with her husband, Brian, just before he left for work. Later that morning, he was critically injured in a car accident. Brian remained in intensive care for a month but was never lucid enough for Laura to tell him she was sorry about the argument before he passed away. Laura battled painful feelings of guilt for a very long time. Then one day Laura was blessed with a deep, heart-felt impression that Brian would have forgiven her just as readily as she would have forgiven him if the situation had been reversed. Feeling the sweet comfort of this knowledge finally allowed Laura to forgive herself.

Forgiving yourself is not easy, but certainly you did not intend the loss that occurred. Forgive yourself and heal rather than allowing yourself to be eaten up by sorrow. Ask God to forgive your mistakes and shortcomings, and He will bless you with peace and comfort.

How Forgiveness Can Cleanse Our Wounds

Choosing to forgive can be difficult, but it brings great peace. When we choose forgiveness, we release ourselves from being a victim. To forgive, we have to make a conscious decision to release the resentment, anger, and bitterness we feel. One way to do this is to make a sincere attempt to understand what the other person was thinking and feeling at the time of the incident. Comprehending their thoughts can help us release and let go of our anger. Another thing that can help us forgive is to consciously try to have compassion for others who made mistakes. Each and every one of us is beloved by our Heavenly Father—even the person who caused the death of your loved one.

Forgiveness may not be easy, but it is essential. If we pray sincerely, God can soften our heart and bless us with the strength we need to conquer our anger and let go. Remember that forgiveness does not mean we condone a person's inappropriate actions. Neither does it mean we will forget what happened.

But what forgiveness *can* do is cleanse our deep, innermost wounds and soothe our heart and soul, allowing peace to come— the sublime peace that can come from only God. "Now the God of hope fill you with all joy and peace in believing, that ye may abound in hope, through the power of the Holy Ghost."[38] Jean Paul Richter said, "Humanity is never so beautiful as when praying for forgiveness, or else forgiving another."[39]

---

38 Romans 15:13.

39 Martha Tarbell quoting Jean Paul Richter, "Sentence Sermons" in *Tarbell's Teachers' Guide to the International Sunday School Lessons for 1907* (Indianapolis: The Bobbs-Merrill Company Publishers), 1906, 221.

CHAPTER 3
GRIEF AFFECTS EVERYONE DIFFERENTLY

Have mercy upon me, O Lord; for I am weak:
O Lord, heal me; for my bones are vexed.
My soul is also sore vexed. . . . O Lord, how long? . . .
Because thy mercy is good, deliver thou me.
For I am poor and needy, and my heart is wounded within me.
I am gone like the shadow when it declineth. . . .
My knees are weak.[40]

THE PAIN OF LOSING A loved one is inevitable and eventually confronts everyone. However, because of individual circumstances and personalities, not everyone experiences grief the same way. Just as no two snowflakes falling in winter will ever be alike, no two survivors adapt to loss in exactly the same way. Grief is highly individual. There are a number of factors that affect how a person reacts to loss, including gender. Grief can have a great impact on our emotional and spiritual states and can also affect our physical bodies because our mental and physical states are intrinsically linked. It can be helpful to know the common symptoms of grief so we can better deal with them.

---

40 Psalm 6:2–3, 106:21–24.

Factors That Influence How a Person Copes with Loss

Feelings of grief and the degree of their intensity depend on the individual, the circumstances surrounding the loss, how close you were to the departed, and the nature of the loss. Psychiatrists Thomas Holmes and Richard Rahe developed the Holmes and Rahe Stress Scale, which studied more than five thousand patients to determine what life events cause the most stress. They found the death of a spouse or child ranked number one on the list.[41] There are a number of factors that influence a person's ability to cope with loss.[42]

1. **Age of the Deceased.** The age of the deceased makes a difference in our reaction to loss. When death involves a child or a young adult, there are often greater feelings of sorrow and pain. With an older person, such as a parent or grandparent, there is an expectation of death, which can soften the loss.

2. **Degree of Intentionality.** While many car crashes are simply accidents, some drivers face culpability because of driving recklessly, while drowsy, or while under the influence of drugs or alcohol. These and other types of death caused by the above factors are generally considered preventable, and the perpetrator is often blamed for the death. These kinds of death can cause survivors to struggle with anger toward the person they see as causing the death.

3. **Unexpected Death.** After a sudden death, family and friends frequently feel shock and experience more intense mourning. There is often sorrow at not being given the opportunity to say goodbye.

4. **Violent Death.** Violent deaths create circumstances far different from other types of loss. When a person is murdered, either individually or during a mass shooting or some other type of terrorist action, those left behind struggle and often feel their

---

41 The Pain Doctor; March 2, 2018. Accessed April 13, 2021. paindoctor.com/top-10-stressful-life-events-holmes-rahe-stress-scale/

42 "Factors that Influence the Ability to Cope with Loss," *Mission Hospice Society*, missionhospice.bc.ca/wp-content/uploads/2018/03/Factors-that-influence-the-ability-to-cope-with-losses.pdf

lives have been turned upside down in an unimaginable way. Anger at the perpetrator is common.

5. **Relationship with the Deceased.** Typically, the closer one is to the person who died, the more difficult the loss is to accept and process. Parents often feel there is no loss as devastating as when they lose a child. Losing a spouse can be nearly as distressing.

6. **Coping Ability.** An individual's response to loss depends in part on their personality. Some people seem predisposed to feel grief more deeply at distressing life circumstances.

7. **Current Stressors.** If one is already facing other challenging and stressful situations, the ability to cope with death can be greatly reduced. Such stressors can include the loss of employment, a health crisis, sending a child to college, losing multiple loved ones within a short time frame, or when facing other challenging situations.

8. **Social Support.** Having a strong support network of family and friends can be vital to helping a person cope with loss. Dr. Patricia A. Thomas said, "Those receiving support from their family members may feel a greater sense of self-worth, and this enhanced self-esteem may be a psychological resource, encouraging optimism, positive affect, and better mental health."[43]

9. **Religious Beliefs.** The degree to which a person believes in a divine being is a strong factor in determining how he or she manages loss. People who believe in God and that life continues beyond the grave typically cope much better than those who believe life ends with the physical death of the body. "Wherefore, whoso believeth in God might with surety hope for a better world, yea, even a place at the right hand of God, which hope cometh of faith, maketh an anchor to the souls of men."[44]

Spiritual Loss

One factor that can add to the pain of loss is if your departed loved one turned away from the gospel before passing. It helps to

---

43 Patricia A. Thomas, Hui Liu, and Debra Umberson, "Family Relationships and Well-Being," *Innovation in Aging*, Nov. 11, 2017, 1(3). ncbi.nlm.nih.gov/pmc/articles/PMC5954612/

44 Ether 12:4.

know repentance and redemption are possible on the other side of the veil. Continue to love and pray for your loved one with all of your heart and wait for the Lord's hand to be revealed in His own due time. Seek the peace that comes from trusting God and have faith in His ability to rescue your loved one but remember that the plan of happiness includes agency. You couldn't force him or her to choose to follow the gospel plan, and neither will God. Rest assured that God will do anything He can to save your loved one in the spirit world if he or she will turn to Him. Trust in God and lay the burden of "saving" your loved one at the Savior's feet, where it belongs. Find solace in prayer, scripture study, and temple attendance as you continue to walk along your own path of discipleship.

President Henry B. Eyring said,

> We have all felt the hope that someday we could feel again the warm affection of that family member we loved so much. . . . For some, that eternal joy may seem a faint or even a fading hope. Parents, children, brothers, and sisters may have made choices that seem to disqualify them from eternal life. . . . A prophet of God once offered me counsel that gives me peace. I was worried that the choices of others might make it impossible for our family to be together forever. He said, "You are worrying about the wrong problem. You just live worthy of the celestial kingdom, and the family arrangements will be more wonderful than you can imagine."[45]

Grief Often Comes in Waves

When we lose someone close to us, waves of sadness, loneliness, and yearning can wash over us with astounding intensity.

---

45 Henry B. Eyring, "The Hope of Eternal Family Love," *Ensign*, August 2016, 4–5. churchofjesuschrist.org/study/ensign/2016/08/the-hope-of-eternal-family-love.html?lang=eng#series_title1

Grief can be cruel because it doesn't just hit once and go away. Rather, it comes back again and again. Just when we feel like we're doing better, we can be flooded again with despair and pain. When that happens, it can feel like all the progress we have made vanishes as heartbreak once again descends. However, it is actually fortuitous that grief comes in waves because relentless grief would be overwhelming. Grief hits, then eases, which allows our spirits to temporarily lighten and reconnect with life. This is the back-and-forth fluctuation of the grieving process, and each wave moves us a little bit further along the path of recovery.

Because grief tends to fluctuate, there may be times when you are in the midst of a normal, pleasant activity when grief unexpectedly hits. This is common, as are mood swings. It's not out of the ordinary to feel speechless with grief one moment and angry the next. You might be filled with anxiety that will not let you sit still, then suddenly lethargic and barely able to move.

Typically, these cycles of sadness are most common during the first six months and lessen during the next three to nine months. The time between moments of grief will gradually lengthen, allowing you to return to a state of equilibrium. However, even years later, episodes of sadness can still occur when you least expect them. Some predictable triggers can set off grief, especially holidays, birthdays, anniversaries, or visiting a familiar location. Ask for support from family and friends during these times. Unpredictable triggers are more difficult—even impossible—to plan for, and you may be blindsided by sights, sounds, smells, and experiences that catch you off guard.

Losing a loved one is a human experience and is not meant to be overwhelming. Of course, even the most resilient person will have difficult moments, but patience can help as you ride through this roller coaster of emotions. Anchor yourself in a regular schedule and normal activities. Do your best to maintain acquaintances and friendships. Taking care of yourself physically and spiritually will allow you to find a healthy balance in life. In time, the oscillating pattern of deep grief and being able to cope with life will even out. You may still vacillate between moments of tranquility and mourning, but eventually you will gain control over your emotions. After a time, that which once seemed bleak and bottomless will give way to rays of sunshine peeking from behind the clouds.

Men and Women Often Grieve Differently

Grieving can be complicated by gender differences because men and women often respond differently to loss. While women tend to grieve openly, men are generally more inhibited about expressing their feelings and tend to grieve privately, preferring to work through their pain by themselves. Men often distract themselves by helping others, becoming more involved in their work, or by engaging in other activities. Many men are action-oriented, and even if they are struggling with the loss themselves, they feel more comfortable if they can actively *do* something to help others who are bereaved. However, when a woman is in a weakened emotional state due to her loss, it can be hard to grasp the complexity of her husband's emotions.

Generally, women tend to grieve in a more intense way and for longer periods of time. Women can be more emotional and display more overt signs of grief through crying, listless behavior, and eating either too little or too much. One of the ways women work through loss is to talk with others. Women typically form close relationships and grow up confiding in friends and family, which makes them comfortable turning to others for help and support after a loss. Since women are able to vocalize their pain, they tend to lean on their closest family members and friends as they process their grief.

Men often suppress their feelings because they don't want to "burden" others. It's not unusual for men to consciously choose to hide their intense sorrow so they don't place additional burdens on a wife, mother, or daughter who is already struggling. Additionally, men often put "thinking and fixing" before "feeling and expressing." In our society, men are expected to fix things, and when a dear one dies, a man is confronted with the reality of knowing this is not something he can fix. Because of that, he will often look for physical ways to relieve another's burdens by mowing the lawn, fixing a cabinet, changing furnace filters, repairing a fence, or changing the oil in a car.

For a couple to cope with shared loss, it is helpful to validate your spouse's feelings. It's also important to work on communicating your needs. Strive to understand what the other is saying. Don't expect your partner to be a mind reader—tell them plainly and clearly what you want and need. Then discuss the best way to help you get your needs met. Compromise is vital. One spouse may want to socialize and attend family activities while the other doesn't feel ready. To compromise, one person may need to push to be more social while the other needs to pull back a little. It's all right if the more social person occasionally attends events on his or her own. Finally, each of you will need to work at staying connected. Even though you will manage your grief in your own way, make an effort to stay involved in each other's lives. Spend time with each other. Talk to each other about your day. Share your feelings and the challenges you're facing.

Common Symptoms of Grief

After a death, cataclysmic feelings may cause us to sorrowfully wonder, "What now?" There is only one remedy for grief, and that is to grieve. To heal, we need to process our grief, and while that may seem a tremendous task when the pain is nearly unbearable, it is possible. One thing that can help is to be aware of some of the common symptoms of grief that you may experience.

Shock

Immediately after losing a loved one, you may feel shock, which causes a merciful numbness. Shock can be thought of as God's way of anesthetizing us until we can gather our bearings and stand up under the pain. Although shock causes life to feel surreal, divine help is available. "I will lift up mine eyes unto the hills. . . . My help cometh from the Lord, which made heaven and earth. . . . The Lord shall preserve thee from all evil: he shall preserve thy soul. The Lord shall preserve thy going out and thy coming in from this time forth, and even for evermore."[46]

---

46 Psalm 121:1–2, 7–8.

Anxiety and Fear

Grief can manifest itself in feelings of anxiety and fear. Although any loss can be heartbreaking, for some it is nothing short of devastating and can seem like the end of everything. Older widows and widowers who have relied on their spouse for years may become fearful and wonder if they can handle living on their own. Young widows and widowers can be anxious about the future and question their ability to raise their children alone. Although fear and anxiety are common, they can occasionally lead to panic attacks or other disorders. If this happens, see a doctor or a therapist.

Staying Excessively Busy

Sometimes the newly bereaved postpone their mourning by keeping their mind and body busy, throwing themselves into their work, hobbies, yard work, or household projects such as cleaning out closets, painting, or redecorating so there is no time to feel grief and pain. Unfortunately, refusing to experience pain can numb you from positive emotions that make life enjoyable, such as love, happiness, and laughter. While it's good to remain active, the key is balance. Monitor yourself and consider cutting back if you find yourself trying to fill every spare minute.

Sleeplessness

A common complaint is having one's normal sleep patterns disrupted. Lack of sleep can result in mental sluggishness, forgetfulness, and fatigue. One natural solution is to take a small dose (1–3 mg) of melatonin one hour before bedtime. If this doesn't work, a higher dosage (4–8 mg) might be needed. If melatonin doesn't help, talk to your doctor about how to increase the amount of sleep you get.

Mood Swings

It's normal to feel a wide range of emotions when in pain. You may become overly concerned about certain matters, be irritable, or find yourself easily distracted. Expect these variations and realize that shifting moods are a natural byproduct of grief. It isn't unusual for friends and family to be the ones who alert you to these problems. If they approach you, accept their concern without becoming defensive. Remember they love you and have your best interests at heart. Then work on managing your emotional swings. You might find it helpful to talk with a therapist, who can teach you how to deal with fluctuating emotions.

Forgetfulness

After a significant loss, some people have difficulty remembering things. Part of this arises from an inability to concentrate with all that is going on. It can also arise from mental fatigue caused by having to adjust to the myriad changes that occur after a loss. If you have a hard time remembering, keep a pad of paper handy to write things down or use your phone to write a reminder list. Put sticky notes everywhere. At this time of upheaval, taking time to write things down will pay big dividends.

Isolating Yourself

Grieving people tend to withdraw from others. It's natural to want some time alone to catch your breath, but when you are newly bereaved, you really need the company of other people. It may take a strong act of will on your part to avoid isolating yourself, but being with others will curb loneliness, provide needed support, and allow you to connect with others, which will enrich your life.

Withdrawing from God

Some people interpret a personal tragedy as proof that God either does not exist or that He doesn't care about them. Satan loves to attack people whose defenses are low and is behind both of these lies. He whispers twisted and damaging lies to make people bitter and blame God for the death. Satan's sole desire is to make all people as miserable as he is: "And because he [Satan] had fallen from heaven, and had become miserable forever, he sought also the misery of all mankind."[47] Refuse to give into these lies. Pray for strength and hold fast to your faith. You can receive crucial spiritual strength and comfort by using your grief to grow closer to, instead of away from, God.

Stress

Almost universally, the death of someone close to us produces a high level of stress, which affects us emotionally and socially.

---

47 2 Nephi 2:18.

Stress is an automatic, biological function that reacts to changes in our environment and acts as a personal warning alarm. If stress and strain continue over a long period of time, exhaustion and mental difficulties can result. Work to make necessary adjustments to thwart the harmful influence of stress before it causes additional problems in your life.

Crying

Some people feel a need to be strong and hold back tears, but crying is a natural response to loss. "Thou shalt live together in love, insomuch that thou shalt weep for the loss of them that die."[48] The Apostle Francis M. Lyman said crying comes not from a lack of faith but from love.

> We mourn, we sorrow for our loved ones that go—our wives, our husbands, our children, our parents; we sorrow for them; and it is well and proper that we should mourn for them and shed tears for the loss, for it is our loss; but it is their gain, for it is in the march of progress, advancement and development.[49]

Tears are essential to relieve tension and let sadness out. Tears contain leucine-enkephalin—one of the brain's natural pain relievers—as well as prolactin, which help cleanse the body of toxic substances. If you feel like crying, you ought to, because studies show that releasing tears helps people process their emotions. While it's healthier to weep than bottle up your grief, it's not helpful to weep so excessively that you are pulled down into hopeless despair. Allow yourself to have a good cry when needed, then move on. Hold on and know that the sun rises even after the darkest night.

Feeling Sad or Depressed

The profound changes and challenges that arise from losing someone you love can cause you to feel depressed. Sometimes

---

48 D&C 42:45.

49 Francis M. Lyman, *Conference Reports*, October 1909, 19. archive.org/details/conferencereport1909sa/page/n19

friends and family may conclude that you are suffering from clinical depression when you are merely struggling with sadness—a normal symptom of grief. If you cry frequently after losing a loved one, you are sad—not depressed. If for a few weeks you feel lost in a fog, are unable to concentrate, sleep too much or too little, have no appetite, or feel anxious at times, you are grief-stricken, not depressed.

Clinical depression is not just feeling sad, low, and blue after a death; it is more intense and lasts longer. Depression amplifies sadness, anxiety, hopelessness, and despair, taking them to a much deeper level and making you feel that your entire life is dark and empty. Typically, the pain of grief ebbs and flows, lessening in intensity as time goes on, but with clinical depression, low feelings remain constant or worsen. Depression is a disease of the mind— just like diabetes and asthma are diseases of the body—and has nothing to do with one's personal character or faithfulness. Monitor your emotions. If you find yourself feeling depressed longer than six weeks, see your doctor or a therapist. You may be suffering from clinical depression. A doctor may recommend medication that can help remedy any chemical imbalances that may be responsible for your depression.

Grief Can Affect the Body

Strong emotions such as grief can manifest themselves in the body through a variety of physical symptoms and ailments. Dr. Stephanie Hairston says, "Stress links the emotional and physical aspects of grief. The systems in the body that process physical and emotional stress overlap, and emotional stress can activate the nervous system as easily as physical threats can. When stress becomes chronic, increased adrenaline and blood pressure can contribute to chronic medical conditions."[50] Elizabeth Hartney, PhD, explains why this happens:

> While physical pain and emotional pain are dif-
> ferent, there is research that suggests that both

50 Stephanie Hairston, "How Grief Shows up in Your Body," *WebMD*, July 11, 2019; News Special Report Reviewed by Neha Pathak. webmd.com/special-reports/grief-stages/20190711/how-grief-affects-your-body-and-mind

types of pain may share some neurological similarities. Both emotional and physical pain are linked to changes in the prefrontal cortex and cingulate cortex. . . . Emotional pain can often feel as strong as physical pain and at times can even cause symptoms of pain throughout the body.[51]

Some commonly reported physical symptoms arising from grief are chest pain, digestive disturbances, dizziness, exhaustion, feeling numb or disoriented, headaches or migraines, inability to concentrate, listlessness, loss of appetite, overeating, and muscular aches and pains. Because many of these symptoms can be caused by medical problems, it's a good idea to consult a physician, even if your symptoms are mild. Going through the grieving process is similar to having a physical illness, and you can expect to be emotionally and physically depleted for a time. Biologically speaking, after a period of deep stress, the human system usually adapts and returns to normal within six to eight weeks.

---

51 Elizabeth Hartney, "How Emotional Pain Affects Your Body," *verywell mind*, July 7, 2020. verywellmind.com/physical-pain-and-emotional-pain -22421#citation-9

CHAPTER 4
THE GRIEVING PROCESS

Be merciful unto me, O Lord:
for I cry unto thee daily. . . .
Unto thee, O Lord, do I lift up my soul.
For thou, Lord, art good . . . and plenteous in mercy unto all
them that call upon thee.
Give ear, O Lord, unto my prayer;
and attend to the voice of my supplications.
In the day of my trouble I will call upon thee:
for thou wilt answer me.[52]

ALL DEATH INVOLVES LOSS, AND grieving is the work that must be done to process that loss and adjust to a new life. Most people suffer acutely after the loss of a dear one, but there are steps you can take to deal with your loss. Recovering can be difficult, but you can do what others have done: heal slowly with God's help. Alma tells us, "I do know that whosoever shall put their trust in God shall be supported in their trials, and their troubles, and their afflictions, and shall be lifted up at the last day."[53]

---

52 Psalm 86:3–7.
53 Alma 36:3.

Losing a loved one has been likened to what happens to a house during an earthquake. After the shaking stops, you feel shocked while surveying the wreckage that used to be your home. Then comes the work as you begin dealing with the mess. Some items may be damaged and need repair. Other things are usable, so you put them back where they belong. You may have to attend to structural damage, perhaps even repairing and restoring the foundation or load-bearing walls.

Similarly, after the loss of a loved one, you face a metaphorical earthquake. First, you must stop and survey how the death has changed your life. You will then begin to deal with and adapt to the changes that come from your loss. Perhaps you'll strive to pray more sincerely or work to improve your ability to receive personal revelation. Other things in your life may remain unchanged, such as love for family, gratitude for the gospel, and trust in God's promise that one day we will again be with those we love.

Next you may need to tend to structural damage and strengthen your personal foundation by building your testimony, increasing your faith, or enlarging your knowledge of God's plan for you. The work may be long and demanding, but step by step, you will be able to pick up the pieces and put your life back together. After surviving the "earthquake" of losing a dear one, you can emerge a better person, having learned many important lessons. You may have developed a deeper understanding of the Lord's mercy and kindness, a stronger commitment to following Christ, a heightened love and concern for others, and an ability to focus on the many blessings God has given you instead of the things that have been taken away.

When working with terminally ill patients, Elisabeth Kübler-Ross developed a list of what she called the five stages of grief. Since then, it has been acknowledged that these stages do not necessarily occur in any specific order and that people often do not experience all of them.[54] More recent developments in the study of bereavement indicate that processing the loss of a loved one has three general stages, which are similar to Kübler-Ross's theory.

54 See Julie Axelrod, "The 5 Stages of Grief & Loss," *PsychCentral*, July 8, 2020. psychcentral.com/lib/the-5-stages-of-loss-and-grief/

Stage one has to do with acknowledging and accepting the reality of your loss. Stage two is processing your grief, which means working through your emotional pain. Stage three is adjusting to the changes in your life. This involves integrating your past with the present and moving forward toward a new future.

After a loss, your spirit needs to heal just as your physical body needs to heal after an injury. No medication, support group, book, or counselor can get you through your heartache—although they can certainly help. At some point, you will have to decide that you *want* to heal. There is an old saying that people do not drown because they fall into the water; they drown because they do not pull themselves out. At this difficult time, you must choose to pull yourself up and move forward. You make this choice because you want to do more than survive. Despite your heart-wrenching loss, you want to process your grief; learn how to change and grow; and lead a productive, fulfilled, and happy life.

Stage One: Accepting Your Loss

When first learning of the death of someone you love, you may feel a sense of numbness, which provides a protective cushion that temporarily obscures and lessens the pain. This shock can help you get you through those first awful minutes, hours, and days. It keeps you in a safer place and allows a needed pause—letting life swirl around you without touching you.

At this time, when you are too stricken to fully function, family and friends may step in and help by calling the funeral home, assisting in planning the service, and purchasing a cemetery plot. As reality sinks in, you may feel that your life has come to a grinding halt. Stay close to God and keep your heart open so you can receive His comfort: "I cried unto God . . . and he gave ear unto me. In the day of my trouble I sought the Lord . . . and ceased not: my soul refused to be comforted. . . . I am so troubled that I cannot speak."[55]

In this early stage of grief, people often find it hard to accept what has happened. Sometimes the most you can do is acknowledge that death has occurred. Acknowledging the death will allow you to recognize that although the life of the person you loved is

---

55 Psalm 77:1–2, 4.

over, yours is not. William James, an eminent nineteenth-century American psychologist, said, "Acceptance of what has happened is the first step to overcoming the consequences of any misfortune."[56]

All loss needs to be accepted in order to move along the healing pathway, and while acceptance may seem an obvious choice, it is not an easy one. Authors Raymond Moody Jr. and Dianne Arcangel said, "Grief is not an emotion but a process with a host of emotions. At the core of grief is deep sorrow and a longing to have the loved one back."[57] As you try to accept that the person you love is actually gone, you may feel like a parachutist in a free fall. But at some point, you will pull the cord, open your parachute, and be able to acknowledge what has happened. This is a turning point, as you begin to find a direction other than down.

Although saying goodbye is never easy, there comes a time when you have to close that door and move on. Being able to say goodbye to your loved one plays a huge part in how we feel and how we process the loss of someone we care about. Joshua shares the following experience:

My grandpa passed away in 2012 from complications of leukemia. We knew his time was growing short, and most of my family was with him. I had planned to join them the next day, but he passed away before I could make it to the hospital. It was surreal, the first time as an adult that I had lost someone close to me. The funeral was beautiful, but I wanted to cry all the time. I felt guilty and also disappointed that I wasn't with my family when he passed away and because I didn't have the chance to say goodbye.

My grandma passed away in March 2017. Once again, we knew it was coming. I coached an afternoon lacrosse game in a rainstorm, and although soaking wet after the game, I ran to my car and drove four hours to her house. My grandma was barely conscious, but I was able to spend a day and a half with her, talking with and playing the guitar for her.

---

56 "William James" in Influential Past Teachers, *Awaken*. awaken.com /2013/07/william-james/

57 Raymond Moody Jr. and Dianne Arcangel, *Life After Loss: Conquering Grief and Finding Hope* (Harper Collins, San Francisco, 2001), 48.

Then I had to leave and go home because of school. My grandma passed away shortly after I left, but I was ok. I had been able to say goodbye and tell her a few things I wanted to say. I didn't cry at her funeral—but then crying isn't necessarily a gold standard for how much you are grieving.

The difference in grieving the deaths of my grandma and grandpa was like the difference between night and day, which I feel was due primarily to my being able to talk with Grandma and say goodbye before she passed.

At this first stage of the grieving process, you'll begin to reevaluate your life and think about how to proceed without having the person you care about in your life. It is common to spend a lot of time wrangling unruly emotions. Sadness over loss often dampens your biological systems, slowing you down, and you may wake earlier than normal, have a harder time falling asleep, or wake during the night. Some people find themselves sleeping more than usual. Sleep is more than just emotional escape. Your body needs more rest, and extra sleep gives your subconscious more dream time to process your loss.

Any major loss changes your life. While it can be difficult to face the future, there are adjustments you can make as you adapt to a new life. When former Church Historian Leonard Arrington lost his wife Grace as a result of heart failure, he said, "There were only two occasions when I broke down and sobbed." Arrington explained that one of those times was when "O Holy Night" was sung at his wife's funeral; the other was when he kissed her goodbye just before closing the coffin. "Other than that, I stood the experience well," Arrington said. "I realize the lonely moments ahead, but am trying to be sensible about the adjustments I have to make."[58]

There will be many adjustments to make, and we are responsible for our attitude toward those changes. If life hands us lemons,

---

58 Bob Mims, "New Collection of Leonard Arrington's vast journals," *The Salt Lake Tribune*, May 9, 2018, A1, A5). sltrib.com/religion/2018/05/09/new-collection-of-leonard-arringtons-vast-journals-shows-battles-the-mormon-historian-had-with-lds-leaders-over-telling-the-truth-about-the-churchs-past/

it is our job to make the best lemonade we can. What cannot be changed must be accepted, even the loss of someone we love dearly. As we do our best to reconcile ourselves to it, we can then strive to rise above it and push forward with a new chapter in our life.

Part of accepting loss is saying goodbye. One of the rituals that helps accomplish this is having a funeral or memorial service. Viewings and funerals bind mourners together in a common grief and helps the bereaved process and accept their loss. These events offer survivors an opportunity to reflect on the deceased person's life, mourn for the temporary separation they must now endure, embrace tender memories, and receive love and support. Going to a funeral home and seeing the departed one's body, sharing sorrow with friends and family, then going to where the body will be interred or the ashes scattered unite those left behind, lighten their burdens, and are important rituals that help us psychologically acknowledge the death.

In her book *A Journey through Grief,* Alla Renée Bozarth, PhD, relates an analogy about accepting your loss—the first stage of the grieving process. Bozarth has a flowering crab tree in her backyard, and one autumn, the small, red fruit did not fall off the tree as usual, even after the leaves had fallen. During the cold and snowy Minnesota winter, the fruit held on stubbornly. However, when spring arrived, the tenacious fruit was finally pushed off the tree by the growth of new shoots.

Bozarth said:

> Ultimately, life takes the place of death. Dead things get pushed away to make room for more life. . . . [That] tree taught me something. . . . No matter how stubbornly I cling to my pain, refusing to let go of my actual loss, to give up my grief, sooner or later if I'm to go on living at all, I will have to give it up. The life inside me will push it all away in its own natural and right time.[59]

59 Alla Renee Bozarth, *A Journey Through Grief: Gentle, Specific Help to Get You Through the Most Difficult Stages of Grieving* (Center City: Hazelden Foundation, 1990), 31–32.

Stage Two: Processing Your Grief

Grief is a journey to a new phase in your life. The goal is not to forget but to reconcile yourself to your loss. You will always have a special bond with your loved one, but the relationship will be different. Your current grief is a testament of the love you have for him or her, and after a great loss, it takes time for the shock and numbness to wear off. It's much like when you wake up after surgery—once the anesthetic wears off, pain and suffering set in. Loss often breaks your heart and can seem like the end of everything. Initially, managing your grief may seem to be as unconquerable as scaling Mount Everest, but in time and with God's help, you will be able to process your grief. "God is our refuge and strength, a very present help in trouble. Therefore will not we fear, though the earth be removed, and though the mountains be carried into the midst of the sea."[60]

In stage two of the grief process, don't worry about choking back tears or swallowing down surging emotions. A good cry can help you work through your sadness and will often help you feel better. If you feel uncomfortable crying in front of others, go somewhere private. As you weep, you might want to cuddle a cat or stroke a dog. The presence of a pet can provide warm comfort. Don't run from the pain and don't worry about your tears—this is only a stage and will not last forever.

When you cut a finger, it bleeds, and that action cleans the wound and enables healing to begin. The same thing happens with grief. You process it by acknowledging the pain, feeling it, then living past it. It will be hard, but you *will* get through it. Talking about your loss and allowing yourself to grieve are fundamental ways of cleaning your inner wound so healing can begin.

Don't worry about feeling sad—it's all right to be sorrowful that the person you love is no longer with you. Your sadness is one way of recognizing how blessed you were to have that person in your life for a time. Remember, though, that acknowledging your sorrow doesn't mean forcing everyone around you to be sad too. Realize that you won't always feel the way you do right now.

60 Psalm 46:1–2.

Try to be graciously present with your loved ones, and do not weigh them down unduly with your sorrow.

Grieving involves a lot of work, but it's not necessary to do it all on your own. Turn to your Father in Heaven, who loves you and watches over you as any tender parent would. He stands ever ready to bless and help if you will but ask. "Let us therefore come boldly unto the throne of grace, that we may obtain mercy, and find grace to help in time of need."[61] God will always be right at your side to support, encourage, and help whenever you are afraid. You can always rely on Heavenly Father to be there during your trials. "And it came to pass that the Lord did visit them with his Spirit, and said unto them: Be comforted. And they were comforted."[62]

After a death, there will be both dark and bright moments. Unfortunately the reality of loss means you may fight debilitating sorrow at a time when you feel weaker than ever. While you need time to process your grief, you don't want to remain in a constant state of sadness for too long. Choose to move on, or you run the risk of becoming engulfed in a darkness from which it will be difficult to escape. Grief is like the ocean—sometimes the water is calm, and sometimes there are enormous waves—but you can learn how to swim. Find comfort and support in those around you and in the wonderful memories you carry in your heart. Press on through the darkness, and eventually you will break into sunshine.

While processing grief in stage two of your loss, strive to maintain perspective. Realize that although you are in great pain, there are still many good things in your life. Be of good courage and know that in time, you will be able to do more than just survive. Courage isn't so much having the strength to go on as it is going on when you don't have the strength. Grief work can hurt, but it pays.

---

61 Hebrews 4:16.
62 Alma 17:10.

Marlene shares the following experience: Years ago, I began having pain whenever I tried to raise my left arm. The doctor diagnosed me with "frozen shoulder." I began physical therapy—a painful process of working the shoulder joint to "unfreeze" it. At the conclusion of my second visit, my shoulder was throbbing painfully. Wondering how much torture I had to look forward to, I asked my therapist how many therapy sessions I would need until my shoulder returned to normal.

He replied cryptically, "Until it doesn't hurt so much."

So it is with grief work. You continue with the process until it doesn't hurt so much.

As you work through your sorrow, you will begin to feel relief. The more you deal with your feelings, the better you will feel. Grief happens to everyone. Allow yourself to process your emotions with the aim of moving forward. You can be stricken by grief, endure it, rail against it, and even become stuck in it. *Or* you can process your grief, have patience, and trust in God—knowing that with His help, you *will* get through it. "I can do all things through Christ which strengtheneth me."[63]

Stage Three: Adjusting to Life without Your Loved One

In the beginning, everything will remind you of the departed. But gradually you will become less sensitive about certain places, sounds, music, and events. Be aware that time by itself does not heal—it only gives you room and an interval to recover. Care for yourself by ensuring you have the basics: food, sleep, and social interaction. Be sensitive to your needs and don't let others push you to move faster than you are able just because they are uncomfortable with your grief. Adjusting to changes in your life will take time. The greater the loss, the longer your recovery may take. Pace yourself and know that the pain won't last forever. Healing will come as you gradually ease into a new life. Don't be concerned if you feel you aren't making any headway—most likely you are progressing but are unable to see it.

---

63 Philippians 4:13.

Occasionally, people may feel they are honoring the memory of the departed by refusing to resume normal, enjoyable activities, but this is unproductive and unhealthy. Happy moments give the bereaved a short break from the pain of loss, and such emotions are not out of place. Your loved one will always be part of you, whether or not you begin participating in life again. If you feel guilty when resuming some enjoyable activity, stop and consider whether your dear one would want you to participate. Do you actually think they would prefer that you stay home and feel miserable?

During this stage, if you haven't already, you can resume a normal work schedule. While remaining actively engaged is a crucial part of the healing process, it can be difficult to resume a full workload. Be accepting if you function below your normal level for a time, and allow your job performance to gradually return to normal without chastising yourself. Know your limits. You may need to occasionally take a day off during the first months of bereavement. Be patient with yourself and let things go that are not priorities. Right now, your well-being is your main concern.

Avoid Getting Trapped by False Beliefs

In stage three of the healing process, you'll want to avoid negative thoughts that can keep you stuck. Here are a few false beliefs that can slow the healing process:

- **Processing my grief will hurt too much.** Some people are afraid that if they let the pain out, it will only make them feel worse. While it is possible that working on your grief *can* make you feel worse, it will do so only *temporarily*. Think of it as lancing a boil. Initially, lancing a boil can be very painful, but letting out the infection is the only way real healing can begin. Locking the pain deep inside only prolongs your suffering, and denying hurt and sorrow can cause those very feelings to stay with you.

- **I shouldn't feel sad because, after all, my loved one is with God.** Just because the person you love is with God doesn't mean you don't miss that person. Yes, the separation is temporary, but it is still a separation. Although you are happy your loved one is in a better place, you certainly don't have to feel guilty if you miss him or her.

- **Putting the pain behind me quickly is the best course of action.** Don't force yourself to act as if everything is fine when it isn't. Allow yourself time to heal, even if well-meaning friends tell you it's time to pull yourself together. Your healing timeline is personal, and you're the only one who knows your limits. It's okay *not* to be okay and to allow yourself a period of mourning. There's no deadline. Work through your feelings in a way that is best for *you*.

- **If I laugh or feel happy, I'm forgetting about my loved one.** Some people feel that if they allow themselves to smile, laugh, and be happy, they are starting to forget their loved one. Remind yourself that Satan is twisting the situation and making it seem like recovering from loss is a bad thing. You *know* you will never forget your loved one, so don't allow Satan to make you feel guilty. You will *always* hold the one you love in your heart, and it's all right to go on with your life and take pleasure in living. Letting go of the deepest parts of your grief has nothing to do with how much you loved that person.

- **I must lack faith because I seem unable to rise above my grief.** This is another ploy of Satan, who wants to convince you that because you are grieving, you must not have faith in God. And yet even Jesus wept over Lazarus. When the Lord arrived in Judea, Lazarus had been dead for four days. Upon seeing Jesus, Martha and Martha wept and told the Savior that if He had come sooner, Lazarus would not have died. When Jesus saw their grief, He wept.[64] Think of that—the Lord of all creation wept with His friends, even though He would soon be breaking the bands of death and ushering in the Resurrection for all mankind.

- **I have no right to mourn because others have greater sorrows.** We've all thought this at times, but suffering is suffering. Having your son die is still painful, even when someone else loses a son *and* a daughter in a car accident. Just because other people suffer greater losses doesn't mean your own anguish is a walk in the park. Don't discount your suffering. Although you can be

---

64 See John 11:1–35.

grateful your suffering is not worse, don't compare it to others. Your suffering *is* real and it hurts. A lot.

Whenever negative thoughts spring up, you *must* stop them. You do this by first realizing they *are* harmful. With recognition comes the power to change. To modify harmful thoughts, come up with a positive statement to replace the negative one. It isn't enough to simply push the undesirable thought away; you must replace it with something positive. For example, if you think, "I shouldn't feel this way; my wife wouldn't want me to grieve so much," change that thought to, "I am working to overcome my sorrow, and my wife will understand I'm doing the best I can."

Helping Children Cope with Loss

Parents play a crucial role in guiding children through a loss because little ones can struggle with the difficult concept of death and have misconceptions about what happens after someone dies. Parents are often reluctant to talk about death because they don't want their children to worry or feel sad. However, children may worry more if *not* given an explanation. Before children can begin to understand death, they typically need to be around five or six years old, comprehend the meaning of time, and understand the word *never*.

Children who suffer the loss of someone close, such as a parent or sibling, may (but don't always) regress emotionally and physically, have nightmares, or have problems sleeping. Some children become needy and fearful of separation. To help them, one of the most important things you can do is to talk to your child and listen to what he or she has to say.

Some common questions children have about death include *What makes people die? What happens to people when they die? Where do people go when they die? And why do people have to die?* Do your best to answer your child's questions in age-appropriate terms. Keep things simple—there is no need to overexplain or go into details. Encourage your children to come to you with any further questions. Help them understand that their loved one's physical body has died, but their spirit—the person they love—is still alive and has gone to live in the spirit world and that the children will see that person again.

It's all right for your children to see you grieve. Explain that you cry at times because you love and miss the person who died. Don't hide your tears, but do avoid dramatic displays of grief in front of your children. Keep children on a regular schedule as much as possible. Having a set routine can be comforting during times of stress. Allow your children to attend the funeral, but tell them beforehand what they can expect. Gently explain that their loved one will not look the same as before.

Things to Remember While Processing Grief

Be sure to give yourself time to process your grief. Be kind to yourself. Don't push yourself to do more than you are able. Be patient and remember that time is a healer. It doesn't erase events, but it allows gaping wounds to slowly close. Accept your current limitations without judging yourself. It doesn't matter where you are on the ladder of recovery—all that matters is that you're facing the right direction.

Stay close to God while adjusting to your loss. Pray always to your loving Father, who wants to bring your soul out of the darkness. Heavenly Father sincerely wants to help you cope with your grief. Express gratitude for your blessings; discuss your worries; ask for peace, comfort, and guidance; and pray for the companionship of the Holy Ghost. "I cried unto the Lord with my voice; with my voice unto the Lord did I make my supplication. I poured out my complaint before him; I shewed before him my trouble. When my spirit was overwhelmed within me, then thou knewest my path."[65]

After losing a loved one, it's not uncommon for people to turn to medication or other addictive substances to blunt the pain. If you feel a need for medication to help you sleep or to calm your emotions, be sure to talk with your doctor first and discuss your concerns. If your doctor prescribes medication, take only as directed. Drugs have their place, but avoid becoming dependent on them. Especially avoid opioids, which are extremely addictive.

---

65 Psalm 142:1–3.

How Long Does It Take to Heal?

Although it's normal to wonder how long it will take before finding relief, there is no set timetable. The length of time depends largely on the circumstances of your loss. People sometimes speak of "the first year" as if it were some sort of milestone, but there is no timeline to indicate when you will start to feel better. Take heart in knowing that as weeks and months go by, grief will gradually lessen its hold. Speaking generally, six months to a year is typically needed for a person to feel back in control. However, some aspects of the grieving process may continue beyond the first year.

You may run into people who wonder why you are not "moving on" and who appear faintly irritated when you're not "better" when they think you should be. Some may feel you're being self-indulgent by "hanging on" to your unhappiness, but pay them no mind because there is no right way or wrong way to mourn. Grief is not a problem to be solved; it is a process to be lived. Healing doesn't come just because you've gone through the first year.

As you work to pull your life back together, support groups can be a great source of strength. Some people attend such groups for extended periods of time because of the warm support and empathy that fellow members provide. One widow who attended a support group for more than a year felt vaguely criticized when a friend, upon finding out she was still attending, asked in surprise, "Are you *still* going to that support group?"

The widow responded, "Well, my husband's still dead."

Be aware that healing from a traumatic death can take longer. Social worker Janice Harris Lord said, "Most research about anticipatory grieving and death following long illness or injury tells us that the expected recovery period ranges from two to four years, based on numerous variables. Research about sudden violent death tells us to expect a four- to seven-year recovery period, acknowledging that recovery is never complete."[66]

---

66 Janice Harris Lord, "America's Number One Killer: Vehicular Crashes," in Kenneth J. Doka, PhD, (Ed.), *Living with Grief After Sudden Loss* (Bristol: Hospice Foundation of America, Taylor & Francis, 1996), 36.

An important thing to know about the grieving process is that your sorrow will have its own timetable, and it usually does not follow a steady upward progression, although in general you should note an overall upward trend. Gradually you will begin having grief-free minutes, hours, and then days. In time, you will notice that you don't have painful bursts of grief as frequently, and when you do, they don't last as long. Take as long as you need, but don't get stuck. Remember that suffering does not make you noble and has no value in itself. When you are able, let the pain go.

Although the fabric of your life has been torn by the death of your beloved one, you *will* mend, and in time, you will be stronger than before. Turn to God, whose arms are always outstretched to you. Kneel in humble prayer to Heavenly Father, who is anxiously waiting to help. Pray for divine counsel to guide you during this difficult time. "But if ye will turn to the Lord with full purpose of heart, and put your trust in him, and serve him with all diligence of mind, if ye do this, he will, according to his own will and pleasure, deliver you out of bondage."[67]

Heavenly Father understands your anguish and can bless you with inspiration, provide much-needed personal revelation, and comfort your heart. In Psalms, we read, "Then they cried unto the Lord in their trouble, and he saved them out of their distresses. He brought them out of darkness and the shadow of death, and brake their bands in sunder. Oh that men would praise the Lord for his goodness, and for his wonderful works to the children of men!"[68]

The Goal of Recovery

The goal of recovery is to learn how to adjust in ways that will allow us to live a full life despite our loss. Life can go on, and we can find meaning in living. When embarking on this journey, we learn much about ourselves. We find out that what goes on *inside* of us matters more than what goes on *around* us. We can't always control what happens to us, but we can decide

67 Mosiah 7:33.
68 Psalm 107:13–15.

what we will do about it. We work to heal because we don't want to continue struggling—always teetering on the brink of tears, fearful of falling apart. The death of someone close to us can cause great suffering, but if we are patient and keep moving forward, we will see improvement, even if it comes only in small increments. You may never be the same person you once were, but you can work to incorporate the reality of your loss into a new life.

Grief is a process to be worked through. If we don't learn how to manage our grief, it will manage us. We may never fully get over our sorrow, but we can rise above it and learn lessons that we can't learn in any other way. It is our goal to become better, not bitter. We can decide what this separation will teach us. When separated for a time by death, we may choose to reevaluate our lives and ask ourselves, "What has losing my dear one taught me? What opportunities for growth has it brought my way? How am I different after this loss? Is there anything more I can learn from this experience?"

Recovery doesn't happen overnight. Sometimes our progress may seem so slight as to be imperceptible, but if we keep trying, we will progress. How does one move a mountain? One shovel-ful at a time. Recovery will come when we have processed our loss, are involved once again in life, and mostly have control over our emotions. There will be setbacks, but you will eventually feel capable of steering your way through them.

Recovery is not linear. The journey may be long, but it pays dividends in the end. Although life is never going to be the same, it will go on, and so can we. If we are willing to process our grief, there can be an end to acute sorrow. Healing doesn't mean we won't mourn anymore—we will just feel it less acutely. In our new life, we will learn to live in healthy, fully functioning ways. Recovery doesn't mean that we no longer miss those we love, for we will never forget them. We will always wish they were with us to share the joy of the day, but as we have patience with ourselves, we'll be able to enjoy a life that will be once again bright and full.

"Have patience, and bear with those afflictions, with a firm hope that ye shall one day rest from all your afflictions."[69]

---

69 Alma 34:41.

CHAPTER 5
LOSING A SPOUSE

The Lord is nigh unto them that are of a broken heart;
and saveth such as be of a contrite spirit. . . .
The Lord redeemeth the soul of his servants:
and none of them that trust in him shall be desolate.[70]

ADJUSTING TO LIFE WITHOUT YOUR spouse can be one of the hardest things you will ever do. The loss of a spouse is devastating on many fronts. Your partner is your confidant and best friend. Some people think of their spouse as their "better half," and to have this "half" of yourself taken away can leave you feeling incomplete, confused, and alone. Losing your mate is, in a way, like losing part of yourself. You can feel bewildered, frightened, and vulnerable when you no longer have a spouse to walk beside you and share your goals, dreams, and daily life. President Henry B. Eyring said:

> One of the great trials of life is losing to death a beloved husband or wife. President Hinckley described the hurt when Sister Hinckley was no longer at his side. The Lord knows the needs

---

70 Psalm 34:18, 22.

of those separated from loved ones by death. He saw the pain of widows and knew of their needs from His earthly experience. He asked a beloved Apostle, from the agony of the cross, to care for His widowed mother, who would now lose a son. He now feels the needs of husbands who lose their wives and the needs of wives who are left alone by death.[71]

It is of great comfort to know that even though temporarily parted, one day you can be with your beloved spouse again. After President Joseph Fielding Smith lost his young wife, Louie, he wrote:

> During this month which has been one of constant anxiety and worry for me, I have passed through trials and experiences of the deepest and most painful kind. And through it all I have depended on the Lord for strength and comfort. After suffering most excruciating pain for three or four weeks and after an illness covering a period of nearly two months my beloved wife was released from her suffering . . . and departed from me and our precious babies, for a better world, where we patiently and in sorrow await a meeting which shall be most glorious.[72]

In time, you can learn to move forward, keeping a heart full of hope for an eventual reunion. When the loss of the one you love is fresh, it can be difficult to focus on your blessings, but it helps

71 Henry B. Eyring, "Adversity," *Ensign*, May 2009, 25–26. churchofjesuschrist.org/study/ensign/2009/05/adversity?lang=eng
72 *Teachings of the Presidents of the Church: Joseph Fielding Smith* (Salt Lake City: The Church of Jesus Christ of Latter-day Saints, 2013), 14. churchofjesuschrist.org/study/manual/teachings-of-presidents-of-the-church-joseph-fielding-smith/the-life-and-ministry-of-joseph-fielding-smith?lang=eng

if you ponder them. Happy are those who, instead of asking why they had to lose their dear one, are thankful for the years they had together and rejoice to know they will be together again. Asking for a priesthood blessing invites the power of heaven into your life in tangible ways.

It will help if you are fortunate enough to have family and friends to support you. Still, you are the one who has to work through your grief. Be gentle with yourself during this most difficult of times and remember progress isn't always moving forward but can include simply maintaining your position. Continue to live and to love, and as you do, healing will come.

Becoming a Single Parent

If your companion dies when you still have children to raise, it can feel as though your world has crumbled into pieces and that you are caught in a nightmare from which you cannot awaken. After such a loss, your concern will center on your children, who need you now more than ever. Your children will look to you for guidance since they, too, are suffering. Talk to them about the loss and encourage them to communicate their feelings.

At this time, you will need to shoulder additional responsibility in making decisions about home rules, finances, curfews, college, and other issues. Children need a stable base if they are to thrive, so you will want to create a solid foundation of love and care, along with setting boundaries and consistently enforcing them. If you will put your hand in God's and pray for comfort and guidance, He will bless you with the strength to help your children even when you're feeling alone and frightened.

When in need, we are counseled, "Pray unto the Father with all the energy of heart."[73] By consistently approaching Heavenly Father in humble, sincere prayer, you will draw closer to Him and He will come nearer to you, providing much-needed comfort and counsel. You can obtain great blessings if you will pray sincerely and in faith, pleading with Heavenly Father to comfort and console you.

---

73 Moroni 7:48.

Be sure not to neglect your own needs. It is common for new widows and widowers to spend so much time focused on their children that they neglect to take care of themselves. However, your needs and issues will not go away simply because you ignore them. During airline flights, flight attendants tell parents that, in case of emergency, they are to put on their own oxygen mask first and then help their children put theirs on. This is because you cannot help others unless you first take care of yourself. Make time to work on healing, for it is only when you are feeling whole that you can truly be of help to your children. You will be working through your grief as your children work through theirs. It's all right for them to see your tears. If they ask what's wrong, tell them you miss their daddy or mommy. If your children want to comfort you, let them.

Adjusting to a New Life

After losing a spouse, you may feel numb, which is one way your mind insulates you from pain. Numbness temporarily anesthetizes you until you can begin to handle your loss. Coming to grips with the reality that your mate has died causes a shock to your body and your mind. In the beginning, it may be almost too overwhelming to think that you will no longer be able to talk to, hug, and share daily experiences with your loved one.

Allow yourself to feel the full measure of your grief and sadness. It's natural to mourn when you've shared years of good times and think about what could have been still ahead of you in the coming years. Feeling these emotions won't harm you, but it is best to move forward when you are ready. Be assured that healing will come, and you will gradually be able to leave the intense sorrow behind.

After your spouse passes away, you will take on new responsibilities. Often, it is only when losing a spouse that the surviving partner becomes fully aware of how dependent he or she was on the other. Tasks that were typically done by your spouse will now be your responsibility. It can take time to learn how to pay the bills online, spray for weeds, paint a fence, clean rain gutters, and change the ink cartridge in your printer. Instead of discussing things with your spouse, you will need to make decisions on your own. If you were dependent on your partner to arrange travel plans, you will need to learn how to make plane and hotel reservations. You'll have to decide if it's time to replace the furnace, who to have repair your sprinkler system, what to look for when purchasing a new cell phone, and other such things. The internet can be a great resource, but so can friends, neighbors, or family members. Don't be afraid to ask for advice and assistance. You're not alone—lots of people love and care about you and would be happy to help.

Added stressors that can accompany the loss of a partner may include significant financial changes, the need to move, and comforting your children even when you have few people to comfort you. Your social world may change. Widowers and widows sometimes note that when they lose their spouse, they also lose their circle of friends. While living as a couple, there is a tendency to make "couple friends," and they may find it awkward to include a newly "single" person. Often it will be necessary to reach out to others and make new friends.

Losing a spouse also means the shape of your day will change. You will miss sharing the inconsequential things that happen during the day. The weeks and months after your spouse's death can be difficult in unexpected ways, so be kind to yourself and do what you can to comfort yourself and move forward. Life will go on with all its small and large beauties, and so will you.

Lifestyle Changes

After your spouse dies, your lifestyle will change. The once common and ordinary acts of eating a meal or going to bed can create a longing for life the way it used to be. Daily tasks and simple everyday chores of washing clothes, mopping the floor, and preparing meals can seem challenging. Then there are more complicated tasks of buying a new computer or laptop, hiring someone to reroof your house, and signing up for Medicare and supplemental insurance. These tasks are why it's vital to have a support system in place to help you adjust to new changes. Some people strive to be fully independent, but as John Donne said, "No man is an island."[74] Everyone needs help at times.

One of the things you may want to do after losing your spouse is find a good financial advisor. Some people hesitate to spend money on a consultant, but in the end, a good advisor will save you money by evaluating your budget, insurance needs, and investment plans, advise you about how to save on taxes, and help you with your retirement plans. Your assets will grow, rather than diminish. A good financial advisor can look at your financial resources, help formulate goals, and come up with a plan to achieve them. You can find a good financial consultant by asking friends, relatives, and colleagues to recommend someone they know and trust.

Graciously accept assistance during this time of emotional strain and be grateful for those willing to support you and lighten your load. Developing a support network will serve to ground you and relieve your worries. Cultivate friends with whom you can talk about your feelings regarding the death of your spouse. Expressing your feelings will help you process your grief and make life easier to manage. Remember, you can face just about anything with the loving support of others.

Ponder the Blessings of Jesus Christ's Atonement

To help us rise above our sorrow, we can ponder the blessings of the Atonement of Jesus Christ. Our Savior broke the bands of death, making it possible for us to be with those we love again. Knowing this fills us with thankfulness and a desire to praise Christ for His goodness and mercy and loving kindness forever and ever.[75] President Ezra T. Benson said:

> Sadness comes to all of us in the loss of loved ones. But there is gratitude also. Gratitude for the assurance we have that life is eternal. Gratitude for the great gospel plan, given freely to

---

74 John Donne, "No Man Is an Island," PoemHunter. poemhunter.com/poem/no-man-is-an-island/

75 See D&C 133:52.

all of us. Gratitude for the life, teachings, and sacrifice of the Lord Jesus Christ.[76]

Speaking of how Jesus Christ's Atonement blesses our lives, President Dallin H. Oaks said:

> Our Savior's Atonement does more than assure us of immortality by a universal resurrection and give us the opportunity to be cleansed from sin by repentance and baptism. His Atonement also provides the opportunity to call upon Him who has experienced all of our mortal infirmities to give us the strength to bear the burdens of mortality. He knows of our anguish, and He is there for us. Like the good Samaritan, when He finds us wounded at the wayside, He will bind up our wounds and care for us.[77]

Even when we are filled to the brim with suffering, we can be filled with gratitude for Jesus Christ and His love for us, which brought to pass His great atoning sacrifice. In regard to the pain we feel at being parted from our loved ones, President Gordon B. Hinckley shared this poignant plea:

> Lord, when we walk in the valley of the shadow of death, give us faith to smile through our tears, knowing that it is all part of the eternal plan of a loving Father, that as we cross the threshold from this life we enter another more glorious, and that through the atonement of the Son of God all

---

76 Ezra Taft Benson, "Life Is Eternal," *Ensign*, June 1971, 33. churchofjesuschrist.org/study/ensign/1971/06/life-is-eternal?lang=eng
77 Dallin H. Oaks, "Strengthened by the Atonement of Jesus Christ," *Ensign*, November 2015, 64. churchofjesuschrist.org/study/ensign/2015/11/saturday -afternoon-session/strengthened-by-the-atonement-of-jesus-christ?lang=eng

shall rise from the grave and the faithful shall go on to exaltation. Give us faith to pursue the work of redemption of the dead that Thine eternal purposes may be fulfilled in behalf of Thy sons and daughters of all generations. Father, grant us faith to follow counsel in the little things that can mean so very much. . . . Lord, increase our faith in one another, and in ourselves, and in our capacity to do good and great things.[78]

Dealing with Loneliness

Loneliness is one of the top mental health issues for people who lose their partners. You will be reminded of your loss every time you cook a meal and eat it alone and every time you tidy up the house, knowing that no one is there to appreciate it. Loneliness can descend when you want to talk to your deceased partner about everyday matters, whenever you have to make an important decision, and when you must attend social functions by yourself.

However, it is possible to rise above loneliness by making an effort to be with people. This is not always easy. When feeling down, it may be easier to crawl into a hole and languish there, but refuse to succumb to such detrimental actions. Go out and join the world without waiting to be invited. Seek to make and maintain friendships by actively reaching out to others. Initiate conversation at church, school concerts, social events, and the grocery store. Listen to what others have to say—they may be feeling as lonely as you. Establish a network of friends and plan activities with them. This will take determination and effort, but you can do it. Do your best to be cheerful and positive. Everyone enjoys the company of people who are happy and optimistic.

There are a number of other ways to alleviate loneliness. You can plan a dinner for friends, invite someone to attend a concert with you, sign up for an exercise class, or take an adult education

---

78 Gordon B. Hinckley, "Lord, Increase Our Faith," *Ensign*, November 1987, 53–54. churchofjesuschrist.org/study/ensign/1987/11/lord -increase-our-faith?lang=eng

class. Get involved in your ward or stake single adult group activities. Many people counter their loneliness by getting a pet. Animals can be a great comfort by reducing feelings of isolation while fulfilling fundamental needs such as love, security, and solace. Attend the temple and consider serving there as a volunteer. Serve a full or part-time Church mission. You might want to find something creative to do, something that brings you joy. After Camilla Kimball (Spencer W. Kimball), Amelia McConkie (Bruce R. McConkie), and Helen Richards (Franklin D. Richards) lost their husbands, they all learned to paint, something that sparked a special interest and brought each of them great joy.

The Gospel Gives Hope for a Brighter Tomorrow

Despite the darkness of life without your spouse, the gospel provides comfort and hope for the future. President Thomas S. Monson spoke of his sorrow after losing his wife, Frances. "Her loss has been profound. . . . She was the love of my life, my trusted confidant, and my closest friend. To say that I miss her does not begin to convey the depth of my feelings." He then spoke of the peace the gospel brought to him.

> Of utmost comfort to me during this tender time of parting have been my testimony of the gospel of Jesus Christ and the knowledge I have that my dear Frances lives still. I know that our separation is temporary. We were sealed in the house of God by one having authority to bind on earth and in heaven. I know that we will be reunited one day and will never again be separated. This is the knowledge that sustains me.[79]

Although you miss your spouse, you can rejoice in knowing that you will be reunited with your spouse and will never again be separated. Elder Richard G. Scott spoke of this when he lost his wife:

79 Thomas S. Monson, "I Will Not Fail Thee, nor Forsake Thee," *Ensign*, November 2013, 85. churchofjesuschrist.org/study/ensign/2013/11/sunday -morning-session/i-will-not-fail-thee-nor-forsake-thee?lang=eng

Fourteen years ago the Lord decided it was not necessary for my wife to live any longer on the earth, and He took her to the other side of the veil. I confess that there are times when it is difficult not to be able to turn and talk to her, but I do not complain. The Lord has allowed me, at important moments in my life, to feel her influence through the veil. . . . I know that I will have the privilege of being with that beautiful wife, whom I love with all my heart, and with those children who are with her on the other side of the veil because of the ordinances that are performed in the temple. What a blessing to have once again on the earth the sealing authority, not only for this mortal life but for the eternities. I am grateful that the Lord has restored His gospel in its fulness, including the ordinances that are required for us to be happy in the world and to live everlastingly happy lives in the hereafter.[80]

---

80 Richard G. Scott, "Temple Worship: The Source of Strength and Power in Times of Need," *Ensign*, May 2009, 45. churchofjesuschrist.org/study/ensign/2009/05/temple-worship-the-source-of-strength-and-power-in-times-of-need?lang=eng

CHAPTER 6
LOSING A CHILD

Little children are alive in Christ,
even from the foundation of the world.[81]

THE DEATH OF A YOUNG child is perhaps the ultimate loss for a
parent to endure. Nothing can come close to the indescribable
pain one experiences at a child's death or the hopelessness that
follows. Those who experience such a loss embark on a lifelong
healing process. Every time you wake and remember, pain shoots
through your heart as you wonder how your child can be gone
and how you can still be here, when in the natural course of life,
you would have been the first to go.

In 1898, President Joseph F. Smith lost his little daughter,
Ruth. Although he had prayed earnestly for her recovery, it was
not to be. President Smith said:

> But O, our prayers did not avail! At last I took
> her in my arms and walked the floor with her
> and helplessly, powerless to aid my darling, dying
> child, I watched her feeble breath depart to come
> no more in time, and her glorious intelligence, her
> bright angelic spirit took her flight to God from

81 Moroni 8:12.

whence she came. . . . With her was swept away all our fond hope and love and joy of earth. Oh! how I loved that child! She was intelligent beyond her years; bright, loving, choice and joyous! But she is gone. . . . O my soul! . . . My darling little petling [is] in her own bright home with those of her brothers and sisters who had preceded her. How blessed, how happy is she! How sorrowful are we!82

Knowing your separation is only temporary and that one day you can be with your beloved child again can bring a measure of comfort. President Wilford Woodruff spoke of this after Brother and Sister Wheeler lost two of their young sons:

I pray my Heavenly Father that he will bless Brother and Sister Wheeler [after losing their four-year-old and six-year-old] in their bereavement, and give them his Holy Spirit, that, when they lie down at night and rise in the morning and miss their children, they may feel to commit themselves into the hands of the Lord, and realize that their separation from their little ones is not for ever, but that in a little time they will be restored to them. This applies to us all in the loss of our children. We lay them away in the grave, but they will come forth in the morning of the resurrection, and if we are faithful to the truth, we shall receive them and rejoice with them.83

A Word about Miscarriage and SIDS

Statistics regarding pregnancy and infant loss state, "Almost one in four pregnancies end in miscarriage and one in 160

82 Joseph Fielding Smith, ed., *The Life of Joseph F. Smith* (Salt Lake City: Deseret News Press, 1938), 463. Used with permission.
83 *Teachings of the Presidents of the Church: Wilford Woodruff*, 86. churchofjesuschrist.org/study/manual/teachings-wilford-woodruff/chapter-8?lang=eng

pregnancies end in stillbirth—23,385 babies annually. Another 4,084 are lost to prematurity and 1,568 are lost to Sudden Infant Death Syndrome (SIDS)."[84]

When a miscarriage occurs, a mother- or father-to-be often feels tremendous grief. This pain may not be fully understood by family and friends, who may think that because the death occurred before birth—and that you never really "knew" the baby—the loss is of no great significance, but this is rarely the case. Losing an unborn child causes great pain.

Carroll and Brent Haddock were looking forward to the birth of their fourth child when, in March of 1976, Carroll began having cramps and developed a fever. It was a frightening time, for Caroll was only four-and-a-half months pregnant. Then she was visited by Aaron, the son she was carrying. Carroll relates:

> I felt this child's presence so strongly. I was doing the dishes when he walked up to my left side and put his right arm around my shoulders and squeezed my right shoulder. He was so close that I felt his shoulder by the top of my head.
>
> I heard him clearly say, "Mama, I'm okay. I am okay."
>
> I answered back, "I know, son. I know."

The next day, Carroll's condition worsened, and she was admitted to the hospital with an infection that caused her temperature to climb as high as 107. When Brent and Carroll's branch president, Arthur Jackson, came to the hospital, Carroll told him the baby was a boy and that everything that was happening had been planned before she had come to Earth. President Jackson gave her a priesthood blessing and in it pronounced, "Your son has been called home on high for a reason that you will not now understand."

Carroll underwent surgery, and the doctors told her the fetus had been a perfectly formed boy. During the next few days, Carroll

---

84 Holly Richardson, "There are ways to get through the grief of a miscarriage," *The Salt Lake Tribune*, October 5, 2019, A11.

suffered great pain from the infection and swelling in her hands and arms from the IV, which had to be painfully repositioned every few hours. One afternoon, feeling extremely weak and discouraged, Carroll began to weep. Suddenly she felt a soft hand on her shoulder and heard a woman say, "It's okay. It's okay." Carroll said that the sense of this woman's love calmed her soul. Sometime later, Carroll wrote about the loss of her unborn son in her journal:

> During my pregnancy, the paramount thing to me was that this child, this son of ours, would be granted mortality, however brief that might be. I wanted this phase of his progression to be accomplished according to the Lord's plan. I never felt anything but peace through all this, and I *know all* of this was according to our Heavenly Father's will. . . . Our son tasted mortality and was called on to celestial life, of this I have absolutely NO doubt. This son has a great calling and is now fulfilling his duties according to his Father's will. I feel humble and blessed to have been called as his mother. He is our son for all eternity and is now with our Heavenly Father. All is well.[85]

SIDS—sudden infant death syndrome, also known as crib death—occurs after a child is born. This type of death is particularly heartbreaking because there are no warning signs. One minute the baby is healthy, and the next the baby is gone. The shock and disbelief are enormous. Parents may search for an answer, but doctors are usually unable to find one. Afterward, parents must face the daunting task of putting away infant clothes, toys, and other belongings. Grieving the loss of a child or unborn child is a heart-wrenching process, and patience is essential. Don't try to rush through the grieving process. Take as much time as necessary. Everyone heals in different ways and at a different pace, and while you may never fully get over the death, you can find ways to survive it.

---

85 Carroll Haddock, personal experience shared with Marlene Bateman via email, interview, and journal entry. Used with permission.

Losing a Child Changes Your Life

In the first weeks, months, and years after suffering a loss of a child, pain is often raw, and there seems to be no way of escaping it. At times, life may seem to hold little or no meaning simply because your son or daughter—your reason for being—is now gone. You may hear your child's voice in your head and ache to reach out and touch him or her. Some parents lose interest in their personal appearance and in the world around them. It's common for the bereaved to neglect their health by failing to eat properly or get enough sleep or exercise. At times, sorrow can become physical and manifest itself in headaches, panic attacks, and stomach pains.

You will need time—lots of it—to get back on your feet. Try to move forward, no matter how small the steps you take, and be patient with yourself and others. Don't feel guilty about what you can or can't do. You will find there can still be some sweet moments—the arrival of a bouquet of flowers from a neighbor, the beauty of a sunset, a visit from a friend. As time passes, you will slowly be able to move beyond the acute pain. Yes, there will still be days when your heart will break in half, but you will manage. Take solace in the words of the Prophet Joseph Smith, who stated:

> All children are redeemed by the blood of Jesus Christ, and the moment that children leave this world, they are taken to the bosom of Abraham. The only difference between the old and young dying is, one lives longer in heaven [the spirit world] and eternal light and glory than the other, and is freed a little sooner from this miserable wicked world. Notwithstanding all this glory, we for a moment lose sight of it, and mourn the loss, but we do not mourn as those without hope.[86]

Grief at the loss of a child can be overwhelming. Although death comes to all, when death hushes the laughter of your

86 Joseph Fielding Smith, ed., *Teachings of the Prophet Joseph Smith* (Salt Lake City: Deseret Book, 1976), 197. Used with permission. scriptures.byu.edu/tpjs/STPJS.pdf

child, it can change you in profound ways. After the loss of his firstborn son, Hyrum, President Joseph F. Smith wrote, "I am speechless—[numb] with grief! . . . My heart is broken; . . . O! I loved him! . . . I will love him forever more. . . . O! God help me!" After another son, Albert Jesse, died, President Smith wrote and told his sister, Martha Ann, that he had prayed that his son would be allowed to live. Instead, little Albert died. In his sorrow, President Smith cried out, "Why is it so? O God why had it to be?"[87]

After your loss, you may not be able to bring yourself to even think about celebrating special events. Family rituals you cherished in the past that marked holidays or other occasions now become difficult events to survive rather than times to rejoice. Your child's birthday is no longer a day of joy and happiness but a time of sad remembrance. You might want to gather as a family or extended family at the gravesite on your child's birthday. Bring balloons in your child's favorite color to release and float toward heaven. Bring permanent markers for family members to write a special message on their balloon. Another idea is to give gifts in the name of your child to a hospital or to needy children at Christmas or on your child's birthday.

After the death of a child, relationships with your spouse, parents, and surviving children can undergo changes. Such an emotionally wrenching experience can place stress on a marriage. Staying close—even in grief—can be the lifeline each needs so desperately. Each partner can offer support and understanding for the other by actively working to keep the relationship strong. A child's legacy should not be the destruction of his or her parents' relationship. It is a tribute to the child you both love to work on your relationship. Make a list of things you both like to do and start doing them. Seeing a marriage counselor can often help couples navigate through this difficult time.

Do your best to maintain and preserve your marriage. You may not be the same person you were before your loss, but

---

87 As quoted in M. Russell Ballard, "The Vision of the Redemption of the Dead," *Ensign*, November 2018, 72. churchofjesuschrist.org/study/ensign/2018/11/sunday-morning-session/the-vision-of-the-redemption-of-the-dead?lang=eng

husbands and wives need the strength and support that come from a loving relationship. Organized support groups are a tremendously helpful resource. Meeting with other parents who have experienced the same loss can be validating and gives you permission to experience the full range of your emotions without feeling censured by others.

It's not uncommon for bereaved parents to want to know more about death and the next life, seeking reassurance that their beloved child is happy and thriving. It's comforting to read personal accounts of the spirit world being a place of beauty, peace, and joy. When eleven-year-old Mitchell Dalton returned to his body after having died for a short time, the account states, "He opened his eyes and said, 'Oh, Papa and Mama, why did you call me back. I have been to such a beautiful place.'"[88]

When Ella Jensen was critically ill from scarlet fever, she visited the spirit world, returning to mortality after a blessing from President Lorenzo Snow. Ella told her aunt Harriet Wight about her experience in the spirit world. Having lost two young daughters, Harriet was deeply touched and began to cry. Ella told her, "Why, Aunt Harriet, what are you crying for. You need not cry for your girls who have gone. I saw and talked with them, and they are very happy where they are."[89]

Children Will Not Be Denied Any Blessings

Part of mourning the loss of a child involves feeling regret for all the special occasions that are lost—going to prom, graduating from high school, getting married, and having children. For your lost child, there will be no first day of school, no swimming lessons, no dating, and no attending college. It's natural to mourn what might have been. Elder Quentin L. Cook spoke about this, saying:

> A unique challenge for those who have lost loved
> ones is to avoid dwelling on the lost opportunities

---

88 Joseph Heinerman, *Spirit World Manifestations* (Salt Lake City: Magazine Printing and Publishing, 1978), 118.
89 Marlene Bateman Sullivan, *Gaze into Heaven: Near-Death Experiences in Early Church History* (Springville: Cedar Fort, 2013), 170.

in this life. Often those who die early have demonstrated significant capabilities, interests, and talents. With our limited understanding, we lament the things that will not be accomplished. . . . The lost opportunity might relate to family, occupation, talents, experiences, or others. . . . But when we look through the wide and clear lens of the gospel instead of the limited lens of mere mortal existence, we know of the great eternal reward promised by a loving Father in His plan.[90]

Heavenly Father's plan of happiness reassures grieving parents that their child will have the privilege of courtship, marriage, bearing children, and receiving all blessings which they may have obtained had they remained on Earth. President Melvin J. Ballard spoke of this:

You mothers worry about your little children [who have died]. We do not perform sealings for them. I lost a son six years of age, and I saw him a man in the spirit world after his death, and I saw how he had exercised his own freedom of choice and would obtain of his own will and volition a companionship, and in due time to him, and all those who are worthy of it, shall come all of the blessings and sealing privileges of the house of the Lord. Do not worry over it. They are safe; they are all right. Now, then, what of your daughters who have died and have not been sealed to some man? . . . The sealing power shall be forever and ever with this Church, and provisions will be made for them. We cannot run faster than the Lord has provided the way.

90 Quentin L. Cook, "The Songs They Could Not Sing," *Ensign*, November 2011, 106–7. churchofjesuschrist.org/study/ensign/2011/11/sunday-afternoon-session/the-songs-they-could-not-sing?lang=eng

Their blessings and privileges will come to them in due time. In the meantime, they are safe.[91]

President Joseph Fielding Smith bore strong testimony that infants and children will not lose any blessing by dying at a young age:

> The Lord is just and will not deprive any person of a blessing, simply because he dies before that blessing can be received. *It would be manifestly unfair to deprive a little child of the privilege of receiving all the blessings of exaltation in the world to come simply because it died in infancy.* The same thing is true of the young men who were deprived of these blessings and laid down their lives during the war. The Lord judges every soul by the intent of the heart. . . . Children who die in childhood will not be deprived of any blessing. When they grow, after the resurrection, to the full maturity of the spirit, *they will be entitled to all the blessings which they would have been entitled to had they been privileged to tarry here and receive them.*[92]

Why Do Some Children Die Young?

Speaking at the funeral of his infant granddaughter, Elder Bruce R. McConkie talked about why some children may be taken at a tender age:

> There are certain spirits who come into this life only to receive bodies; for reasons that we do not

---

91 Bryant S. Hinckley, *Sermons and Missionary Services of Melvin J. Ballard* (Salt Lake City: Deseret Book Company, 1949), 260. familysearch.org/library/books/records/item/20024-sermons-and-missionary-services-of-melvin-joseph-ballard?viewer=1&offset=0#page=263&viewer=picture&o=info&n=0&q=

92 Bruce R. McConkie, ed., *Doctrines of Salvation: Sermons and Writings of Joseph Fielding Smith*, vol. 2 (Salt Lake City: Bookcraft, 1955), 54.

know, but which are known in the infinite wisdom of the Eternal Father, they do not need the testing, probationary experiences of mortality. We come here for two great reasons—the first, to get a body; the second, to be tried, examined, schooled, and tested under mortal circumstances, to take a different type of probationary test than we underwent in the premortal life. There are some of the children of our Father, however, who come to Earth to get a body—for that reason solely. They do not need the testings of this mortality.[93]

When Bryan's first child, Holland, turned three, Bryan and his wife were expecting another baby "when doctors discovered a tumor the size of a golf ball in [Holland's] brain." Bryan wondered why this was happening and thought, "We're good people. We've done everything God's asked us to do and yet this is still happening. I tried to pray. I tried reading the scriptures. I tried doing all these things to try to find peace and I couldn't." Finally, through earnest prayer, Bryan received a comforting assurance that his daughter would survive. The doctors removed the tumor, but it returned. Another surgery was performed, but the tumor grew back, running along Holland's spine. As Bryan prayed, the Lord told him that his daughter was going to die.

Dismayed, Bryan asked why God had allowed him to think for over a year that Holland would be all right. Gently, Heavenly Father revealed that if He had told Bryan in the beginning that his daughter was going to die, Bryan would have started to grieve too soon. Bryan and his wife lay on either side of their daughter in her hospital bed as she passed away. Bryan said, "That was the worst feeling I've ever had in my life. I felt hopeless. I felt angry toward

93 Bruce R. McConkie, as quoted in Robert L. Millet, "Alive in Christ: The Salvation of Little Children," in Monte S. Nyman and Charles D. Tate Jr., eds. *The Book of Mormon: Fourth Nephi, From Zion to Destruction* (Provo, UT: Religious Studies Center, Brigham Young University, 1995), 1–17. rsc.byu.edu/archived/book-mormon-fourth-nephi-through-moroni-zion-destruction/1-alive-christ-salvation-little

God." Over time, as he worked through his grief, Bryan said he came to understand that God was a true friend during this painful time. "A friend is there for you when nobody else can be and He [God] was there for me and my family. . . . Nobody else could understand the pain and the grief and the sorrow that we felt."[94]

It is natural to struggle to understand why a sweet child is taken at a young age. However, it can be helpful to consider Nephi's response when an angel asked him a question to which he had no answer—"Knowest thou the condescension of God?" Nephi did not know but replied humbly, "I know that he loveth his children; nevertheless, I do not know the meaning of all things."[95] If we can be humble like Nephi, we can acknowledge that while we do not know all the reasons behind the loss of a child, we do know that God loves us. President Wilford Woodruff said:

> The question may arise with me and with you— "Why has the Lord taken away my children?" But that is not for me to tell, because I do not know; it is in the hands of the Lord, and it has been so from the creation of the world all the way down. Children are taken away in their infancy, and they go to the spirit world. They come here and fulfil the object of their coming, that is, they tabernacle in the flesh. . . . Our children will be restored to us as they are laid down if we, their parents, keep the faith and prove ourselves worthy to obtain eternal life; and if we do not so prove ourselves our children will still be preserved, and will inherit celestial glory.[96]

94 "Finding Hope After Losing a Child," *YouTube*, uploaded by The Church of Jesus Christ of Latter-day Saints, December 21, 2017. youtube.com/watch?v=gCH_s7BB3fs&t=368s; "Line Upon Line," *Meridian Magazine*, latterdaysaintmag.com/video-finding-hope-after-losing-a-child/
95 1 Nephi 11:16–17.
96 *Teachings of the Presidents of the Church: Wilford Woodruff*, 84–85. churchofjesuschrist.org/study/manual/teachings-wilford-woodruff/chapter-8?lang=eng

Church doctrine tells us God created this earth so His children could gain a physical body and have opportunities to grow spiritually. Elder Bruce R. McConkie explains that children who die young are pure, while most of us need further trials and testing so we can learn, grow, and develop.

> We may rest assured that all things are controlled and governed by Him whose spirit children we are. He knows the end from the beginning, and he provides for each of us the testings and trials which he knows we need. President Joseph Fielding Smith once told me that we must assume that the Lord knows and arranges beforehand who shall be taken in infancy and who shall remain on earth to undergo whatever tests are needed in their cases. . . . It is implicit in the whole scheme of things that those of us who have arrived at the years of accountability need the tests and trials to which we are subject and that our problem is to overcome the world and attain that spotless and pure state which little children already possess.[97]

Children Are Saved in the Celestial Kingdom

After receiving a glorious vision, President Joseph F. Smith declared, "And I also beheld that all children who die before they arrive at the years of accountability are saved in the celestial kingdom of heaven."[98] Abinadi also testified of this, saying, "Little children also have eternal life."[99] When Elder Bruce R. McConkie was asked if children are saved in the celestial kingdom, he stated:

---

97 Bruce R. McConkie, "The Salvation of Little Children," *Ensign*, April 1977, 6. churchofjesuschrist.org/study/ensign/1977/04/the-salvation-of -little-children?lang=eng
98 D&C 137:10.
99 Mosiah 15:25.

To this question the answer is a thunderous *yes,* which echoes and re-echoes from one end of heaven to the other. Jesus taught it to his disciples. Mormon said it over and over again. Many of the prophets have spoken about it, and it is implicit in the whole plan of salvation. If it were not so the redemption would not be infinite in its application.[100]

In August 1839, President Wilford Woodruff was called to serve a mission in the British Isles, leaving behind his wife, Phoebe, and his only child, one-year-old Sarah Emma. The following year, while still in Great Britain, he learned of his daughter's death. His wife wrote him:

> My dear Wilford, what will be your feelings when I say that yesterday I was called to witness the departure of our little Sarah Emma from this world? Yes, she is gone. . . . The Lord hath taken her home to Himself for some wise purpose. It is a trial to me, but the Lord hath stood by me in a wonderful manner. I can see and feel that He has taken her home and will take better care of her than I possibly could for a little while until I shall go and meet her. [101]

Little Children Are Redeemed by Christ

The scriptures tell us that children who die before the years of accountability are redeemed by our Savior and will be saved in celestial glory through His sacrifice. "Little children are whole, for they are not capable of committing sin. . . . Little children are alive in Christ, even from the foundation of the world."[102]

100 Bruce R. McConkie, "The Salvation of Little Children," *Ensign,* April 1977, 4. churchofjesuschrist.org/study/ensign/1977/04/the-salvation-of-little-children?lang=eng

101 *Teachings of the Presidents of the Church: Wilford Woodruff,* 79. churchofjesuschrist.org/study/manual/teachings-wilford-woodruff/chapter-8?lang=eng

102 Moroni 8:8, 12. (See also D&C 74:7; Mosiah 3:16; Moroni 8:11–22; and D&C 29:46–47.)

Because children are not accountable for sins, they do not fall spiritually and do not need to be redeemed. They are said to be alive in Christ because He saves them through His Atonement: "Little children are redeemed from the foundation of the world through mine Only Begotten."[103] Although the pain of losing your precious child can feel too great to bear, take solace in knowing your child is safe and alive in Christ. Elder Bruce R. McConkie offers the following words of comfort:

> Among all the glorious gospel verities given of God to his people there is scarcely a doctrine so sweet, so soul satisfying, and so soul sanctifying, as the one which proclaims—*Little children shall be saved. They are alive in Christ and shall have eternal life. For them the family unit will continue, and the fulness of exaltation is theirs. No blessing shall be withheld. They shall rise in immortal glory, grow to full maturity, and live forever in the highest heaven of the celestial kingdom*—all through the merits and mercy and grace of the Holy Messiah, all because of the atoning sacrifice of Him who died that we might live.[104]

Parents Can Be Reunited with Their Children

Although the repercussion of your child's death will echo forever in your life and the life of your spouse, it is good to remember that family ties can endure beyond the grave. Ordinances and covenants performed in temples can enable worthy family members to be sealed together for eternity. President Joseph F. Smith was comforted to know that one day he would be reunited with his children:

> I take consolation in the fact that I shall meet my children who have passed behind the veil;

---

103 D&C 29:46.

104 McConkie, "The Salvation of Little Children," 3. churchofjesuschrist.org/study/ensign/1977/04/the-salvation-of-little-children?lang=eng

I have lost a number, and I have felt all that a
parent can feel, I think, in the loss of my children. I have felt it keenly, for I love children, and
I am particularly fond of the little ones, but I
feel thankful to God for the knowledge of these
principles, because now I have every confidence
in his word and in his promise that I will possess
in the future all that belongs to me, and my joy
will be full.[105]

Elder Richard G. Scott and his wife, Jeanene, found great solace in their temple sealing after their third child, a daughter, died
shortly after birth. Six weeks after this death, their second child, a
son, had surgery to repair a heart defect. After the operation, the
surgeon told the worried parents the surgery had been a success.
But he returned a short time later and told them their little boy
had died. Elder Scott said of this experience:

Later, during the night, I embraced my wife and
said to her, "We do not need to worry, because
our children were born in the covenant. We have
the assurance that we will have them with us in
the future. Now we have a reason to live extremely well. We have a son and a daughter who have
qualified to go to the celestial kingdom because
they died before the age of eight." That knowledge has given us great comfort. We rejoice in
the knowledge that all seven of our children are
sealed to us for time and all eternity.
    That trial has not been a problem for either
of us because, when we live righteously and have
received the ordinances of the temple, everything
else is in the hands of the Lord. We can do the

105 Joseph F. Smith, *Gospel Doctrine: Sermons and Writings of President Joseph
F. Smith* (Salt Lake City: Deseret Book, 1939), 454. archive.org/details/
gospeldoctrine009956mbp/page/n473

best we can, but the final outcome is up to Him. We should never complain, when we are living worthily, about what happens in our lives.[106]

Parents Will Raise Their Children in the Resurrection

There can be no more comforting doctrine to grieving parents than to know they will be reunited with their departed child and have the opportunity to raise them in the Resurrection. Children who die will come forth in the First Resurrection as children. President Joseph F. Smith said:

> Joseph Smith taught the doctrine that the infant child that was laid away in death would come up in the resurrection as a child; and, pointing to the mother of a lifeless child, he said to her, "You will have the joy, the pleasure and satisfaction of nurturing this child, after its resurrection, until it reaches the full stature of its spirit." There is restitution, there is growth, there is development, after the resurrection from death. I love this truth. It speaks volumes of happiness, of joy and gratitude to my soul. Thank the Lord he has revealed these principles to us.[107]

The Prophet Joseph Smith further stated: "They [children] must rise just as they died; we can there hail our lovely infants with the same glory—the same loveliness in the celestial glory, where they all enjoy alike."[108]

---

106 Richard G. Scott, "Temple Worship: The Source of Strength and Power in Times of Need," *Ensign*, May 2009, 45. churchofjesuschrist.org/study/ensign/2009/05/temple-worship-the-source-of-strength-and-power-in-times-of-need?lang=eng

107 Joseph F. Smith, "Status of Children in the Resurrection," *Improvement Era*, May 1918, 571. archive.org/details/improvementera2107unse/page/570

108 Joseph Smith, in *History of the Church of Jesus Christ of Latter-day Saints* (Salt Lake City: Deseret News, 1950), 6:366. Used with permission. byustudies.byu.edu/content/volume-6-chapter-17

President Joseph F. Smith taught more about this doctrine, relating what the Prophet Joseph Smith said at the funeral of his niece, Sophronia:

> In 1854, I met with my aunt [Agnes Smith], . . . who was the mother of that little girl [Sophronia] that Joseph Smith, the Prophet, was speaking about, when he told the mother that she should have the joy, the pleasure, and the satisfaction of rearing that child, after the resurrection, until it reached the full stature of its spirit; and that it would be a far greater joy than she could possibly have in mortality, because she would be free from the sorrow and fear and disabilities of mortal life, and she would know more than she could know in this life. I met that widow, the mother of that child, and she told me this circumstance and bore testimony to me that this was what the Prophet Joseph Smith said when he was speaking at the funeral of her little daughter.[109]

The Prophet Joseph Smith gave grieving parents hope when he told the Saints in Nauvoo:

> A question may be asked—"Will mothers have their children in eternity?" Yes! Yes! Mothers, you shall have your children; for they shall have eternal life. . . . As the child dies, so shall it rise from the dead, and be for ever living in the learning of God. . . . It will still be the child, in the same precise form [when it rises] as it appeared before it died out of its mother's arms, but possessing all the intelligence of a God. Children dwell in the mansions of glory and exercise power, but appear in the same form as when on earth. Eternity is

109 Smith, "Status of Children in the Resurrection," in *Improvement Era*, May 1918, 571. archive.org/details/improvementera2107unse/page/570

full of thrones, upon which dwell thousands of
children, reigning on thrones of glory, with not
one cubit added to their stature.[110]

Parents may wonder if their departed children will remain
children in the spirit world or if they will assume an adult-
sized body. President Joseph F. Smith relates an experience that
occurred to Bishop Hunter after his young son died. When the
son visited Bishop Hunter, he appeared as a full-grown man,
which perplexed his father. President Smith said:

> Bishop Hunter did not understand it. He went
> to my father [Hyrum Smith] and said: "Hyrum,
> what does that mean? I buried my son when he
> was only a little boy, but he has come to me as
> a full-grown man—a noble, glorious, young
> man, and declared himself my son. What does it
> mean?" Father [Hyrum Smith] told him that the
> Spirit of Jesus Christ was full-grown before he was
> born into the world; and so our children were full-
> grown and possessed their full stature in the Spirit,
> before they entered mortality, the same stature
> that they will possess after they have passed away
> from mortality, and as they will also appear after
> the resurrection, when they shall have completed
> their mission. Joseph Smith taught the doctrine
> that the infant child that was laid away in death
> would come up in the resurrection as a child.

Speaking more on this subject, President Joseph F. Smith said:

> The spirits of our children are immortal before
> they come to us, and their spirits, after bodily

---

110 Joseph Smith, in *History of the Church of Jesus Christ of Latter-day
Saints* (Salt Lake City: Deseret News, 1950), 6:316. Used with permission.
byustudies.byu.edu/content/volume-6-chapter-14

death, are like they were before they came. They are as they would have appeared if they had lived in the flesh, to grow to maturity, or to develop their physical bodies to the full stature of their spirits. If you see one of your children that has passed away it may appear to you in the form in which you would recognize it, the form of childhood; but if it came to you as a messenger bearing some important truth, it would perhaps come as the spirit of Bishop Edward Hunter's son (who died when a little child) came to him, in the stature of full-grown manhood, and revealed himself to his father, and said: "I am your son."[111]

---

111 Smith, *Gospel Doctrine*, 455. archive.org/details/gospeldoctrine009956mbp /page/n473

CHAPTER 7
SUICIDE

My soul melteth for heaviness:
strengthen thou me according unto thy word. . . .
Wait on the Lord: be of good courage, and he shall strengthen
thine heart: wait, I say, on the Lord.[112]

SUICIDE IS ONE OF THE most devastating types of loss. If someone you love dies by suicide, you will face a variety of painful emotions—shock, confusion, guilt, rejection, and anger. Suicide is usually seen as avoidable, and because of that, family and friends may feel they are at fault in some way for not thwarting the death. Survivors may ask themselves, "How did I miss the warning signs?" "Why didn't he tell me how badly he was feeling?" "Why didn't I receive an inspired prompting so I could have prevented this?"

The fact is that the person made the decision to end his or her life and you are not at fault. You must remind yourself that as you much as you would like to, you cannot control other people's actions. A saying in some recovery programs is "I didn't cause it, I can't control it, and I can't cure it." This is a useful, practical statement that can help you maintain your personal sanity during this difficult time.

---

112 Psalm 119:28; 27:14.

However, if the one who died by suicide is your child, emotions can skyrocket. When the great love parents have for their child is not enough to prevent suicide, they may feel like they've failed. If this is the case for you, fight the feelings of guilt and tell yourself that your child's decision to end their life was just that—their decision. All you can do is your best, and you will need to accept that you are not responsible for anyone making the decision to end his or her life.

The "Why" of Suicide

When someone we love decides to end their pain with suicide, it causes family and friends to begin a painful mourning process. Grieving survivors often have a great need to know *why* the person chose suicide and what could have prevented it. Unfortunately, those questions are often unanswerable. It is common for people in crisis to believe that suicide is their only option. Often victims aren't choosing death as much as they are choosing to end their unbearable pain. People who contemplate suicide often think they will be relieving their family and friends of the burden they feel they have become. When a depressed mother takes her life, it is often because she believes she is hurting her children more than she is helping and that they would be better off without her.

There are many reasons a person chooses suicide, but often such individuals have mental and biochemical imbalances. Some have endured long periods of mental or physical illness or both. It's not unusual for people to experience intense mental anguish that leaves them feeling lonely, friendless, and cut off from life—trapped in what they believe to be a hopeless situation.

Sister Reyna I. Aburto, second counselor in the Relief Society General Presidency, said that after her father died by suicide, her family searched for answers as to why he took his life.

> Untreated mental or emotional illness can lead to increased isolation, misunderstandings, broken relationships, self-harm, and even suicide. I know this firsthand, as my own father died by suicide many years ago. His death was shocking

and heartbreaking for my family and me. It has taken me years to work through my grief, and it was only recently that I learned talking about suicide in appropriate ways actually helps to prevent it rather than encourage it. I have now openly discussed my father's death with my children and witnessed the healing that the Savior can give on both sides of the veil.[113]

Healing Will Be Difficult, but It Is Possible

Losing someone to suicide can leave those close to them mentally numb. Some report feeling like a robot—if someone tells them to get dressed, they will put their clothes on. If they are told to go someplace, they will go. But without direct orders, they are like a ship without a rudder. Judith M. Stillion, PhD, said, "Evidence is beginning to accumulate that suggests that those who experience the death of a friend or loved one by suicide (i.e., suicide survivors) are more likely to experience different, perhaps more complicated, grief reactions than those whose loved ones die from natural causes or from accidents."[114]

Those "complicated grief reactions" may include feelings of guilt, confusion, and shame. Family and friends must also cope with the uncomfortable knowledge that the deceased did not want the help they would have given so willingly. Bewilderment comes from wondering how the person managed to hide their feelings so well. There is a search for motives as survivors try to make sense out of something that makes no sense. With so many painful, swirling feelings, some mourners choose not to reveal the cause of death to those they don't know well. Also some people report feeling less support when death occurs by suicide rather than by natural or accidental causes.

---

113 Reyna I. Aburto, "Thru Cloud and Sunshine, Lord, Abide with Me!" *Ensign*, November 2019, 58. churchofjesuschrist.org/study/ensign/2019/11/3 1aburto?lang=eng

114 Judith M. Stillion, "Survivors of Suicide," in Kenneth J. Doka, ed., *Living with Grief*, 42.

Some may wonder how the person who died will fare in the next life. Elder Dale G. Renlund addressed this issue: "There's an old sectarian notion that suicide is a sin and that someone who commits suicide is banished to hell forever. That is totally false. I believe the vast majority of cases will find that these individuals have lived heroic lives and that suicide will not be a defining characteristic of their eternities."115

When you lose someone you love to suicide, all happiness and peace can be shattered. Grief can feel like a relentless shadow that follows you everywhere. One woman who lost her daughter said, "A few weeks after my daughter's death, the realization and magnitude of what had happened started to creep in. It was like heavy, thick black smoke seeping in at first, followed by all-consuming billows until I was surrounded by complete darkness. Grief in its rawest [form] has its own dimension of blackness."116

Marlene shares the following experience:

Years ago, I traveled to a bookstore for a book signing. The store manager, Andrea, [name has been changed] told me that she had lost her husband five years earlier. During a lull, we talked further, and Andrea confided she was especially interested in my latest book, *Gaze into Heaven: Near-Death Experiences in Early Church History*, because a few years earlier, her only son had died by suicide.

Heartbreak was still evident as Andrea choked up after admitting she worried how her teenage son was faring in the spirit world. Then Andrea confided that after her son's death, he had appeared to her. He told her that he had been allowed to come back in order to comfort her and to reassure her that he was doing well. He also said he was sorry for having caused her so much pain.

Prior to her son's visitation, Andrea confessed that she'd felt very depressed and had reached a critically low point in her

---

115 Tad Walch, "LDS Apostle: 'Totally false' that suicide leads to permanent hell," *Deseret News*, July 2, 2018. deseret.com/2018/7/2/20648210/lds-apostle-totally-false-that-suicide-leads-to-permanent-hell

116 LeEtta Thorpe, "Saved After My Daughter's Suicide," *Liahona*, September 2017, 68. churchofjesuschrist.org/study/liahona/2017/09/saved-after-my-daughters-suicide?lang=eng

life—so low in fact, that she wondered if she could go on. Her son's brief visit lifted her spirit and gave her the reassurance she so desperately needed. Although still pained at the loss of her son and husband, Andrea said that afterward she was able to hold on to those few precious minutes and be comforted when feeling low. Displaying great faith and strength, Andrea said she knew that one day she would be reunited with her son and husband.

After losing a loved one to suicide, it will be up to you to rebuild your life, moment by moment, breath by breath. Try to dwell on the positive as you go from day to day, and strive to enjoy the good things in your life. Look up to God for help while looking outward to friends and family for support, and know that in time healing will come. Every day will bring a new lesson because every day your loved one will still be gone, yet somehow, your life must go on. After Judy Collins, the folk singer, lost her son to suicide, she advised others who had suffered a similar loss: "You must believe that you will recover, that you will smile, that you will thrive. You are here. You are alive, breathing, yearning, weeping. . . . You are the mother, the daughter, the father; you are the son, the brother. You are a perfect being, you are a perfect person, simply grieving."[117]

Young children can have an especially difficult time after losing a parent to suicide. Ever since three-year-old Winnie Bates lost her father to suicide, she has been afraid of being separated from her mother. If her mother needs to go somewhere without her, Winnie cries and throws tantrums. During one meltdown, Winnie screamed that she wanted to go to heaven to be with her daddy.[118] It's important for the surviving parent or guardian to make sure children grow up knowing two very important things: that the deceased parent loved them and that the suicide was not the children's fault.

It is natural and human to be hurt, wounded, and even angry at your loved one for choosing suicide. It may help to know that people who take their own life are in such emotional pain that they are unable to comprehend how devastating their death will

---

117 Judy Collins, *The Seven T's: Finding Hope and Healing in the Wake of Tragedy* (New York: Penguin, 2007), 54.
118 See Becky Jacobs, "This Is Real Life for Us," *The Salt Lake Tribune,* September 15, 2019, A4.

be to those left behind, and most often, they truly believe their loved ones will be better off without them.

Forgive them.

You'll also want to forgive anyone you feel played a part in the death. Perhaps you feel your spouse was overly harsh on your son before he died by suicide or that your son-in-law should have shown your daughter more love or insisted she get counseling for her depression. You may want to blame friends or your surviving children for not telling you how profoundly your child was struggling. And you may blame yourself for all you feel you should or shouldn't have done. Even though your heart is broken, try not to blame yourself or others, for that will only intensify your pain. Pray for understanding and forgiveness. Accept that your loved one chose his or her own path.

Do your best to focus on the present. You can't undo what happened, but you can change how you think and what you do about it. Don't dwell on the final months of the person's life, when he or she was most likely withdrawing from you and the world. Try also not to think too much on the future and all the things your loved one would be doing if still alive. It's difficult to remain in the here and now, but that is what you must try to do. While time won't erase what happened, it can allow your wound to begin to heal. And most of all, remember that one day you will see your loved one again.

Suicide Prevention

Globally 800,000 people die from suicide every year, and suicide is one of the leading causes of death in young people.[119] In Utah, suicide rates have increased every year since 2008 and now outnumber homicides by a ratio of eight to one, according to a study conducted by researchers from Harvard's T.H. Chan School of Public Health.[120]

In 2018 The Church of Jesus Christ of Latter-day Saints released a video series to promote suicide awareness and provide resources for suicide prevention. In this series, Elder Dale G. Renlund said:

---

119 See Hannah Ritchie, Max Roser, and Esteban Ortiz-Ospina, "Suicide," OurWorldInData.org. ourworldindata.org/suicide.

120 See Benjamin Wood, "Suicide rates in Utah outnumber homicides," *The Salt Lake Tribune*, November 15, 2018, A7.

What we need to do as a church is to reach out in love and caring for those who have suicidal thoughts, who have attempted suicide, who feel marginalized in any way. We need to reach out with love and understanding. You do that in concert with health-care professionals, and with ecclesiastical leaders, with friend and family support.[121]

One particularly harmful and common myth is that talking about suicide makes things worse by putting ideas in people's heads. Nowadays, top mental health professionals say that simply is not the case. "'Some professionals once discouraged talking about suicide for fear it would lead to more people killing themselves—which is untrue,' said Donna Schuurman, senior director of advocacy and training at The Dougy Center in Oregon, which works with grieving children and families." Taryn Hiatt, American Foundation for Suicide Prevention area director over Utah and Nevada, agrees, saying, "'Losing a loved one to suicide should be talked about as openly as losing someone to cancer or another health issue.'"[122]

Asking about suicide in an open and caring way opens the doors of communication and lets your loved one know it's all right to talk to you. Most people considering suicide feel very alone, and having someone ask them directly about suicide can help break down the walls of their loneliness.

To prevent suicide, it's important to have honest and direct conversations with anyone who begins to show warning signs. Elder Dale G. Renlund suggests taking a friend or loved one's hand, looking that person in the eye, and asking directly if he or she is thinking about suicide. Elder Renlund encourages people

---

121 Tad Walch, "LDS Apostle: 'Totally false' that suicide leads to permanent hell," *Deseret News*, July 2, 2018. deseret.com/2018/7/2/20648210/lds-apostle-totally-false-that-suicide-leads-to-permanent-hell
122 Becky Jacobs, "Lehi mother shares the impact of husband's suicide to get people talking," *The Salt Lake Tribune*, September 15, 2019. sltrib.com/news/2019/09/15/lehi-mother-shares-impact/

to take time to listen carefully to their loved one's response, come up with safety plans, and then help him or her find professional help.[123] Most young people who are considering suicide will give one or more warning signs. Take action if someone does one or more of the following:

- Talks about suicide
- Says he or she wants to die
- Physically hurts himself or herself
- Says things will never get better
- Appears to be in emotional pain
- Struggles to cope after a recent loss
- Stops doing activities he or she used to enjoy
- Seems more worried, anxious, or prone to anger than usual

Parents of teenagers can be unsure if their child is acting out because of hormonal changes or if the situation indicates something more serious. One thing that can help is to stay involved in the teen's life and have honest communication. If problems last more than two weeks, parents are encouraged to seek out a counselor for their child or themselves. Support groups can be helpful, as can priesthood blessings. If someone you know is considering suicide,

1. Take the person seriously.
2. Stay with the person.
3. Help the person remove things they could use to hurt himself or herself.
4. Urge the person to call the twenty-four-hour National Suicide Prevention Hotline at 1-800-273-TALK (8255). You can also text TALK to 741741 to communicate with

---

123 Walch, "LDS Apostle: 'Totally false' that suicide leads to permanent hell." deseret.com/2018/7/2/20648210/lds-apostle-totally-false-that-suicide-leads-to-permanent-hell

a trained crisis counselor from the Crisis Text Line, which is available 24/7 at no cost.

5. Escort the person to mental health services or an emergency room.

CHAPTER 8
THE FIRST DAYS, WEEKS, MONTHS, AND YEAR

Out of the depths have I cried unto thee, O Lord.
Lord, hear my voice: let thine ears be attentive to the voice
of my supplications.[124]

GRIEF OVER THE LOSS OF a loved one is universal because love is universal. The death can be devastating and the recovery a genuine struggle. After a loss, there will be a period of transition that lasts until you are able to cope with your feelings. Author Raymond Moody said, "Grief is an instinctive response to loss; it is a process with a host of feelings. New grief is continuous; that is, it consumes the body, mind, and soul around the clock, for many days or weeks."[125]

The sadness that comes from loss turns your attention inward, giving you time to reflect, take stock of where you are in life, turn to God in prayer, and recalibrate your life to the reality of your loss. Someone once described this process as slogging through molasses. This slowing down period is actually a good thing since it provides you time to recover from the shock of losing someone you love. You might feel as though you are living in a surreal state.

124 Psalm 130:1–2.
125 Moody and Arcangel, *Life After Loss*, 36.

All of this allows you a chance to gather your bearings while you take life one step and one day at a time.

The First Days

When you first get the news that your loved one has died, it is common to feel stunned. Just as the body goes into shock after being physically injured, the mind goes into shock to deal with emotional upheaval. It's common to think things like, "I can't believe it!" "He can't be dead!" or "This can't be happening!"

Shock is a defense mechanism that can last a few hours to a few months. The numbness you feel is natural, although it may not seem that way at the time, and occurs when your emotional system shuts down to provide temporary insulation from the full impact of your loss. Some people describe this as feeling like they are on autopilot or as if they were going through life in slow motion. It's common to have memory lapses and difficulty concentrating. When awakening in the morning, you might briefly forget that your dear one is gone. During the day, you may tell yourself to remember to tell him or her the joke you just heard. You might even start to call for him or her—until reality hits.

In the first days, excruciatingly raw pain may plague you. There may be a hollowness in your stomach as if someone has punched you, an ache in your heart making you wonder if it is breaking in two, or a lump in your throat. Some people lose their appetite; others find themselves eating too much. Normal sleeping patterns can be disrupted. Some people want to sleep all the time, while others find it hard to fall asleep. Still others find themselves waking constantly.

Immediately after a death, you must focus on pressing demands, such as making decisions regarding organ donation, a postmortem examination, the disposition of the remains, and funeral plans. It helps to have family members step in and assist you in making decisions because you can't get away from these responsibilities even when caught up in grief. In addition, you must face emotional challenges such as handling the abrupt disruption of your life, redefining responsibilities and roles of family members, addressing challenges to faith, and coping with financial changes.

Shortly after a loss, family members are often bombarded with visitors, food, offers to help, phone calls, and flowers. This is compassion at its highest level. Alma told his people to help "bear one another's burdens, that they might be light . . . to mourn with those that mourn; . . . and comfort those that stand in need of comfort."[126] However, once the funeral is over and the flowers have withered, you will no longer ask "Why?" but "What do I do now?" As time goes on, calls, condolences, and offers gradually decrease. Some survivors are relieved, while others may feel vaguely disturbed at the reminder that other people have a life to return to while theirs has stopped. At this time, you must, out of necessity, learn how to pick up what's left of your life. When your loss is new and the pain sharp, it may seem unthinkable that life can go on, but it will. There will be people who will continue to give you support. Don't be shy in asking for help as needed—not just now but in the coming weeks and months. Let people be there for you, and in the future, you can be there for others.

The First Weeks

During the first weeks, an unexpected loss can turn your world into an unfamiliar place. People can feel stunned and overwhelmed. Some feel numb for a while. Part of the reason is that when you lose someone, it can feel as if you are losing a piece of yourself. Much of a person's identity comes from their relationships to others. If you lose a husband, you may feel that you've lost your identity as a wife. A man who loses his only child may wonder how to define himself now that he is no longer a father. If this is the case for you, remember that redefining yourself is a process. You don't have to let go of who you were; you just need to adapt for the future. The sudden absence of a loved one can leave a large hole in your life, making you wonder how to face your loss. Take it slowly, moving forward one step at a time.

---

126 Mosiah 18:8–9.

Grief affects people differently. Some people become extra active and busy, while others turn lethargic and find themselves sleeping constantly. During the first weeks, you will go through one of the most traumatic experiences a person can have, so treat yourself kindly. If you feel tired, sleep. If you feel like crying, cry. Coping with routine tasks can be not only daunting but exhausting. Grief can affect a person not only emotionally but also physically. One of the most commonly reported symptoms of grief is exhaustion. This exhaustion makes small tasks like driving to the grocery store and getting a gallon of milk or stopping to gas up your vehicle seem like monumental tasks. This lack of energy can be worrisome, but it is normal. A great loss has nearly the same effect as if you had undergone surgery. Be patient and give yourself time to recuperate.

During these initial weeks, some people report having difficulty focusing. It's common to misplace your glasses or keys, fail to remember appointments, or forget your shopping list when going to the store. Difficulty remembering comes from being distracted as you work to process your loss. Grieving can also cause emotions to be unpredictable and unstable. Mood swings may be wide and deep. Such emotions are simply manifestations of grief, but if you stop eating, become dehydrated, are unable to sleep more than a few hours, or begin having suicidal thoughts, seek professional help immediately.

When you feel able, it is often helpful to return to your job. Most survivors return to a daily schedule within a few weeks, while others need more time. Having a routine during times of stress can speed healing. Mothers and fathers will need to get up and prepare breakfast for their children, pack lunches, do laundry, go grocery shopping, make evening meals, and help with homework. Resuming normal activities does not mean you are denying your loss; it simply means you are dealing with the present.

For the first few weeks when you are physically and emotionally vulnerable, try not to concern yourself with what lies in the future. There will be time to cope, to understand, and to process *later*. Right now, you need only take care of yourself, your dependents, and others who are close to you. Turn to friends and relatives for help if you find yourself unable to care for yourself or your children.

Your loss will change you, but you don't have to let it push you into an abyss. The Apostle Paul counseled us to turn to God, "Who comforteth us in all our tribulation."[127] Hold on to the comfort that God gives you. Realize that love never ends and the one you love is not gone forever. He or she has only moved to a new place—a place where you will one day join them, never to be parted again.

The First Months

During the first months after your loss, there will continue to be moments of suffering, although they may not be as intense. It's normal at this point to still feel unable to fully accept the loss and wonder if you will ever be able to adjust to a world without your loved one, but do what you can to move forward. If you can, put off selling your house or changing jobs. This is a tender time, and grief can cause you to make unwise decisions—ones you may regret. Wait until the fog of mourning has lifted and you can see more clearly the options before you.

During this time, you might notice a change in your physical health. You might have more headaches than normal, get a cold or the flu, have increased blood pressure, or have difficulty stabilizing your diabetes. There can also be mood changes, an inability to focus, or irritability. Sleep can be restless, absent, or full of disturbing dreams.

Some days may be long and challenging, but trust in God and know that, in time, you will be able to reestablish your place in a new, changed world. As you continue to grieve, heartbreak and sorrow may remain frequent companions. Sadness will ebb and flow as you ride continuing waves of grief. You may have bouts of crying, but there is no shame in shedding tears—they are simply a manifestation of your grief and can be cathartic. However, if you continue to feel sad most of the time, find nothing that gives

---

127 2 Corinthians 1:4.

you pleasure, and neglect to take care of yourself, see a doctor or a therapist. You might find it helpful to join a support group. Hearing other people's experiences can provide solace. As you share your own experience, it can be comforting and empowering to hear counsel from those who have walked the same path you are now on.

In the first months, it's not uncommon to feel lethargic and lack interest in the world around you. At times, sadness may seem like a bottomless pit with no way out, making you wonder if you will feel this way for the rest of your life. Rest assured, this is not the case. Healing will come in time. For now, treat yourself as tenderly as if you are recovering from a major illness. Stay close to God, the master healer, who will succor you during this time of need. "Look unto God with firmness of mind, and pray unto him with exceeding faith, and he will console you in your afflictions."[128] Pray often, and trust in Heavenly Father's great love for you. In time, the clouds will part, and light will come.

The First Year

The first year has special challenges and can be characterized by a continued sense of fluctuating pain and a sense of disorientation. A scab may form over your wound but can be reopened by the slightest trigger. During this time, you will experience a number of firsts, such as the first Easter, Christmas, birthday, and anniversary. Each of these events can be emotionally challenging and physically draining. All of these events present new challenges and cause new pain as you awaken to the profound sorrow of knowing your loved one will never again be present for these events.

You are not the first person to find these occasions challenging. People have always had to learn how to cope with the pain and grief of losing someone dear to them, and that means you can too.

Marlene shares the following experience: Once, when I was battling depression, a friend advised, "Don't be so afraid of pain— it won't kill you." Although this comment was not appreciated at

---

128 Jacob 3:1.

the time, since I was completely flooded with pain and anguish, I was grateful for it later. When bowed down with sorrow, it's good to know that although your loss hurts—enormously at times—the pain will not kill you. Rely on and trust Heavenly Father. Pray for His help, and He will send angels who can support you in countless ways. "For he shall give his angels charge over thee, to keep thee in all thy ways. They shall bear thee up in their hands."[129]

Remind yourself that you have made it this far and are beginning to engage in life once more, which means you are making progress. Hold on to those precious moments when you feel genuinely content. Let them give you hope for the future.

During the first twelve months, you may still occasionally experience numbness, which serves to cushion some of your continuing pain. Occasionally, you might go into overdrive, staying busy as a way to push your pain into the background. It's also common to still feel off-kilter and have raw feelings spill out now and then. Rest assured that, with time, you will learn how to moderate your life.

Toward the end of the first year, you may feel a need to reexamine your life. As you do, you may find that your priorities have shifted. Take time to ponder on what matters to you *now* and how to implement these new priorities in your life. At this stage, some people are ready to make new plans and ponder various questions such as *Where do I want to live? Should I change jobs? How will I support myself?* Monitor your feelings and avoid making impulsive decisions.

The first year is a busy time that affords little opportunity for sitting still in one's grief. Don't expect complete recovery by the end of the first year, but do expect your days to be brighter. Hopefully you'll be able to cast off some of your sorrow and realize that life will continue, although in an altered state. Your pain will ebb, and light will come into your life—so slowly you may not even notice the incremental brightening. Although emotion may still overwhelm you at times, you will feel longer periods

---

129 Psalm 91:11–12.

of relief in between. Keep working on healing your wounds. As authors Brook Noel and Pamela D. Blair advise, "It is essential that you set aside some time to feel your grief and sadness as this is the most necessary part of the healing process."[130]

Rest assured that God is on our side as we navigate our way through our healing process. President Thomas S. Monson said:

> Let us be of good cheer as we go about our lives. Although we live in increasingly perilous times, the Lord loves us and is mindful of us. He is always on our side as we do what is right. He will help us in time of need. Difficulties come into lives, problems we do not anticipate and which we would never choose. None of us is immune. The purpose of mortality is to learn and to grow to be more like our Father, and it is often during the difficult times that we learn the most, as painful as the lessons may be.[131]

---

130 Noel and Blair, *I Wasn't Ready to Say Goodbye*, 54.
131 Thomas S. Monson, "God Be with You Till We Meet Again," *Ensign*, November 2012, 210–11. churchofjesuschrist.org/study /ensign/2012/11/sunday-afternoon-session/god-be-with-you-till-we-meet-again?lang=eng

CHAPTER 9
HANDLING HOLIDAYS AND SPECIAL OCCASIONS

Be strong and of a good courage . . .
for the Lord thy God, he it is that doth go with thee;
he will not fail thee, nor forsake thee.[132]

DEATH HAS A WAY OF changing one's perspective, and once-happy celebrations can present a real challenge after the death of a loved one. While the rest of the world relishes holidays, special events can bring your loss to the forefront, making you feel vulnerable and fragile. Instead of a heart overflowing with joy, yours might be filled with sadness. It is necessary at such times to rely on the Lord, remembering that "the Lord is good to all: and his tender mercies are over all his works."[133]

After losing a loved one, the first of everything is often the hardest. People often dread the first birthday, the first Christmas, the first death anniversary, and so on because these firsts cause you to feel your loss anew. If you lost a child, Mother's Day or Father's Day can now be a day of heartbreak. Trying to celebrate under such circumstances is difficult. Trying to enjoy special occasions and provide a joyful experience for your surviving family can be

132 Deuteronomy 31:6.
133 Psalm 145:9.

like riding a roller coaster—full of cresting happiness one moment and sinking sorrow the next. And that's okay. Those hard moments remind you of how much you loved the departed and wish he or she were still with you.

Christmas is a special season that brings up wonderful memories of years past. At this time, it is only natural that you remember your loved one's favorite Christmas carol, how much he loved Christmas cookies, and how eager she was to decorate the Christmas tree. Such memories, although treasured, can force you to deal with sharp feelings of loss.

There is no easy answer for how to get through holidays. Some people find the best way to survive is to allow special occasions to pass as quietly as possible, but that can be difficult if you have children or are spending the holidays with family. It will be difficult, but try not to dwell on what once was. Instead, focus on the blessings you currently have in your life.

Sometimes people dread upcoming holidays more than they need to and find that the days and weeks leading up to the holiday cause more pain than the occasion itself. Don't spend what little energy you have worrying—chances are the actual event won't be as bad as you fear. With patience and healing, you will once again be able to celebrate these occasions with joy. Be gentle with yourself and allow time to adjust. Accept that the holidays will not be the same as in years past but that you will do your best and that is enough. Following are suggestions that can help you not just get through special occasions but enjoy them.

Let Yourself Mourn

Don't force yourself to put on a happy face when you feel wretched inside. If you want to sit alone and cry, allow yourself some time, but don't stay in that dark spot. Let your feelings out and then move on. Call someone for support, or pray and discuss your feelings with your Father in Heaven. God is always there for you. "Hear my prayer, O Lord, and let my cry come unto thee. Hide not thy face from me in the day when I am in trouble; incline thine ear unto me: in the day when I call answer me speedily."[134] If you feel sad when you're with other people, it's all right to let them know—they will understand. If you need to cry, you may want to find a quiet spot to be alone. After, make an effort to gather yourself and return to the group. Don't be embarrassed at your red eyes—again, those who care for you will understand.

Plan Ahead

Birthdays, anniversaries, and holidays are often charged with emotions, leaving you more likely to feel teary and sorrowful. Knowing this gives you a chance to plan how to get through these events. Take charge of what happens that day—don't just sit back and let it happen. Perhaps you can arrange to be with close friends or family members who understand the special challenges the day may bring. For birthdays or anniversaries, some people prefer to take the day off from work, while others prefer to go to work and stay busy. Think about what activities would make you feel better and decide on a course of action. Making plans ahead of time will eliminate stress, help you get through the day, and allow you to cope with your feelings.

Balance Solitude with Sociability

On special days, you may need some alone time, but do your best to balance that with spending time with others. Some people rely on friends who have experienced the same kind of loss because they can better understand what you are going through. Accept offers of help from family members and friends, whether it's to go shopping, bake cookies, attend a concert, or help wrap gifts. If you're having a hard time coping, call someone. Mention the loss and tell them, "Today is a hard day and I could use a distraction. Could we go shopping, see a movie, or go out to dinner?"

Don't turn down invitations because you are afraid of crying; people will sympathize if you shed a few tears. There may be times—when faced with special events such as a wedding—that you don't feel like celebrating because you're so awash in sorrow. If you want to avoid certain celebrations at this point, your feelings

---

134 Psalm 102:1–2.

are telling you that you have more healing to do. Try not to feel guilty or ashamed, and rest assured that you won't always feel this way. Recovering is a process. Be patient with yourself. Once you rebuild your life, you'll be able to delight in joyful events once more.

Make the Holiday a Special Time for Children

If you are newly widowed and have young children, the holidays will be difficult. Don't be shy about asking for help with your children's holiday shopping, wrapping, baking, or other holiday-related activities that will brighten your children's lives. Ask a few family members or friends to come and help you and the children decorate the tree. People will be delighted to know you thought of them. Think of ways to make special occasions bright and happy for children who have lost someone. You might want to take them shopping or to a favorite restaurant. Make Christmas cookies together, go sledding, or go see Christmas lights. Think of fun outings they might enjoy, such as playing miniature golf, riding go-karts, going on an Easter egg hunt, delivering Valentines, going trick-or-treating, or visiting a farm that has animals and fun activities.

Simplify and Make New Traditions

Because your life has changed, it's okay to modify the way you have traditionally celebrated. Holidays can be stressful because of the abundance of activities available, so simplify your life and think about what events mean the most to you and which ones will fit your new life better. Don't hold on to old traditions simply because that's the way you've always done things.

You may want to create new traditions for your family. One family decided to rent a cabin by a lake for their yearly family reunion instead of having a barbecue at the local park as they'd done for years. Another family decided to go out to dinner for their grandparent's birthday instead of cooking their usual elaborate meal at home. Instead of having your traditional Easter dinner at your house as you've always done, you could ask someone else to host it.

Talk about Your Loved One

Sometimes your family and friends will avoid mentioning the deceased on holidays and special occasions because they fear it might upset you. But departed loved ones should be remembered and talked about. You can help break the ice by mentioning the deceased and including them in normal conversation. Relive happy memories and don't push away all thoughts of "what used to be." While you won't want to dwell on memories if they cause too much pain, in time you'll be able to share happy ones that all of you can smile about.

Think of special ways to remember your loved one. One idea is to ask each family member ahead of time to take a few moments before Thanksgiving dinner or at a Christmas gathering to relate a favorite memory of your dear one. Another idea is to light a candle and place it in a prominent location, letting everyone know it is there in your loved one's memory. A candle represents light and warmth, which is just what the person you loved gave you. Marlene shares a friend's way of remembering a loved one: When a friend of mine hosts Thanksgiving dinner for her extended family, she sets up dining tables in her front room next to her piano, on which she displays numerous pictures of her departed daughter. It's a loving reminder of someone who is still so dear to her and her family.

Take Charge of Your Thoughts

One of the hardest things in the world is to push away feelings of sadness, but it can help if you actively work to push out negative and unhelpful thoughts. Focus on your mercies rather than your miseries. Think on your blessings instead of your burdens. Striving to be positive and grateful is especially appropriate at Thanksgiving and when celebrating Christmas and the Savior's birth. Remind yourself that although it will be painful at times, you *will* survive birthdays, anniversaries, and holidays. For those who have lost a spouse, wedding anniversaries can be especially difficult. Although you can't help but mourn your loss on this special day, try to think of the things for which you are grateful—the happy and fun things you did together, and how blessed you are that you had as much time together as you did. And, most of all, remember that one day you will be together again.

If you begin to feel stressed, take time to sit quietly and read, play music, or listen to uplifting talks. Another way to relieve stress is to go for a walk. Any kind of exercise is beneficial because it releases neurochemicals called endorphins that help elevate your mood. If you have dogs, take them along, or arrange to go walking with a friend. Take time to notice the beauty of the world around you. To help take care of yourself, you may want to set an appointment with a therapist, arrange to spend time with a close friend, or plan a special activity to give yourself something to look forward to.

CHAPTER 10
IDEAS FOR COPING WITH GRIEF

And I will also ease the burdens which are
put upon your shoulders, that even you cannot feel
them upon your backs, even while you are in bondage; and this
will I do that ye may stand as witnesses for me hereafter,
and that ye may know of a surety that I, the Lord God,
do visit my people in their afflictions.[135]

AT TIMES, IT MIGHT SEEM impossible not to give in to sorrow, but
with God's help, you can rise above those painful feelings. Life
may still be filled with anguish, but each day you can rise and
pray for the strength to do what needs to be done. If you turn to
God, He can provide you with strength beyond your own. "The
Lord is my strength and song, and is become my salvation."[136]

Those who have lost a loved one may wonder, *Will my life ever
seem normal again? When will I stop feeling this way? What can I
do to speed my recovery? How can I feel whole again?* These are all
legitimate questions. Your best hope at managing grief is to turn to
the Savior—the ultimate source of all comfort and healing. He has
promised, "I will not leave you comfortless: I will come to you. . . .

135 Mosiah 24:14.
136 Psalm 118:14.

Peace I leave with you, my peace I give unto you: not as the world giveth, give I unto you. Let not your heart be troubled, neither let it be afraid."[137]

Although healing will take time, there are many useful ideas and techniques that can help you manage your grief and move forward. As you work to cope with your grief, keep your loved one close—speak their name often, bring them into your dreams, and hold him or her tightly in your heart.

Nurture Yourself

Losing someone you love can leave you deeply changed. During this difficult time, you'll want to nurture yourself because taking care of yourself is not only okay, it's *vital*. Paying attention to your needs will fortify you for the challenging journey ahead, which is to integrate the death of your loved one into your new reality.

At times it can be hard to find a reason to get out of bed. To compensate for these feelings, give yourself something to look forward to. Plan in advance to do something every day that you enjoy. This will help you heal. Decide what things you'd like to do. You might enjoy spending time reading, baking, or garden-ing. Perhaps you like going for walks, having lunch with friends, or getting a pedicure or a massage. Simple things can make you feel good, such as changing into comfortable clothes when com-ing home, taking a long bath, or sitting outside when the weather is nice. Buy a bouquet of cut flowers for yourself. Rent a movie you'd like to see. Be sure to take care of your spiritual needs by praying daily, studying the scriptures, attending church meetings, and visiting the temple. Whatever you choose, know that you are keeping your life in balance by nurturing yourself and attending to your physical, emotional, social, and spiritual needs.

Be Physically Active

The health benefits of being physically active are tremendous and cannot be overemphasized. Although being physically active can be difficult when you are grief-stricken and lacking in energy, exercise is probably one of the most therapeutic activities you

---

137 John 14:18, 27.

can undertake. American singer Judy Collins talked about how exercise helped after her son died by suicide:

> On many days after my son's death, I had to run until I practically dropped; walk until I was exhausted; swim until I had swum out the anger, the hurt, the pain, the denial. Endorphins . . . give us energy and a change of mood. Many days, when I was so angry I was in tears, or unable even to think about moving, I would start a slow workout and find myself feeling hopeful by the time a half hour or forty-five minutes had gone by.[138]

Exercise is a natural way of energizing yourself. When you get your body moving and your blood flowing, your brain's hypothalamus and pituitary gland produce neurochemicals called endorphins, which bring about feelings of euphoria and well-being. Low levels of neurotransmitters like serotonin and norepinephrine are linked to depression and anxiety; when you exercise, these neurotransmitters are released into your body, combatting stress and increasing feelings of contentment. Exercise regularly by bicycling, hiking, or hitting the gym. Swim a few laps at the local pool, work out to an exercise video, or jog around the neighborhood. Yoga is good for quieting the body and the mind while you stretch, focus yourself, and become limber. Walking is one of the best, least expensive, and most beneficial exercise methods. In case of inclement weather, invest in a treadmill or stationary bicycle to ensure you have your daily dose of exercise.

Postpone Making Major Decisions

When facing a significant loss, the first year of bereavement is usually not the best time to make significant decisions. Avoid making far-reaching decisions hastily. Unless unusual circumstances warrant it, it's best to avoid moving when it will uproot you from your family, friends, and the familiarity of your living

---

138 Collins, *The Seven T's*, 108–9.

space. This is not the best time to change jobs, remarry, move out of your home, or make other major decisions. If the mortgage is too burdensome, seek counsel from people who are experts in this field. If you cannot maintain the house and yard on your own, ask family members to help with chores. You can also ask around and find young people who might be willing to do chores at a reasonable rate.

If you are older and one of your children asks you to move in with them, take time to consider all the ramifications. It can be difficult to adjust to no longer being the queen or king of your own castle and feeling pressed to do things the way other family members want. An alternative might be to move to a retirement center or an assisted living center where you can get help with meals, housecleaning, and other necessities.

Get Enough Sleep

Sleep plays an essential role in health, and yet the majority of people do not get enough sleep, seriously impacting their well-being. Lack of sleep can have detrimental long-term effects, including increased risk of heart disease, kidney disease, high blood pressure, diabetes, and stroke. During sleep, important physical and mental processes are carried out that can

- keep your body temperature and metabolism at a proper level.
- control brain functioning and improve memory.
- keep your immune system working.
- repair tissues and stimulate growth in children by releasing a growth hormone.
- keep your heart and blood vessels healthy.
- regulate your appetite, weight, and blood glucose levels.

Research recommends that adults get seven to eight hours of sleep each night to be well rested. Since regular, good-quality sleep is restorative for the brain and important for both emotional and physical health, it's important to establish a regular sleep routine. Try to go to bed at the same time each night, and limit your screen time beforehand.

Cultivate an Attitude of Gratitude

Although we are naturally saddened when losing someone we love, one of the greatest reasons we can be grateful is the knowledge that this separation is only temporary. Happiness is everlastingly eternal because of our Savior, Jesus Christ, and His Atoning sacrifice, which allows us to be reunited with those we love.

One of the grandest blessings of the gospel is knowing that those we have lost are in a better place. While we miss them dreadfully, we are thankful to know that even if they suffered from illness, disease, bodily infirmity, or the effects of old age, they are now free from *all* pain and suffering. When resurrected, all of us will have perfected and immortal bodies, unburdened by age, sickness, and disability. When we return to heavenly realms, tears of sadness and loss will be replaced with an abundance of happiness and joy, "good measure, pressed down, and shaken together, and running over."139 President Ezra Taft Benson taught:

> Through the resurrection of our Lord and by revelations given to the Prophet Joseph Smith and other modern prophets, we know that life does not end at death when our bodies are buried in the earth. But our spirits, which give life to our bodies, continue to live in the spirit world, where we may associate again with family and friends. . . . Even though death may come to our loved ones and friends, we know that in the spirit world, they are happy, removed from the sorrows and tears of mortal life. They now understand much more clearly the purpose of our Heavenly Father's plan and that they will live eternally. Someday we will

---

139 Luke 6:38.

know them again, for we all will come forth as Jesus did with perfected bodies.[140]

Resist thinking that because your loved one is gone, you have nothing to be grateful for. We all receive innumerable daily blessings, and personal and spiritual growth is accelerated when we express gratitude for those blessings. Joseph F. Smith said, "The grateful man sees so much in the world to be thankful for, and with him the good outweighs the evil. Love overpowers jealousy, and light drives darkness out of his life."[141] Gratitude can work miracles in our lives. Being grateful has the power to bless our souls with peace, comfort, and joy. Sister Bonnie D. Parkin, past general president of the Relief Society, said, "Gratitude is our sweet acknowledgment of the Lord's hand in our lives; it is an expression of our faith."[142]

The Healing Power of Animals

Having a pet can help families and individuals heal from grief. Pet ownership has been linked to many physical benefits, including reduced risk for heart disease, lower stress levels, fewer doctor visits, a decrease in cholesterol levels, and lower blood pressure. In addition, statistics show that people who have a pet to care for live longer and have fewer health problems than those living without a pet.[143]

Living, breathing animals who trust us with their lives provide emotional support and help us heal. How? Through hormones.

---

140 Ezra Taft Benson, "He Is Risen!" *Friend*, April 1981, 6–7. churchofjesuschrist.org/study/friend/1981/04/friend-to-friend-he-is-risen?lang=eng

141 Smith, *Gospel Doctrine*, 263. archive.org/details/gospeldoctrine009956mbp/page/n281

142 Bonnie D. Parkin, "Gratitude: A Path to Happiness," *Ensign*, May 2007, 35. churchofjesuschrist.org/study/ensign/2007/05/gratitude-a-path-to-happiness?lang=eng

143 Alexandra Gekas, "10 Health Benefits of Owning a Pet," *Woman's Day*, February 11, 2011. womansday.com/life/pet-care/a2352/10-health-benefits-of-owning-a-pet-116238/

Studies have proven that petting a dog or cat increases levels of the vital brain chemicals such as dopamine and serotonin, which improve a person's mood and reduces stress, anxiety, and depression. Stroking a dog lowers blood pressure and provides comfort for those who feel lonely, which is why animals are being used to visit patients in hospitals and for companionship in retirement villages. Studies have shown that "playing with your pet increases the levels of the feel-good chemicals serotonin and dopamine in your brain. Maybe that's why people recover from a stressful situation more quickly when they're with their pets than with their partners or friends, a study done by the National Institutes of Health (NIH) found."[144]

Not only that, but Lynette Hart, PhD, associate professor at the University of California, Davis, School of Veterinary Medicine says, "Studies have shown that Alzheimer's patients have fewer anxious outbursts if there is an animal in the home."[145] If you hesitate to make a long-term commitment, you can consider becoming a "foster" parent, taking in animals who are waiting to be adopted. Check with your local animal shelter or humane society.

For those who can provide a good home, there are many types of pets to consider, from outside pets—such as horses, ponies, and pygmy pigs—to indoor pets, such as dogs, cats, birds, guinea pigs, bunnies, tropical fish, lizards, ferrets, gerbils, or hamsters.

Cats and dogs are popular because they are loyal and fairly self-sufficient. "Studies show that dogs [or cats] reduce stress, anxiety and depression, ease loneliness, encourage exercise and improve your all-around health. . . . Just *playing* with dogs has been shown to elevate oxytocin and dopamine, creating positive feelings and bonding for

144 "Are People with Pets Happier and Healthier?" *Music City Scale.* scalemusiccity.com/are-people-with-pets-really-healthier-and-happier/#:~:text=Playing%20with%20your%20pet%20increases,of%20 Health%20(NIH)%20found
145 Jeanie Lerche Davis, "5 Ways Pets Can Improve Your Health," *WebMed.* 2004. webmd.com/hypertension-high-blood-pressure/features /health-benefits-of-pets#1

both the person and their pet."[146] Oxytocin is another feel-good chemical that can stimulate many positive feelings. Owning a pet has many therapeutic effects because they offer unconditional love, provide emotional support, and alleviate stress. "Even hardened criminals in prison have shown long-term changes in their behavior after interacting with dogs."[147]

Dogs provide companionship, are overjoyed to see you when you come home, reduce anxiety, add structure to your day, and love to stay by your side. Cats are more independent but also offer comforting companionship. Both cats and dogs must be fed and watered daily, taken to the vet if ill, and given necessary shots. If you are gone for a few days, you'll need to arrange for their care during your absence. Owning a pet is not for everyone. Consider your situation, and determine if a pet would fit into your lifestyle. While owning a pet is a responsibility and definitely takes time and effort, they can nurture and help you heal.

Stay Close to Family and Friends

As you work on processing your grief, your burden can be made lighter by actively connecting with people who can support you. Take the time and effort to stay close to friends, family, coworkers, support groups, and Church members and leaders. Help is all around—you just need to let people in. Accept help when friends and family offer.

Good friends are basic to life and health. During your time of grief, make the time to visit and socialize with supportive friends. Accept their love and concern when they reach out. Bask in the support, comradery, and comfort they bring. Often friends are the ones to help you emerge from the darkness. If you have few friends, reach out to those who might become friends. Reach out and reestablish contact with old friends. And don't

146 Greer Grenley, "How Dogs Can Help with Depression," National Alliance on Mental Illness, February 2, 2018. nami.org/Blogs/NAMI-Blog/February-2018/How-Dogs-Can-Help-with-Depression
147 Lawrence Robinson and Jeanne Segal, "Mood-Boosting Power of Dogs," *HelpGuide.Org*, October 2017. hr.unm.edu/docs/ehp/mood-boosting-power-of-dogs.pdf

overlook your family. Some people count family members among their closest friends. Many times all you need is someone to talk to—you're not looking for someone to solve your problems but someone to simply talk with about life and living.

Finding a few close friends who will listen to and commiserate with you is cathartic because it helps release inner tension. Each time we talk about a painful experience, the pain is eased a little. Don't be embarrassed if tears come. There is healing in remembering and in keeping the best memories alive. It's important to create a support system during dark times because the more isolated you are, the more difficult the grieving and the slower the healing process. It's a form of sabotage to live your life in isolation. Without the comfort and love of other human beings, none of us is very strong, but if we associate with others who accept us and support us, we can survive anything.

Eat Healthy Foods

A nutritious, well-balanced diet is the foundation for good, overall health. It can be difficult to think about food when you are grieving, but if you focus on eating nourishing food, you'll get the nutrients your body needs to stay healthy and strong during this difficult time. Widows and widowers often have an especially hard time eating properly, but your body needs nourishment. If you don't like eating alone, invite a friend to come over and share a meal. Another option is to turn on the radio or TV during your meals. Some people read a book or newspaper while they eat.

To eat healthy meals, eat high-quality proteins, carbohydrates, and heart-healthy fats while reducing your intake of processed foods and saturated fats. Eating properly helps maintain your body's everyday functions, promotes optimal body weight, and can assist in disease prevention. Neglecting healthy eating habits increases the risk of heart disease, diabetes, cancer, bowel complications, and becoming overweight.

Use Humor to Lighten Your Spirits

Smiling and laughing are strong medicines—powerful antidotes to stress, pain, and conflict. Nothing works faster or more consistently to bring your mind and body back into balance than a good laugh. Proverbs states, "A merry heart doeth good like a medicine."[148] The more you can smile and laugh during the first months and year, the better your mental health will be. G. K. Chesterton once wrote: "Angels can fly because they can take themselves lightly."[149]

Dani Bates—who lost her husband, Denny, to suicide—said, "If there's anything that Denny taught me . . . it's that you have to laugh to get through life sometimes. And sometimes it seems way too soon or way too awkward or way too weird. But you still have to make jokes about it, you know? It's how we can survive the hard things in life."[150]

Joshua shares the following experience: When my grandpa passed away, I felt a lot of pain, but the thing that helped the most was recounting memories with family members about the funny things he had said or done. Our reminiscing helped all of us accept that although he was gone physically, his spirit would live on in our memories. I believe laughter is an essential part of the grieving process and can go a long way toward consoling family members by lightening their spirits.

Smiling allows us to pause and come up for air. It also improves our mental health and overall well-being. One of the best things about smiling is that it can boost our mood even if we're feeling sad. Studies have found that even if we fake a smile, it tricks our brain into believing we're happy, which then spurs genuine feelings of happiness, increases positive thoughts, and helps our bodies deal with stress more effectively. Dr. Vanessa Reda, a licensed marriage and family therapist, has conducted "smile therapy" sessions, where participants use smiling to improve their mood. She said, "People overwhelmingly report a more positive mood through the

148 Proverbs 17:22.

149 Gilbert K. Chesterton, "The Eternal Revolution" in *Orthodoxy*, Project Gutenberg. gutenberg.org/cache/epub/130/pg130.html

150 Becky Jacobs, "Lehi mother shares the impact of husband's suicide to get people talking," *The Salt Lake Tribune*, September 15, 2019. sltrib.com/news/2019/09/15/lehi-mother-shares-impact/

experience [of smiling]. There's a tremendous body/mind connection, making smiling an excellent coping and self-soothing technique."[151]

Immerse Yourself in Service

One of the most therapeutic things you can do to help *yourself* is to do something for someone *else*. As we serve, our capacity to love increases. It is impossible to minister to others without receiving something valuable in return. Helping carry someone else's load inevitably lightens our own as it refines our spirits. By thinking of others and serving them, we will be blessed with peace and inner happiness. Elder Dieter F. Uchtdorf said, "To help others *is* the path of discipleship. Faith, hope, love, compassion, and service refine us as disciples. Through your efforts to help the poor and the needy, to reach out to those in distress, your own character is purified and forged, your spirit is enlarged, and you walk a little taller."[152]

We become more Christlike as we strive to help others, and doing so lightens our burden even as we strive to lift the burdens of others. The Lord has said, "Bear ye one another's burdens, and so fulfil the law of Christ."[153] Our Savior taught that the first great commandment is to love God with all of our heart, soul, mind, and strength.[154] This means that everything we do should be motivated by our love for our Heavenly Father and His Son. Poet, writer, and philosopher Kahlil Gibran observed, "Work is love made visible,"[155] and as we study the life of our Savior, it is easy to see the great love He had for others by the way He constantly rendered service.

151 Cari Scribner, "Even a Fake Smile Can Boost Your Mood," *ctPost*, August 7, 2013. ctpost.com/healthyyou/home/article/Even-a-Fake-Smile-Can-Boost -Your-Mood-4621347.php

152 Dieter F. Uchtdorf, "Your Great Adventure," *Ensign*, November 2019, 88. churchofjesuschrist.org/study/ensign/2019/11/43uchtdorf?lang=eng

153 Galatians 6:2.

154 See Mark 12:30.

155 Kahlil Gibran, "Work Is Love Made Visible," *The New York Times*, July 25, 1948. archive.nytimes.com/nytimes.com/books/98/12/13/specials/gibran -secrets.html

Jesus served all of mankind in a deeply personal way in Gethsemane by atoning for our sins and then hanging on the cross at Golgotha, performing the most selfless act of service in the history of the world, which caused Him great personal agony. In this remarkable act of service, Jesus Christ descended below us all, then was lifted up on the cross so He could raise all of us to a higher plane.

King Benjamin declared, "When ye are in the service of your fellow beings ye are only in the service of your God."[156] We become more Christlike if we can work past our sorrow and focus on lifting others up. Learning to lose ourselves in service is to begin to be more like God. His work is to exalt His children, and He strives constantly "to bring to pass the immortality and eternal life of man."[157]

The second great commandment is to love our neighbor as ourselves.[158] Even if we feel lost in grief, our sorrow will ease if we give of ourselves to help someone in need. Simple acts of service can transform our grief into hope, love, and joy as we serve family, friends, and neighbors. President Thomas S. Monson said:

> We are surrounded by those in need of our attention, our encouragement, our support, our comfort, our kindness—be they family members, friends, acquaintances, or strangers. We are the Lord's hands here upon the earth, with the mandate to serve and to lift His children. He is dependent upon each of us.[159]

Performing acts of service allows us to meet and talk with others whose sorrow may be greater than our own and to realize

---

156 Mosiah 2:17.
157 Moses 1:39.
158 See Matthew 22:39.
159 Thomas S. Monson, "What Have I Done for Someone Today?" *Ensign*, November 2009, 86. churchofjesuschrist.org/study/ensign/2009/11/what-have-i-done-for-someone-today?lang=eng

we are all on this path together. There are dozens of worthy orga-
nizations that depend on volunteers to serve the community and
would welcome your help. Even if your health is not good or
your mobility is limited, you can find some type of service suited
to your capabilities.

There are countless opportunities to serve, big and small. To lift
your spirits, take cookies to a neighbor, text a funny joke to a friend,
or babysit for a young mother so she can run errands or attend the
temple. Take an elderly neighbor grocery shopping, or take flowers
to someone who is elderly, ill, or recovering from surgery. You can
organize friends and family members who are musically inclined to
share their talents by singing or playing instruments at an assisted
living center. Pay for the guy behind you in the McDonald's drive-
up line, give your sister a call, put a note in your child's lunchbox,
and—well, you get the idea. Don't forget genealogical work and
ordinance work at the temple for your ancestors, which is a tremendous act of love. Serving others blesses not only other people's
lives but also our own because ministering allows the Holy Ghost
to be our constant companion when we act selflessly.

Create a Memory Book

Some people find comfort in creating a memory book about
their departed loved one. A scrapbook filled with priceless memories, including pictures and commentary, can be a wonderful
keepsake—a memento you and your family will always treasure.

Visit your local craft store for printed and colored paper, as well
as stickers and other items to decorate your pages. Ask a friend to
help you get started, or search online for ideas. Begin by collecting
all the materials you want to include—photos, postcards, articles,
letters, illustrations, quotations, ticket stubs, programs, and so on.
If you are making a book for your child, collect items from various
programs, vacation souvenirs, awards, and other memorabilia.
You can also create a glass-enclosed wall hanging, or shadow box,
with your child's soccer or basketball shirt or other items.

Lay the materials you want on a page, and arrange them until
you're satisfied. Use glue dots or glue sticks to secure them to the

page. You can write in dates and commentary about the occasion. At the end, you may want to include the funeral program, notes from the eulogy, and stories people related at the services. Take your time. There's no need to rush. Once done, you'll have a priceless, treasured memory book to look through when you want to reconnect with your dear one.

Keep a Journal

Keeping a journal can be helpful when recovering from loss. Singer-songwriter Joan Collins started writing a journal after the loss of her son, Clark. Collins said, "I started writing, getting the journals out and doing the work day by day, telling the tale, talking about my rage, my sorrow, my new kittens."[160] Write down all of your feelings, good and bad, so you'll have a written record to look back on and see your progress. If you ever feel that you're not moving forward, your journal can be a written record showing that even if you take a step or two back, you are further along the road to recovery than when you first started. Write your thoughts and feelings about your loved one or any changes you observe in yourself. Be sure to include any bits of inspiration that come to you during prayer or while reading the scriptures. You can include any significant events that occurred that day, your plans for tomorrow, or a story of a person who was helpful to you or that you were able to help.

Do Something Creative

Taking time to be creative can dispel heartache by renewing your soul, igniting a spark of enthusiasm, boosting your spirit, giving you a new zest for life, and helping you find new purpose. You can express yourself creatively through art, music, or countless other pursuits. Rekindle a long-abandoned interest, whether it's karate, painting, ceramics, or music. Perhaps you'll use your creative talents to redecorate a room in your home, make a quilt, sew an article of clothing, write poetry, or do some other project.

Adult education classes—often held in local high schools— have classes in creative endeavors such as woodwork, guitar,

---

160 Judy Collins, *The Seven T's: Finding Hope and Healing in the Wake of Tragedy* (New York: Penguin Group), 2007, 56.

foreign languages, ceramics, photography, metalwork, and others that can bring out your latent talents. Watch for local businesses who may offer classes on cooking, laying tile, or landscaping your backyard. You might want to unleash your creativity by taking voice lessons or a dance class or learning how to work with clay.

Other Activities That Can Help You Feel Better

During a time of loss, your soul needs nurturing. Think about what would make you feel better and write down a list of activities you would enjoy. Here are a few suggestions:

- Get a new cookbook and experiment with new dishes.
- Cut, color, or style your hair differently.
- Take a trip to someplace interesting, near or far.
- Paint a room in your house.
- Go shopping. Buy a book, a new lamp, towels, or some new clothes.
- Go outside! Sunlight and fresh air are good for you. Walk barefoot on the grass, go to a nearby lake or river and walk along the shore, hike a trail in the mountains, or go to a nearby park.
- Watch the sun rise or set.
- Set an appointment and talk with your bishop.
- Buy some colorful flowers and plant them in your yard or in a pot by your door.
- Watch your favorite TV show or rent a movie you've been wanting to see.
- Ask for a priesthood blessing.
- Plan a special activity for your children or grandchildren. They will welcome a chance to spend time with you in a fun activity.
- Join a book club or take an adult education class.
- Find a new hobby, or immerse yourself in one you already enjoy.
- Go to the library and pick out a good book.
- Go back to college.
- Start a new career or business.

Find Comfort in Honoring Your Loved One

Some people find solace in paying tribute to their loved one through a special act of service that blesses the lives of others. There are hundreds of humanitarian projects that you, your family, and your friends can do to assist others and honor your loved one's memory. Here are a few ideas:

- Start a scholarship fund in your child's name and award a one-time or yearly scholarship to someone who has the same interests as your child. The scholarship can be for any amount.
- Collect food or money and give to a local food bank.
- Organize a blood drive.
- Contact your local city. Perhaps you can plant a tree in a park or donate a park bench.
- Honor your loved one's memory by using the money you would have spent on gifts for them to help someone in need.
- Volunteer at a hospital, food bank, elementary school, retirement home, or homeless shelter.
- Arrange a neighborhood toy or clothing drive to collect for needy children at Christmas in the name of the person you love.
- Start an annual tournament (tennis, volleyball, or some other sport) in your child's name.
- Collect warm coats, gloves, or socks in the name of your departed loved one for the homeless.
- If you have lost a child, it can be therapeutic and rewarding to donate your child's toys and other belongings to a children's home, hospice, or hospital to brighten the lives of others.
- Organize neighbors and paint an elderly person's home, or do yard work for a neighbor who is ill or disabled.

CHAPTER 11
SEEING A PROFESSIONAL FOR ASSISTANCE

Then they cry unto the Lord in their trouble,
and he bringeth them out of their distresses.
He maketh the storm a calm,
so that the waves thereof are still.
Then are they glad because they be quiet;
so he bringeth them unto their desired haven.[161]

ALTHOUGH THOSE WHO LOSE A loved one are deeply saddened and feel adrift for some time, most people have a natural resilience and are eventually able to find their way again. Such is the nature of grief and human nature. While bereavement is a formidable experience and can dramatically shift your perspective on life, you can turn to God for help, and He can bless you with personal revelation on how to manage your loss.

Circumstances and timing can intensify the severity of your grief. Typically, people suffer more acutely if they have faced a number of losses in the past year, if the death was particularly traumatic, or if they are dealing with other problems. Family and friends can be a great support but usually don't have the training or experience a professional can provide, which is why many people turn to counseling to work through their sorrow.

161 Psalm 107:28–30.

Why See a Therapist?

If your car isn't running correctly, you take it to a mechanic—an expert in their field—and explain the problem. The mechanic will perform diagnostic tests to find out what the problem is and what needs to be done to fix it. Likewise, if your abdomen hurts, you go to a doctor and explain your symptoms. The doctor—an expert in physical ailments—will do tests to find out what is causing the pain and advise you what needs to be done to alleviate it.

Seeing a professional to get help when you are grieving is comparable to seeing a mechanic when your car needs fixing or visiting your doctor when suffering physical problems. If you are struggling after the death of a dear one, you can get help by seeing a therapist—an expert in their field. Therapists are trained to help with grief and many other mental health issues. You can feel reassured that when you see a therapist, you're dealing with a specialist—someone who has seen countless people go through what you are now facing and who has the knowledge and skills to help you. Don't think you have to be desperate or facing a crisis to seek professional help. You can get help whether you are hurting a little or a lot. Seeking help is a sign that you have the strength and resolve to take care of yourself.

Sometimes Church members think all they need to do to resolve emotional issues is read the scriptures, pray, and attend church. But frequently, it takes more than that. Elder Jeffrey R. Holland advised:

> If things continue to be debilitating, seek the advice of reputable people with certified training, professional skills, and good values. . . . Prayerfully and responsibly consider the counsel they give and the solutions they prescribe. If you had appendicitis, God would expect you to seek a priesthood blessing *and* get the best medical care available. So too with emotional disorders. Our

Father in Heaven expects us to use *all* of the marvelous gifts He has provided in this glorious dispensation.[162]

Healthy and Unhealthy Grief

Healthy grief has a function. It allows survivors to acknowledge, feel, and integrate the loss of their loved one and to move forward with life. However, becoming fixated on the loss can lead to unhealthy grief, which prolongs suffering, interrupts normal activities, and prevents people from living life to the fullest. Unhealthy grief can also morph into depression, anxiety, and other mental disorders.

To prevent this, it's important to create a support system. The more isolated you are, the more difficult the grieving and the slower the healing process. Cherishing and holding on to some possessions that belonged to the deceased is normal, but holding on to every piece of clothing, furniture, or possession for more than a year is a sign of unhealthy grief.

Unhealthy grief can manifest itself in various emotional and physical forms. Some physical symptoms include ulcers, headaches, frequent nightmares, stomach upsets, and exhaustion. Unhealthy grief can show itself in behaviors such as dependence on alcohol or medications, overspending, overeating, self-harm, and violence. If you begin to experience these negative behaviors, it's important to seek professional help immediately.

Chronic Grief

Recovering from grief can be a genuine struggle, but usually the process is not overwhelming or never-ending. However, when grief persists for a long period of time, it can turn into chronic grief and adversely affect everything in your life.

Chronic grief occurs when the pain of loss overwhelms a person and interferes with their ability to function, making it

---

162 Jeffrey R. Holland, "Like a Broken Vessel," *Ensign*, November 2013, 41. churchofjesuschrist.org/study/ensign/2013/11/saturday-afternoon-session/like-a-broken-vessel?lang=eng

nearly impossible to return to a normal daily routine even after years have passed. Prolonged grieving is caused by an insatiable desire to have the deceased person back with them. People overwhelmed by grief often stop participating in life because their only interest lies in the past. Therapy can be very beneficial in such cases. Joshua shares the following experience:

> I've done a fair amount of grief counseling, and it's always interesting to see how differently people handle death. Once I saw a fifty-year-old client who had really been thrown after losing his sister. We began discussing the situation, and as the client talked about his feelings, I sensed that some things weren't quite adding up. Then I learned that this client's sister had passed away more than ten years ago. We discussed that while it's good to keep the memory of those you love in your heart, it's also necessary to move on with your life. Obviously, this client had suffered great trauma over losing a sibling, but I felt it was important, for the client's mental health, to dedicate more time to the present and future rather than hold on to the past.

How to Find a Counselor

When seeking a therapist, ask for personal recommendations from your friends, family, doctor, bishop, local hospital, or school psychologist. Check your insurance to find out which therapists are covered under your plan. Help is available even if your insurance does not have good mental health coverage or if you don't have insurance. Some family service agencies and mental health clinics charge according to a person's financial circumstances. Talk to your bishop to see if Church social services are available in your area. Often those payments are adjusted to your ability to pay. Once you have a list of counselors, do some research online to familiarize yourself with their specialties and help you decide which one might be a good fit for you.

When setting an appointment, explain what kind of help you are seeking, such as with depression, anxiety, or grief. Be sure to find a therapist with whom you feel comfortable. The patient-therapist relationship is a significant one, so if you're not satisfied after a few visits, keep looking until you find someone compatible—someone you can trust. It may take time to find a therapist with whom you feel comfortable, but the right one is worth their weight in gold.

Joshua learned about the importance of having a good therapist-client relationship while he was studying to become a therapist. Many times the success of counseling depends on whether a client is able to trust their therapist. If clients don't have confidence in their counselor, they are less likely to open up about the challenges they're facing, which can limit their progress. Trust usually accelerates therapy because patients are more likely to do as the therapist advises when they trust their therapist. Dr. John Mayer agrees it is essential for patients to trust their therapist. "One of the most important steps that helps [the patient] is to build a trusting relationship. With empathy, genuineness, and trust, a strong rapport can be built, and therapists are able to communicate and direct their patients in a way that facilitates healing."[163]

Sometimes people drop out of counseling because they feel they are not getting better as quickly as they hoped or because it hurts too much. Have patience. Feeling better is a process that takes time. It's common for people to feel worse before they get better, so don't give up. Equate this to having surgery to correct a painful physical problem; it may be necessary to hurt more for a short time in order to feel better for the rest of your life.

What Do the Initials Mean?

A therapist is a licensed mental health professional who helps clients improve their lives, develop better cognitive and emotional skills, and cope with various challenges. When searching for a therapist, it's helpful to understand the initials behind a therapist's name.

---

163 John Mayer, "3 Important Elements of a Good Therapist Relationship," Dr. on Demand. blog.doctorondemand.com/3-important -elements-of-a-good-therapist-relationship-901bfc7e352c

- **Clinical Psychologist.** A clinical psychologist at a doctorate level can have *Dr.* before their name and can have *PhD*, *PsyD*, or *EdD* after it. A psychologist at a master's level can use the initials *MA*, *MS*, *LGPC*, or *LCPC*.
- **Psychiatrist.** A psychiatrist has gone to medical school and will have *Dr.* before his or her name. Psychiatrists can prescribe medications.
- **Social workers.** A clinical social worker has at least a master's degree in social work and can have the initials *MSW*, *LGSW*, *LCSW*, *LMSW*, *LISW*, *LSW*, *CSW*, and others.
- **Marriage and Family Therapists.** Marriage and family therapists can use the initials *MA*, *MFT*, *LMFT*, or *LCMFT*. They have completed a master's program in marriage and family therapy.

Medication

Most grieving people don't need antidepressant medication. In the first days and weeks following a death, grievers will usually have a great deal of support and be able to feel and express all their emotions. If you still are in pain as time goes by and support from others lessens, you may be tempted to self-medicate, but this is not advisable. Do not take medication prescribed for someone else, and it is *never* a good idea to take illegal drugs.

Sometimes an individual's depressed mood is so profound or overwhelming that it interferes with normal day-to-day actions. If this happens, see your doctor and follow his recommendations. If your doctor prescribes a sleep aid or some other medication, take it as directed; do not take more than the recommended dosage. If after six weeks you are still feeling persistently sad or irritable or have little interest in life, you may be suffering from clinical depression. Make an appointment with a physician or a psychiatrist, who may prescribe an antidepressant medication to help you during this difficult time.

Support Groups

Many people find it helpful to attend a support group. There are many professionally led support groups organized and facilitated by therapists, social workers, psychologists, and other mental health professionals. Such groups can be the ideal place to inexpensively explore your feelings and receive encouragement and help. While some people rely solely on one-to-one counseling, others find support groups provide a valuable supplementary assistance, and still others feel support groups alone meet all their needs.

Support groups assist mourners to recognize they are not alone and allow them to see how others are managing their loss. No one will be able to understand your feelings as well as someone who has traveled the same road. Attendees are often gratified by the understanding, care, and support they receive.

Although your loss may feel like a weight keeping you stuck in the same place, your goal—along with everyone else's in your group—will be to move forward. What you will learn by sharing your memories, your sadness, and your victories is that it's okay to feel sad. And lost. And angry. It's okay to feel a whole lot of things that other people might not understand. You will also learn that it may take time to overcome your loss. Finally, you'll learn that everyone has their own journey to make.

In a support group, you will see how other people are struggling with the same issues you are, and you'll discover new ways to cope with your loss. When you see someone who is further along in the healing process than you are, you'll realize there is light and hope ahead. After attending for a while, new people will join, and you'll see those who are at the beginning of the mourning process and notice how they are where you used to be. You will have the opportunity to reach out to them with the same love and compassion that others showed you.

To find a group, check with your therapist, doctor, bishop, local hospital, or social services. You can google support groups online and find a group that fits your particular need by using the term *support group* with additional search terms such as *bereavement, newly widowed, young and widowed, loss of a child, suicide,* and so on. If a group doesn't fit you after you've attended a number of meetings, don't give up—try another group.

Turn to Christ, the Ultimate Healer

Although seeking professional help, whether a therapist or a support group, is one of the best steps we can take when beset by grief, it's good to remember that Jesus Christ can help us heal. "Then they cry unto the Lord in their trouble, and he saveth them out of their distresses. He sent his word, and healed them, and delivered *them* from their destructions."[164]

Our Savior has the power to cast out any darkness that veils our life and replace it with light and peace. We can also ask God to fight Satan—who likes to prey on us when we are weak. Although losing a loved one hurts deeply and makes us wonder if we will ever feel like ourselves again, Heavenly Father can lessen our pain. If we pray in faith, God will comfort and bless us with strength and peace. "Whatsoever thing ye shall ask the Father in my name, which is good, in faith believing that ye shall receive, behold, it shall be done unto you."[165]

When we feel an empty place in our heart after losing someone close to us, remember Christ's victory over death. When Christ accomplished His great atoning sacrifice, He irrevocably defeated death and ushered in the Resurrection. Those we love are still alive because of Christ's magnificent gift to all of mankind. The doctrine of resurrection offers comfort and hope to all who mourn. This is why the Savior could tell His disciples—despite their sufferings, trials, and martyrdom—to be of good cheer. We miss our deceased family and friends but know our separation is for only a short time. As we await our reunion, we can direct our thoughts to Jesus Christ and be everlastingly grateful that He broke the bands of death so that all could live.

Part of Christ's mission on Earth is to comfort all who mourn.[166] He is our advocate with the Father and works continually for us, leading us along, blessing our lives, and lightening our load. Although Christ always stands ready to help, we must reach out and ask for His help, for He will not interfere with our agency.

---

164 Psalm 107:19–20.

165 Moroni 7:26.

166 See Isaiah 61:2.

Because of the all-encompassing love that Heavenly Father and Jesus Christ have for us, they will answer the prayers of anyone who prays in humility and faith. The Apostle Paul wrote, "We trust in the living God, who is the Saviour of all men, specially of those that believe."[167] When we follow the Savior with a humble heart and a contrite spirit, He can comfort our hearts, lift us up, and fill our grieving souls with abiding peace and joy.

---

167 1 Timothy 4:10.

CHAPTER 12
THE POWER OF PRAYER

Praying always with all prayer and supplication in the Spirit, and watching thereunto with all perseverance and supplication for all saints.[168]

PRAYER CAN BE A POWERFUL source of comfort when we feel overwhelmed by our loss. By reaching out and asking for help, God can enfold us in the arms of His love and comfort us. Prayer is a blessing from God—a wonderful, sacred means of conversing with Deity that pierces the veil. In Alma, we are instructed to pray continually. "Yea, cry unto him for mercy; for he is mighty to save. Yea, humble yourselves, and continue in prayer unto him. . . . Yea, and when you do not cry unto the Lord, let your hearts be full, drawn out in prayer unto him continually for your welfare."[169] President Ezra Taft Benson said prayer can bring serenity and peace:

> All through my life the counsel to depend on prayer has been prized above almost any other advice I have . . . received. It has become an integral part of me—an anchor, a constant source of strength, and

---

168 Ephesians 6:18.
169 Alma 34:18–19, 27.

the basis of my knowledge of things divine. . . .
Though . . . reverses come, in prayer we can find
reassurance, for God will speak peace to the soul.
That peace, that spirit of serenity, is life's greatest
blessing.[170]

In prayer, we can find the consolation we seek when God
speaks to our wounded heart. The sense of serenity that comes
from heaven is a great blessing in time of need. President Thomas S.
Monson counseled those who were facing trials when he said:

To those within the sound of my voice who are
struggling with challenges and difficulties large and
small, prayer is the provider of spiritual strength;
it is the passport to peace. Prayer is the means by
which we approach our Father in Heaven, who
loves us. Speak to Him in prayer and then listen
for the answer. Miracles are wrought through
prayer.[171]

We were not placed on this earth to walk alone. To help us
while away from our heavenly home, we have been given the gift
of prayer, an amazing source of power, strength, and solace that
is available to each of us. Our Heavenly Father knows us better
than we know ourselves and, since He can see the beginning from
the end, is in the preeminent position of being able to provide
invaluable help if we will only ask. In the scriptures, He gives us
a comforting promise: "Search diligently, pray always, and be
believing, and all things shall work together for your good."[172]

Elder Richard G. Scott taught about the priceless gift of
being able to talk with God:

---

170 Ezra Taft Benson, "Pray Always," *Ensign*, February 1990, 4–5.
churchofjesuschrist.org/study/ensign/1990/02/pray-always?lang=eng

171 Thomas S. Monson, "Be Your Best Self," *Ensign*, May 2009, 68.
churchofjesuschrist.org/study/general-conference/2009/04/be-your-best-
self?lang=eng

172 D&C 90:24.

Prayer is a supernal gift of our Father in Heaven to every soul. Think of it: The absolute Supreme Being, the most all-knowing, all-seeing, all-powerful personage, encourages you and me, as insignificant as we are, to converse with Him as our Father. Actually, because He knows how desperately we need His guidance, He commands, "Thou shalt pray vocally as well as in thy heart; yea, before the world as well as in secret, in public as well as in private" (D&C 19:28).

It matters not our circumstance, be we humble or arrogant, poor or rich, free or enslaved, learned or ignorant, loved or forsaken, we can address Him. We need no appointment. Our supplication can be brief or can occupy all the time needed. It can be an extended expression of love and gratitude or an urgent plea for help. He has created numberless cosmos and populated them with worlds, yet you and I can talk with Him personally, and He will ever answer.[173]

Through Prayer, We Can Receive Personal Revelation

Because Heavenly Father loves us, He wants to hear from us and provide the blessings we need. God will listen as we talk to Him about any sorrows, worries, and troubles that arise from our loss. President Harold B. Lee said:

> The most important thing you can do is to learn to talk to God. Talk to Him as you would talk to your father, for He is your Father. . . . He wants you to cultivate ears to listen, when He gives you the impressions of the Spirit to tell you what to do. If you learn to give heed to the sudden ideas which come to your minds, you will find those

---

173 Richard G. Scott, "Using the Supernal Gift of Prayer," *Ensign*, May 2007, 8. churchofjesuschrist.org/study/ensign/2007/05/using-the-supernal-gift-of-prayer?lang=eng

> things coming through in the very hour of your
> need. If you will cultivate an ear to hear these
> promptings, you will have learned to walk by
> the spirit of revelation.[174]

If we pray in humility, trusting that God will answer our prayers, He will give us gentle promptings and personal revelation that will provide us with direction. In the New Testament, we read, "If any of you lack wisdom, let him ask of God, that giveth to all men liberally, and upbraideth not; and it shall be given him."[175] When Joseph Smith read this verse, it sank deep into his heart, prompting him to go into the woods to pray. As a result, he received the First Vision, which led to the Restoration of the gospel.

All of us can benefit from having personal revelation to guide and direct us. As we pray and ponder, God will bless us with inspired thoughts, feelings of peace, and guidance for our lives. As we take the time to listen when we pray, God will offer counsel on what we can do to help ourselves and those around us.

In the early days of the Church, Sister Eliza R. Snow wanted women to know they could receive divine inspiration to guide them in their personal lives, in their families, and in their Church responsibilities. She said, "Tell the sisters to go forth and discharge their duties, in humility and faithfulness and the Spirit of God will rest upon them and they will be blest in their labors. Let them seek for wisdom instead of power and they will have all the power they have wisdom to exercise."[176]

---

174 *Teachings of the Presidents of the Church: Harold B. Lee* (Salt Lake City: The Church of Jesus Christ of Latter-day Saints, 2000), 55. churchofjesuschrist. org/study/manual/teachings-harold-b-lee/chapter-6?lang=eng
175 James 1:5.
176 *Daughters in My Kingdom: The History and Work of Relief Society* (Salt Lake City: The Church of Jesus Christ of Latter-day Saints, 2011), 45. churchofjesuschrist.org/study/manual/daughters-in-my-kingdom-the -history-and-work-of-relief-society/a-wide-and-extensive-sphere-of-action?lang=eng

When the Spirit of revelation comes, it is *felt* more than heard, which is why it is often referred to as the whispering of the Spirit. The Prophet Joseph Smith explained how to recognize the Spirit:

> A person may profit by noticing the first intimation of the spirit of revelation; for instance, when you feel pure intelligence flowing into you, it may give you sudden strokes of ideas, so that by noticing it, you may find it fulfilled the same day or soon; (i.e.) those things that were presented unto your minds by the Spirit of God, will come to pass; and thus by learning the Spirit of God and understanding it, you may grow into the principle of revelation, until you become perfect in Christ Jesus.[177]

One of the most glorious revelations ever received in the latter days—the vision of the redemption of the dead given to President Joseph F. Smith—provides great comfort to those who have lost a loved one. During his lifetime, President Smith experienced much personal loss. His father died when he was a young boy, and some years after crossing the plains, he lost his mother. He also suffered the loss of a brother, two sisters, two wives, and thirteen children. The vision of the redemption of the dead came at a time when President Smith was mourning personal losses as well as grieving the loss of life from World War I, which ended up killing more than twenty million people, and the 1918 Spanish flu pandemic, which would eventually take the lives of nearly one hundred million people.

All of these losses instilled in President Smith a deep desire to know more about the state of the individual soul after death, and he

---

177 *Teachings of the Presidents of the Church: Joseph Smith* (Salt Lake City: The Church of Jesus Christ of Latter-day Saints, 2004, 2011), 132. churchofjesuschrist.org/study/manual/teachings-joseph-smith/chapter-10?lang=eng

prayed to learn more concerning this matter. Although President Smith prayed in humble faith, months of prayer went by without an answer. But his faith did not waver. He continued to pray, and in October 1918, President Smith received an extraordinary revelation about the spirit world that gives us much comforting information about what happens when our dear ones pass away. This revelation reveals the depth and breadth of Heavenly Father's glorious plan of salvation and demonstrates Christ's love for us—a love so great that Jesus gave His life to bring about the Atonement so that we might live.[178]

Attending Church and the Temple Enhances Our Prayers

To increase the efficacy of our prayers, advance in holiness, increase in favor with God, and more fully receive the power of God in our lives, we need to attend our church meetings and go to the temple as often as we are able. Doing so allows us to draw nearer to God, who will then draw near to us. Attending our meetings will provide an anchor in our lives, a constant source of strength as we learn more of things divine. While caught in the throes of grief, tears often threaten, which can make church attendance difficult. But if we pray for courage and have faith, God can strengthen us. Staying close to the gospel can provide much solace. President Heber J. Grant said:

> We realize that our Father in Heaven can bind up broken hearts and that He can dispel sorrow and that He can point forward with joy and satisfaction to those blessings that are to come through obedience to the Gospel of the Lord Jesus Christ. . . . There will come a time, through the blessing and mercy of God, when we will no more have sorrow but when we shall have conquered all of these things that are of a trying and distressing character, and shall stand up in the presence of the living God, filled with joy and peace and satisfaction.[179]

178 See D&C 138.
179 Heber J. Grant, "In the Hour of Parting," *Improvement Era*, June 1940, 330. archive.org/details/improvementera4306unse/page/n11

Attending the temple can be a great source of strength. Holy temples are a reliable venue of peace and consolation when in need of refuge. Being in the house of the Lord provides refreshment to our spirit—buoying us up when we are laid low by the vicissitudes of life. President Gordon B. Hinckley taught that temple ordinances can bring comfort after losing a loved one. He said:

> I was [once] called to the hospital bedside of a mother in the terminal stages of a serious illness. She passed away a short time later, leaving her husband and four children, including a little boy of six. There was sorrow, deep and poignant and tragic. But shining through their tears was a faith beautiful and certain that as surely as there was now a sorrowful separation, there would someday be a glad reunion, for that marriage had begun with a sealing for time and eternity in the house of the Lord, under the authority of the holy priesthood.[180]

Trust the Lord

President Thomas S. Monson reminded us that when we pray, we should strive to trust the Lord: "As we offer unto the Lord our family prayers and our personal prayers, let us do so with faith and trust in Him. Let us remember the injunction of Paul to the Hebrews: 'For he that cometh to God must believe that he is, and that he is a rewarder of them that diligently seek him' (Hebrews 11:6)."[181]

If we trust in God, we can be led by the Holy Spirit to surmount the problems of the world, grow spiritually, and receive

---

180 *Teachings of the Presidents of the Church: Gordon B. Hinckley* (Salt Lake City: The Church of Jesus Christ of Latter-day Saints, 2016), 313. churchofjesuschrist.org/study/manual/teachings-of-presidents-of-the-church-gordon-b-hinckley/chapter-23-the-blessings-of-the-holy-temple?lang=eng
181 Thomas S. Monson, "Come unto Him in Prayer and Faith," *Ensign*, March 2009, 6. churchofjesuschrist.org/study/ensign/2009/03/come-unto-him-in-prayer-and-faith?lang=eng

divine guidance. "Trust in the Lord with all thine heart; and lean not unto thine own understanding. In all thy ways acknowledge him, and he shall direct thy paths."[182]

Heavenly Father is mindful of us and will answer our prayers when we place our trust in Him and seek divine direction for our lives. The prophet Nephi knew on whom he could rely for divine help. He said, "O Lord, I have trusted in thee, and I will trust in thee forever."[183]

There are times in our lives when our needs are great and our despair high, making it difficult when asking for a special blessing to add the caveat "if it be Thy will." However, even when anguished, we need to trust God and align ourselves with His will. If we pray with faith, humility, and sincerity of heart, God will pour forth blessings from heaven upon our heads and comfort us in our loss. "And whatsoever ye shall ask the Father in my name, which is right, believing that ye shall receive, behold it shall be given unto you."[184]

If we fully place our trust in the Lord, we will also trust His timing: "Behold, God is my salvation; I will trust, and not be afraid; for the Lord Jehovah is my strength and my song; he also has become my salvation."[185] President Joseph F. Smith prayed for many months before he received an answer from God. If we have patience while enduring our trials, Heavenly Father will bless us with strength to face the storms of life that come to all of us. Even if our problems are not immediately resolved, He can bless us with spiritual strength during moments of need and give us the ability to endure our hardships.

Trust and faith go hand in hand. When we have faith in Jesus Christ, we accept His will and trust that He knows what is best for us. As we trust God, we will come to see His tender mercies in our lives—moments when He lifts us through our grief, trials, and challenges. Although there will be times when we stumble and

---

182 Proverbs 3:5–6.
183 2 Nephi 4:34.
184 3 Nephi 18:20.
185 2 Nephi 22:2.

fall, we can exercise trust in Him by getting up on our feet and trying again. God has given us a glorious promise regarding prayer: "Let your requests be made known unto God. And the peace of God, which passeth all understanding, shall keep your hearts and minds through Christ Jesus."[186]

Elder Richard G. Scott said:

> We are like infants in our understanding of eternal matters and their impact on us here in mortality. Yet at times we act as if we knew it all. When you pass through trials for His purposes, as you trust Him, exercise faith in Him, He will help you. That support will generally come step by step, a portion at a time. While you are passing through each phase, the pain and difficulty that comes from being enlarged will continue. If all matters were immediately resolved at your first petition, you could not grow. Your Father in Heaven and His Beloved Son love you perfectly. They would not require you to experience a moment more of difficulty than is absolutely needed for your personal benefit or for that of those you love.[187]

---

186 Philippians 4:6–7.
187 Richard G. Scott, "Trust in the Lord," *Ensign*, November 1995, 17. churchofjesuschrist.org/study/ensign/1995/11/trust-in-the-lord?lang=eng

CHAPTER 13
THERE MUST BE FAITH

Wherefore, there must be faith;
and if there must be faith there must also be hope;
and if there must be hope there must also be charity.
And except ye have charity ye can in nowise be saved in
the kingdom of God; neither can ye be saved in the kingdom of
God if ye have not faith; neither can ye if ye have no hope.[188]

ALTHOUGH LOSING A DEAR ONE causes an emptiness in our hearts
that is real and painful, faith brings comfort by assuring us that
in time, we will see our loved one again. Tears may still overflow,
but they do not arise from despair—they come because of love
and tender feelings at being separated for a season. At such times,
faith enables us to stand firm. President Spencer W. Kimball related
having faith to physical reservoirs that store water from spring rains
for later use. He said that in addition to having physical water
reservoirs, we also need to have spiritual reservoirs, "reservoirs of
faith so that when the world presses in upon us, we stand firm and
strong. . . . We need a storage of faith that can carry [us through] . . .
disappointments, disillusionments, and years of adversity."[189]

When faith is strong, it can transform sorrow into the hope
of a joyful future reunion. Faith gives us strength to withstand our

188 Moroni 10:20–21.
189 Kimball, *Faith Precedes the Miracle*, 110–11. Used with permission.

loss and continue on. "And Christ truly said unto our fathers: If ye have faith ye can do all things which are expedient unto me."[190]

And yet, even if your faith is strong and your testimony deep, it is painful to lose a loved one. The Prophet Joseph Smith mourned his friends and family who had passed away. Speaking at the funeral for a young man named Ephraim Marks, Joseph said:

> It is a very solemn and awful time. I never felt more solemn; it calls to mind the death of my oldest brother, Alvin, who died in New York, and my youngest brother, Don Carlos Smith, who died in Nauvoo. It has been hard for me to live on earth and see these young men upon whom we have leaned for support and comfort taken from us in the midst of their youth. Yes, it has been hard to be reconciled to these things. I have sometimes thought that I should have felt more reconciled to have been called away myself if it had been the will of God; yet I know we ought to be still and know it is of God, and be reconciled to His will; all is right. It will be but a short time before we shall all in like manner be called: it may be the case with me as well as you.[191]

Countless blessings come from having faith. One of the foremost of those blessings is faith that one day we will be saved with our loved ones in the kingdom of God. Alma taught us to live "having faith on the Lord; having a hope that ye shall receive eternal life; having the love of God always in your hearts, that ye may be lifted up at the last day and enter into his rest."[192] This knowledge is especially comforting after losing someone we love.

190 Moroni 10:23.
191 Joseph Smith, in *History of the Church of Jesus Christ of Latter-day Saints* (Salt Lake City: Deseret News, 1950), 4:587. byustudies.byu.edu/content/volume-4-chapter-34. Used with permission.
192 Alma 13:29.

One particular test of faith occurs when a loved one passes away despite our humble prayers and priesthood blessings. At such times, it can be hard to accept that God's answer is no. Because we know God hears our prayers, we must have faith to accept His divine will, knowing that God will do nothing except what is best for us and our loved ones. His sole aim is designed to bless our lives—whether in this life or in the next.

Through faith, we know God can heal the sick and injured, but only if the person is not appointed unto death. If we understand this principle, we can take comfort in knowing that if our loved one passes away after receiving a blessing, it is because it was their appointed time to leave mortality. If God chooses to call our loved one home, we must continue to exercise faith and trust in God, who has promised, "If they die, they shall die unto me."[193]

When Mary and Martha's brother, Lazarus, became gravely ill, the sisters surely prayed fervently for their brother. But despite their prayers, Lazarus died. Although grief-stricken, Mary and Martha continued to hold fast to their faith. When Jesus arrived four days later, Martha told the Savior that she knew if He had been there, her brother would not have died. Then she added, "But I know, that even now, whatsoever thou wilt ask of God, God will give it thee."

Jesus replied, "I am the resurrection, and the life: he that believeth in me, though he were dead, yet shall he live: And whosoever liveth and believeth in me shall never die. Believest thou this?"

Martha replied, "Yea, Lord: I believe that thou art the Christ, the Son of God."

Mary also told Jesus that if He had been there, her brother would not have died. When Jesus saw the tremendous grief Mary and Martha felt at their brother's death, Jesus wept. Then in majesty and power, He commanded Lazarus to come forth. "And he that was dead came forth."[194]

---

193 D&C 42:44.
194 John 11:22, 25–27, 44. See also verses 1–43.

Inspirational Examples of Faith
A Widow in Prussia

During our life, we will experience many tests of faith, and surely one of the most trying is losing a loved one. However, having a firm and unshakable faith in Jesus Christ gives us strength to endure our heartache, hope of better things to come, and the knowledge that one day our dark night will be turned into a brilliant new dawn.

Such was the case for a faithful woman living in Prussia during World War II. Shortly after the war ended, Ezra Taft Benson and Frederick W. Babbel were assigned to assist the Saints in Europe. When they arrived at Karlsruhe, Germany, Elders Benson and Babbel climbed over piles of rubble and eased themselves through blasted walls to make their way to a district conference. In a poorly lit room with no heat, President Benson offered encouragement to a group of 260 Saints.

After the meeting, Max Zimmer, the acting president of the Swiss Mission, pointed out a timid, emaciated sister with red, swollen eyes. She had no shoes—only burlap sacks wrapped around her feet. Her face was purple-gray, and she had the protruding joints that indicated an advanced stage of starvation. President Zimmer related her story to President Benson.

In the final dreadful days of the war, the woman's husband died, leaving her alone to care for their four children. Due to the agreement of the occupying military powers, she was one of eleven million people who had been driven out of their homeland of Prussia in late summer. Although grief-stricken, the young widow journeyed to West Germany, a trek of more than one thousand miles (1,600 km). With no means of transportation, she and her children were forced to walk, taking only whatever bare necessities would fit into a small, wooden-wheeled wagon. She carried her baby in her arms while her other three children—the oldest being only seven—trailed her. With no food or money and facing constant danger from other refugees and marauding troops, the young mother scavenged food each day from the fields and forests they passed in order to feed her children.

As the weeks passed, the weather grew colder, and the temperature dropped below freezing. When their shoes gave out, the mother wrapped burlap around her children's feet. Then the snows came. Occasionally the woman found shelter in a barn or shed, and the little family huddled together for warmth since the few thin blankets they had did little to protect them from the cold. One morning, she woke to find that her three-year-old daughter had died. The grieving mother had nothing with which to dig a grave except a tablespoon.

They traveled on. Then her seven-year-old son died. Again, the mother was forced to dig a grave. When her five-year-old son died, all she had left was her baby daughter. She was nearing the end of her journey when her baby died in her arms. The spoon was gone, so she had to dig a grave in the frozen earth with her bare fingers. After losing her husband and all four of her children, the woman's grief was nearly unbearable, and she considered ending her life, as so many of her fellow countrymen had done.

Then something inside told her, "Get down on your knees and pray."

She did, praying more fervently than she had ever prayed before. The woman was blessed with an outpouring of the Spirit, which gave her the strength to continue her journey until she finally reached Germany. After the conference, Elder Ezra Taft Benson and Elder Frederick W. Babbel talked with her.

Afterward, Elder Babbel stated: "In conclusion, she bore a glorious testimony, stating that of all the ailing people in her saddened land she was one of the happiest because she knew that God lived, that Jesus is the Christ, and that if she continued faithful and true to the end, she would be saved in the celestial kingdom of God."[195]

Heber J. Grant's Daughter

One of the greatest consolations that faith provides is allowing us to trust in God's timing, even when it is not the timing we would have chosen. Author John Bytheway said:

---

195 Frederick W. Babbel, *On Wings of Faith* (Salt Lake City: Bookcraft, 1972), 42.

When we exercise faith in *him*, and in *his* timing, we can be assured that all things will work together for our good, however painful they may be for us at the moment. If someone you love dies, it does not necessarily mean that your faith was lacking. It may just mean that for reasons we may not know in this life, it was the Lord's will that the person pass on. One day we will understand why! (D&C 101:32–36). Real faith is knowing that the Lord loves us with all of his heart so we can trust in him with all of our hearts. One day he will explain all things and wipe away all of our tears.[196]

One example of having great faith occurred in the life of President Heber J. Grant's twelve-year-old daughter, who had faith that her mother would recover, even though she had been seriously ill for some time. Sister Grant had been bedridden for months before it appeared that death was imminent. Elder Grant called his children to gather around her bedside and tell their mother goodbye.

His twelve-year-old daughter objected, saying, "Papa, I do not want my mamma to die. I have been with her in the hospital . . . for six months; time and time again. . . . You have administered to her, and she has been relieved of her pain and quietly gone to sleep. I want you to lay hands upon my mamma and heal her."

Gently, Elder Grant told her and his other children that he felt impressed it was time for their mother to go. After the children filed out of the room, Heber knelt by his wife's bed and prayed. "I told the Lord I acknowledged his hand in life [and] in death. . . . But I told the Lord that I lacked the strength to have my wife die and to have it affect the faith of my little children." Heber then pleaded with the Lord to give his daughter "a knowledge that it was his mind and his will that her mamma should die."

---

196 John Bytheway, *Righteous Warriors: Lessons from the War Chapters in the Book of Mormon* (Salt Lake City: Deseret Book, 2004), 119.

An hour later, Elder Grant's wife passed away. When he told the children, his six-year-old son, Heber, started to cry. Elder Grant's twelve-year-old daughter reached out to comfort her little brother. While hugging him, she said, "Do not weep, Heber; since we went out of this room, the voice of the Lord from heaven has said to me, In the death of your mamma the will of the Lord shall be done."[197]

Daniel Apilado

While attending stake conference in the Philippines, Elder Evan A. Schmutz learned of a tragedy that befell local Church leader Daniel Apilado. In 1974, Daniel Apilado and his wife converted, were baptized members of the Church, and were later sealed in the temple. As the years passed, they were blessed with five beautiful children. Elder Apilado was serving as stake president when a fire broke out in his small home on July 7, 1997. Elder Schmutz related:

> Brother Apilado's oldest son, Michael, rescued his father, pulled him from the burning structure, and then ran back into the house to rescue others. It was the last time Brother Apilado saw his son alive. Taken in the fire were Brother Apilado's wife, Dominga, and each of their five children. The fact that Brother Apilado was living a life pleasing unto God when tragedy struck did not prevent the tragedy, nor did it make him immune from the sorrow that followed. But his *faithfulness* in keeping his covenants and exercising his faith in Christ gave him assurance in the promise that he will be reunited with his wife and family. This hope became an anchor to his soul (see Ether 12:4).

Elder Schmutz continues:

---

197 Bryant S. Hinckley, *Heber J. Grant: Highlights in the Life of a Great Leader* (Salt Lake City: Deseret Book, 1951), 243–44.

During my visit, Brother Apilado, now the stake patriarch, introduced me to his new wife, Simonette, and to their two sons, Raphael and Daniel. Truly, Jesus Christ can and will "bind up the brokenhearted" (see Isaiah 61:1; see also verses 2–3).

In sharing Brother Apilado's story, I am concerned that the enormity of his loss may cause many to think their own sorrows and sufferings are of little consequence in comparison. Please don't compare, but seek to learn and apply eternal principles as you wade through the furnace of your own afflictions.

If I may speak to you individually—"all ye that labour and are heavy laden" (Matthew 11:28)—may I suggest that your personal struggles—your individual sorrows, pains, tribulations, and infirmities of every kind—are all known to our Father in Heaven and to His Son. Take courage! Have faith! And believe in the promises of God!

The purpose and mission of Jesus Christ included that He would "take upon him the pains and the sicknesses of his people," "take upon him their infirmities," and "succor his people according to their infirmities" (Alma 7:11–12).

To fully receive these gifts our Savior has so freely offered, we all must learn that suffering in and of itself does not teach or grant to us anything of lasting value unless we *deliberately* become involved in the process of learning from our afflictions through the exercise of faith.[198]

---

198 Evan A. Schmutz, "God Shall Wipe Away All Tears," *Ensign*, November 2016,   117–18.   churchofjesuschrist.org/study/ensign/2016/11/sunday-afternoon-session/god-shall-wipe-away-all-tears?lang=eng

CHAPTER 14
CULTIVATING DIVINE ATTRIBUTES

Blessed be God, even the Father of our Lord Jesus Christ,
the Father of mercies, and the God of all comfort;
Who comforteth us in all our tribulation, that we may
be able to comfort them which are in any trouble, by
the comfort wherewith we ourselves are comforted of God.[199]

OUR LIVES WILL BE CHANGED after losing a loved one. Although
no one wants to go through the pain that comes from personal
loss, it is possible to become wiser, more understanding, more
appreciative of life, and more spiritual not *in spite* of our grief and
suffering but *because* of it. There are insights we can cultivate from
the trials and hardships we face in mortality. As we turn to God,
we come to understand more deeply that God knows us, loves
us, and is aware of all the pain we experience. We can grow and
cultivate spiritual attributes as we draw closer to Heavenly Father
in times of anguish. "As we learn from the loss something of value
that benefits ourselves and others, our loss is transformed," said
author Ann Stearns. "An event that takes away something precious
becomes an event that gives us something new."[200]

199 2 Corinthians 1:3–4.
200 Ann Kaiser Stearns, *Living Through Personal Crisis* (New York:
Ballantine Books, 1985), 146–47.

Cultivating Increased Compassion

Remembering how gentle and kind other people were in helping us get through our loss, we can become more compassionate and loving when we see someone else in pain. We don't have to look far to see sadness etched on someone's face and feel a desire to reach out and offer compassionate help. We are all in this world together and can offer support and a listening ear to others when times are hard. The Dalai Lama said,

> We must not only learn to recognize the importance of empathy, compassion . . . but we must reinforce these ideas so that they become translated into our actions, into how we interact with other people and with the world around us. . . . If each of us can learn to relate to each other more out of compassion . . . this can go a long way in reducing many of the conflicts and problems that we see today in the world. So, in this way, I believe that we can help create happier individuals and happier society, as well as a more peaceful world.[201]

A compassionate person has learned that no one is perfect and, therefore, refrains from judging. This is what God asks of us. "Be ye all of one mind, having compassion one of another."[202]

Cultivating an Appreciation for Life

The bereavement process can give us a new appreciation for life, for relationships, and for the world around us. Losing a loved one reminds us that our time on Earth is finite and that many circumstances, including death, are beyond our control. When we realize how fleeting life can be, every second becomes precious. Because of this new understanding, we might choose to enjoy life more and spend more time with those we care about. Although

---

201 His Holiness the Dalai Lama and Howard Cutler, *The Art of Happiness in a Troubled World* (New York: Doubleday Religion), 2009, 307–8.
202 1 Peter 3:8.

Heavenly Father created our incredibly complex bodies to function in amazing ways, we are still vulnerable, living organisms. When we realize life is fragile, we can be motivated to make the most of each day and be grateful for the blessings the Lord has given us. "I will sing unto the Lord as long as I live: I will sing praise to my God while I have my being. My meditation of him shall be sweet: I will be glad in the Lord."[203]

Cultivating Increased Spirituality

The solemnity of death can prompt us to take inventory of our life and our devotion to God. Death is a stark reminder that our time on Earth is short and that another life awaits. Coming face-to-face with the transitory nature of mortal life helps us understand more fully what things matter most. At these times, we may begin sorting through our beliefs and reevaluating our priorities. We may have an increased desire to draw closer to our Heavenly Father as we attempt to answer the age-old questions of why we are here and where we are going. Other questions we might ask ourselves are: *Am I headed in the right direction? Am I doing my best to follow the Savior? What can I do to draw closer to God?* We might decide to spend more time praying, reflecting, and studying the scriptures in order to become more like our Heavenly Father.

Cultivating an Increased Sense of Gratitude

Despite our loss, blessings still abound in our life, and we can show gratitude for them. We can be grateful for simple pleasures, such as a cool breeze on a summer day, the cheerful smile of a child, the comfort of a hot shower, and the kindness of a friend who calls to check on us. A grateful heart is an expression of humility and the beginning of greatness. It is the foundation for all other virtues such as faith, courage, contentment, happiness, and love. The Lord has promised, "He who receiveth all things with thankfulness shall be made glorious."[204]

No matter what circumstance we find ourselves in, a sense of gratitude is nourished by these sacred truths we hold dear: that Heavenly Father lives and loves us and that through the Atonement

---

203 Psalm 104:33–34.
204 D&C 78:19.

of Jesus Christ, we can live forever with those we love. Being grateful for whatsoever things we have been given is to show faith in God. By trusting Him, we can look forward with an eye of faith as we "hope for things which are not seen, which are true."[205]

Cultivating Relationships with Others

Losing a loved one often gives us a greater appreciation for friends and family who are still with us. When death reminds us that life is transitory, we better understand that every moment spent with someone we care about is precious. With that insight, we can enrich and enhance our relationships and work to repair any that have been damaged. As we face the fact that eternity lies just around the corner, we better comprehend that *now* is the best time to ask for and give forgiveness. We can show greater love by forgiving others, even as Jesus forgives us. "And be ye kind one to another, tenderhearted, forgiving one another, even as God for Christ's sake hath forgiven you."[206]

Cultivating Inner Strength

While loss hurts and sorrow is an unwelcome companion, continuing to move forward can assist us to cultivate an inner strength. Our goal in life is to grow spiritually and become more like God, and as we learn how to keep moving despite our grief, God can bless us to become stronger. "The Lord will give strength unto his people; the Lord will bless his people with peace."[207]

Learning how to be resilient will bless us throughout our lives, helping us cope with the many trials that come during mortality. Trudging onward despite the pain we experience can help us gain strength, a precious commodity that can assist us the next time we face anguish and sorrow.

Cultivating a Desire to Help Others

After a loss, we may feel a desire to help others. Christ's entire life was one of service. "For even the Son of man came not to be ministered unto, but to minister, and to give his life a ransom for many."[208] A good way to pay tribute to our departed loved one is

---

205 Alma 32:21.
206 Ephesians 4:32.
207 Psalm 29:11.
208 Mark 10:45.

to work to improve the lives of others. There are countless ways we can memorialize our loved one by humanitarian acts, whether it is serving those in our family, our community, our country, or the world. Following are inspirational stories about how people have honored their departed loved ones.

Inspirational Legacies

Thanh Williamson

Ondi and Thanh Williamson were nearing their tenth wedding anniversary when they were involved in a head-on collision on August 14, 2002, in Orderville, Utah. Their seven-year-old daughter, Alexa, was in the back seat. Thanh, thirty-two, was sitting beside her, buckled into a two-point lap belt, the only seat belt available at that position. Ondi, who was driving, had multiple fractures; Alexa had minor injuries. Both were saved because of their seat belts. The high-speed impact caused Thanh to jackknife over her lap belt, causing fatal abdominal injuries.

When Ondi learned it was the seat belt and not the crash that killed his wife, he filed suit against the car manufacturer, alleging the design of the lap-only belt was defective. A long, drawn-out legal battle began, and Ondi suffered from post-traumatic stress disorder and bipolar disorder, making it impossible for him to work. For the next two years, Ondi didn't leave his house.

"I used to take care of everything," he said, "but I couldn't take care of myself." Despite his illness, Ondi was determined to press forward with his suit and endured years of court battles to make seat belts safer. He said, "When a loved one passes away, you want a legacy."

Nine years after Thanh died, the US Supreme Court issued a precedential decision on seat-belt requirements, making them safer. Today, Ondi keeps a brief from his court case on his nightstand as a reminder that some good came out of his tragedy. Ondi said, "This is Thanh's legacy, the Supreme Court decision. A lot of people are protected because of our loss."[209]

209 Pamela Manson, "'A lot of people are protected because of our loss': A Utah woman's death set legal precedent, but her family still feels the pain of her absence," *The Salt Lake Tribune*, January 15, 2018. sltrib.com/news/2018/01/15/how-a-utah-womans-car-crash-death-led-to-a-precedent-setting-us-supreme-court-decision-on-seat-belts-and-continuing-pain-for-her-family/

Hannah Warburton

The last phone call sixteen-year-old Hannah Warburton made was to a suicide hotline, but when her call went unanswered, Hannah took her life. The previous year, Hannah had been struggling to recover from injuries suffered in a car accident and became emotionally stressed when her condition did not improve, even after receiving neuropsychiatric help and physical therapy.

After Hannah's death, her mother, Laura Warburton, wanted to ensure that calls for help would never go unanswered and began working with the Utah State Legislature to ensure that suicide prevention hotlines would always be fully manned. Partly because of her efforts, Utah lawmakers unanimously passed "Hannah's Bill" in January 2018, requiring crisis lines in the state to be available at all hours of the day year-round.

Laura Warburton said she was grateful when the House passed this bill. She then worked to promote suicide prevention and anti-bullying legislation in Utah. Laura was honored by the Legislature for her hard work, but she said all her efforts were meant to honor her daughter, Hannah.[210]

Rachael Runyan

Three-year-old Rachael Runyan was snatched by an unknown assailant from a park fifteen feet away from her home in Sunset, Utah. A ten-year-old witness saw a man entice Rachael away with the promise of bubble gum and ice cream. Rachael's body was found a week later, but the murderer was never found.

After losing her daughter, Elaine worked as an advocate for missing children and their families. On the thirty-fourth anniversary of Rachael's abduction, Elaine and her family joined with a number of people, including their neighbor Allen Glines as well as Ed Smart, whose fourteen-year-old daughter, Elizabeth, had been abducted in Salt Lake City. Together, they worked to

---

210 Dennis Romboy, "Utah House passes 'Hannah's Bill' to ensure suicide crisis lines staffed 24/7," KSL.com, January 26, 2018. ksl.com/article/46246751/utah-house-passes-hannahs-bill-to-ensure-suicide-crisis-lines-staffed-247

rename the park where Rachael disappeared to Rachael Runyan Memorial Park. When the park was dedicated, the family released thirty-four purple balloons, one for each year they'd lived without Rachael. "It's a remembering. It's an honoring," Elaine said. "We still miss our child who was kidnapped by some unknown person, and we've had to live with this. . . . We like to keep her memory alive and leave a legacy with her name on it."[211]

Shanna Osborn

Jason and Clarissa Osborn dreamed of having a large family, but shortly after their first son, Carter, was born in 2013, Clarissa developed brain tumors that required radiation treatment and affected her ability to conceive. Through intrauterine insemination treatments, Clarissa became pregnant, but their baby girl, Shanna, had a rare heart defect and lived for only three months.

Six months later, with the help of fertility treatments, Jason and Clarissa were overjoyed to learn they were expecting quadruplet daughters. Through a series of baby showers and donations from viewers of a local television show called *Random Acts*, they were able to fill their home with four bassinets, four high chairs, four strollers, four car seats, and cases of formula and diapers.

In June 2017, Clarissa went into labor in her twenty-third week of pregnancy and had an emergency C-section. Their four daughters, Kylie, Ellie, Savannah, and Lexi, each weighed less than one pound and all died. Jason said, "After already losing one daughter, to lose another four was heart-wrenching. I kept thinking, 'Why all four? Couldn't just one have made it?'"

Clarissa said that, after having received so much help from others, "it was important to us to pay it forward somehow," and she and Jason donated all their high chairs, bassinets, car seats, and other baby supplies to families who had a baby with the same type of heart defect as their first daughter, Shanna. The Osborns

---

211 Mariah Noble, "Park where 3-year-old Rachael Runyan was abducted in 1982 serves as her memorial," *The Salt Lake Tribune*, September 24, 2016. archive.sltrib.com/article.php?id=4380727&itype=CMSID

also decided to honor the five daughters they had lost by starting the Shanna K. Osborn Foundation, which awards a five-hundred-dollar educational scholarship every year to a college student who has survived a heart defect. Jason said, "We wanted our daughters to go to college, so this is a way for us to follow some other young people through their journey and support them, even though we don't have our little girls. It's a way to keep them in our lives and keep their memories alive."[212]

Lauren McCluskey

Lauren McCluskey, a young athlete attending the University of Utah, was stalked, kidnapped, and killed on campus in October 2018 by a man she had dated. To honor her memory, a red maple was planted alongside the track where she used to run.[213] Also because of Lauren's death, an independent panel looked into what could have been done to protect her and came up with a list of thirty recommendations for changes to make the University of Utah campus safer.

In March 2019, Matt McCluskey, Lauren's father, testified before Utah lawmakers, urging passage of a bill to order state colleges to develop safety plans that would protect victims of sexual assault, stalking, and dating or domestic violence. McCluskey said the bill could remedy the "systemic failures" that led to his daughter's death as well as improve communication between on- and off-campus police agencies. The Utah House passed the bill,[214] and later that month, Utah Governor

---

212 Cathy Free, "Utah couple who lost five babies in 11 months honor their children's memory: We wake up to 'raw hearts and pain,'" *Yahoo! News*, August 7, 2017. yahoo.com/news/utah-couple-lost-five-babies-141048426.html

213 See Christopher Kamrani, "Gifted and intense on the track, U. student and track star Lauren McCluskey is remembered by her community," *The Salt Lake Tribune*, November 5, 2018. sltrib.com/news/2018/11/05/alongside-university/

214 Courtney Tanner, "Campus safety bill spurred by Utah student Lauren McCluskey's killing passes in the Utah Senate," *The Salt Lake Tribune*, February 26, 2019. sltrib.com/news/education/2019/02/26/campus-safety-bill/

Gary Herbert signed the bill, which also improved the response of campus police dealing with cases of sexual assault and relationship violence.[215]

Samantha Josephson

In March 2019, twenty-one-year-old Samantha Josephson was kidnapped and killed after calling a ride-sharing service and getting into the wrong car, thinking it was her Uber ride. At a vigil held for Samantha, her father, Seymour Josephson, said he was going to dedicate his life to improving the safety of ride-sharing services.[216] Seymour Josephson said he wants others to learn from what happened to his daughter and be more careful using services like Uber and Lyft. He also wants to see those companies improve safety for their clients. Josephson said, "I don't want anyone else to go through this again—I can't tell you how painful this is."[217] Samantha's mother, Marci Josephson, added that using ride-sharing companies like Uber has become "natural" and most customers assume they are safe. "'We trust people and you can't,' she told ABC News. 'You have to change the way that the laws are to make it safer.'"

After Samantha's death, South Carolina lawmakers passed the "Samantha L. Josephson Ridesharing Safety Act," which would require ride-sharing vehicles to have illuminated signs while on duty. While Seymour Josephson praised the proposal as a "great start," he suggested other safety requirements, such as ensuring ride-sharing vehicles have front license plates and having

215 See Courtney Tanner, "Utah governor signs campus safety bill—spurred by U. student's death—and a handful of other education measures," *The Salt Lake Tribune*, March 30, 2019. sltrib.com/news/education/2019/03/30/utah-governor-signs/

216 "Dad pushes for safety after daughter's death," *The Salt Lake Tribune*, April 2, 2019, A2.

217 Sheila Vilvens, "Samantha Josephson's father urges USC students to be safe using Uber, Lyft. Here are some tips," *Cincinnati Enquirer*, April 1, 2019. greenvilleonline.com/story/news/local/2019/04/01/samantha-josephson-usc-student-killed-uber-father-urges-rideshare-safety/3330536002/

companies put barcodes on the side of their vehicles so that riders can put their phone up to it and know if it's their ride.[218]

Elsie Mahe

In November 2016, a playmate of three-year-old Elsie Mahe went to the kitchen where Sunny Mahe was washing dishes and told her Elsie was hanging by a string. When Sunny went to see, she found Elsie entangled in the cord of a window blind. Her daughter was not breathing and didn't have a heartbeat. Then the miracles began. Sunny said the first one occurred earlier that morning, when a friend asked if Sunny could babysit her little girl. If it wasn't for that child, Sunny said she wasn't sure how long it would have taken her to find Elsie. Then, when calling 911, Sunny found that paramedics just happened to be three minutes away. Although Sunny had no medical training, she performed CPR perfectly and was able to get Elsie's heart to start beating.

Sunny said with all those miracles, she and her husband, Reno, felt they had good reason to hope for healing. However, Elsie's brain scans showed extensive damage, and when she was placed on a respirator, her condition deteriorated. Elsie rallied briefly, then went back on the ventilator. After praying, Sunny and Reno received promptings that their daughter would not live. Then Reno felt another prompting—about organ donation. When the couple met with the director of the hospital's organ donation team, the pieces behind this tragedy fell into place for Sunny. She said, "As we considered the experience of her miraculous breathing and decline, we cannot help but wonder if someone else's horrible accident had not happened yet and Elsie was holding on to wait for them."[219] Sunny wrote:

---

218 David Boroff, "Samantha Josephson's parents urge ride-sharing companies to keep customers safer: 'We trust people and you can't,'" *New York Daily News*, April 15, 2019. nydailynews.com/news/national/ny-samantha-josephson-parents-urge-safety-20190415-oogyi43sdna75ferummhti2bly-story.html

219 "Daughter of Reno Mahe, BYU running backs coach, dies after accident," ESPN.com, November 30, 2016. espn.com/college-football/story/_/id/18170054/daughter-byu-cougars-running-backs-coach-dies-accident

The miraculous healing we have been praying for is not FOR Elsie, but FROM Elsie. We met this morning with a representative from the hospital organ donation team and feel confident that this is the Lord's will for Elsie—to be a life saving miracle for others. It is not the miracle that we wanted, but it is the one we got. It is still a miracle.[220]

Sunny added, "Faith doesn't protect you from grief or mourning or sadness. . . . Why didn't I hear the prompting to check on her sooner? I don't believe that there was one. That's the part that I have had to work through and learn how to apply His [God's] grace—that . . . the things that aren't right in this world, they will be right in the world to come."[221]

Priscilla Bienkowski and Sophia Hernandez

In May 2020, eighteen-year-old Priscilla Bienkowski and seventeen-year-old Sophia Hernandez were on Utah Lake in inflatable pool tubes when an unexpected storm arose. They were not wearing life jackets when strong winds picked up and swept them away. The bodies of the drowned girls were recovered a week later.[222] The Hernandez and Bienkowski families decided to use the pain of their loss to try and prevent similar tragedies. Priscilla Bienkowski's older sister, Stephanie, came up with the concept of providing a life jacket station after hearing that many teens don't wear them because they consider them expensive. The Hernandez and Bienkowski families worked with the Utah

---

220 "BYU coach's family to donate 3-year-old daughter's organs after tragic accident," Fox News, November 28, 2016. foxnews.com/health/byu-coachs-family-to-donate-3-year-old-daughters-organs-after-tragic-accident

221 "Finding Healing After the Death of a Child, His Grace," *YouTube*, uploaded by The Church of Jesus Christ of Latter-day Saints, July 23, 2020. youtube.com/watch?v=vg8ofUBEQcg

222 Graham Dudley, "Bodies of 2 missing Utah County teens recovered at Utah Lake," KSL.com, May 14, 2020. ksl.com/article/46752932/bodies-of-2-missing-utah-county-teens-recovered-at-utah-lake

Lake Commission to collect life jackets, monetary donations, and volunteers to install life jacket racks on the shores of Utah Lake. "We want everybody to be safe out there," said Santiago Hernandez, father of Sophia Hernandez. "We don't want this to happen to anybody."[223] Both families said they wanted to honor their daughters with their efforts to save the lives of others.

Although the previous stories are exceptional in scope, there are other meaningful yet simple things you can do to honor a loved one's memory. To acknowledge gratitude for their presence in your life, you could plan a memorial in which family and friends send flowers floating down a river, blow bubbles into the wind at a park, share their favorite memory of the deceased, or release balloons at their gravesite. Individually or as a group, you can plant a tree or flowers or work in a community garden. You might choose to donate to your loved one's favorite charity or set up a small yearly scholarship in their name at their high school or college. Another way to pay a personal tribute is to choose one particular trait they embodied, such as honesty, faith, kindness, or love, and resolve to incorporate that virtue more fully into your life.

---

223 Garna Mejia, "Family hopes to avoid future tragedies with new initiative at Utah Lake," KSL.com, September 27, 2020. ksl.com/article/50022193/family-hopes-to-avoid-future-tragedies-with-new-initiative-at-utah-lake

CHAPTER 15
THE TOMB IS EMPTY:
BECAUSE HE LIVES, WE WILL ALSO

O death, where is thy sting? O grave, where is thy
victory? . . . Thanks be to God, which giveth us
the victory through our Lord Jesus Christ.[224]

EVER SINCE MARY LOOKED IN the tomb and saw only emptiness,
the Resurrection of Jesus Christ has brought hope and comfort
to those who recognize in it the prospect of their own. "Yea, and
blessed are the dead that die in the Lord, from henceforth, when
the Lord shall come . . . they shall rise from the dead and shall
not die after, and shall receive an inheritance before the Lord."[225]

When someone we love dies, the Resurrection is a great source
of hope and comfort, assuring us that we will meet again in the
world to come. As Joseph Smith said at a conference in Nauvoo
on April 7, 1844, we will soon meet with our loved ones.

I have a father, brothers, children, and friends
who have gone to a world of spirits. They are only
absent for a moment. They are in the spirit, and
we shall soon meet again. . . . When we depart,

---

224 1 Corinthians 15:55, 57.
225 D&C 63:49.

we shall hail our mothers, fathers, friends, and all whom we love, who have fallen asleep in Jesus. There will be no fear of mobs, persecutions, or malicious lawsuits and arrests; but it will be an eternity of felicity.[226]

Jesus Christ's Atonement is a divine blessing that offers everyone the gift of being resurrected. "For as in Adam all die, even so in Christ shall all be made alive."[227] Focusing on the promise and reality of the Resurrection helps us overcome heartbreak and establishes peace in our hearts. Although we cannot help but feel the pang of loss, it is comforting to know that through the Atonement of Jesus Christ, loving relationships can continue beyond the doors of death.

Be Ye Comforted

Although we weep for departed loved ones, the tears we shed need not be of despair, only of sadness at losing their company for a time. And though we grieve, we do not mourn inconsolably, as those who believe death is the end of all association.[228] Those who believe in Jesus Christ have faith in the promise of the Resurrection and never need to fear that we will not see our loved ones again. The Prophet Joseph Smith said:

> If I have no expectation of seeing my father, mother, brothers, sisters and friends again, my heart would burst in a moment, and I should go down to my grave.
>
> The expectation of seeing my friends in the morning of the resurrection cheers my soul and makes me bear up against the evils of life. It is

---

226 Joseph Smith Jr., "The King Follett Sermon," *Ensign*, May 1971. churchofjesuschrist.org/study/ensign/1971/05/the-king-follett-sermon?lang=eng
227 1 Corinthians 15:22.
228 See 1 Thessalonians 4:13.

> like their [*sic*] taking a long journey, and on their
> return we meet them with increased joy.[229]

Because the Savior broke the bands of death, we know death is not the end. As Samuel T. Coleridge said, "Death but supplies the oil for the inextinguishable lamp of life."[230] With an understanding of gospel doctrine, faith supplants fear and hope replaces despair. The people of Anti-Nephi-Lehi had such great faith in Jesus Christ that they had no fear of death and refused to take up arms to protect their own lives. "They never did look upon death with any degree of terror, for their hope and views of Christ and the resurrection; therefore, death was swallowed up to them by the victory of Christ over it."[231]

Do not feel that you are lacking in faith when you shed tears of sorrow at the death of someone you love. It is natural to mourn being separated. Our Savior said, "Thou shalt live together in love, insomuch that thou shalt weep for the loss of them that die, and more especially for those that have not hope of a glorious resurrection. And it shall come to pass that those that die in me shall not taste of death, for it shall be sweet unto them."[232]

We can always rely on Christ for comfort, even when anguished by the death of a loved one. Though sadness will always accompany death, we can take solace from the Atonement of Jesus Christ and trust that in time, an inner peace and eventual joy can be ours. In Revelation we read, "For the Lamb which is in the midst of the throne shall feed them, and shall lead them unto living fountains of waters: and God shall wipe away all tears from

---

229 Joseph Fielding Smith (ed.), *Scriptural Teachings of the Prophet Joseph Smith*. scriptures.byu.edu/tpjs/STPJS.pdf, 296. Used with permission.
230 Samuel Taylor Coleridge, *Literary Remains*, vol. 1, collected and edited by Henry Nelson Coleridge, Project Gutenberg. gutenberg.org/files/8488/8488-h/8488-h.htm
231 Alma 27:28.
232 D&C 42:45–46.

their eyes."233 Isaiah provides the same tender reassurance when he said that the Savior "will swallow up death in victory; and the Lord God will wipe away tears from off all faces."234

One thing that provides great comfort at a time of loss is to know that our dear ones have gone to a far better place. "Those that die shall rest from all their labors, and their works shall follow them; and they shall receive a crown in the mansions of my Father, which I have prepared for them."235 If we could glimpse the glory and joy that our loved ones surely felt when their eyes closed on this life and opened onto the realm of eternity, our sorrows would lessen and we would feel gladness instead of grief. "May Christ lift thee up, and may his sufferings and death, and the showing his body unto our fathers, and his mercy and long-suffering, and the hope of his glory and of eternal life, rest in your mind forever."236

Because of Christ's Resurrection, our eternal spirit will be reunited with a perfect and glorified body that will be immortal, perfect, and free from pain, disease, or any other earthly impediments.237 Joseph F. Smith spoke of this blessed restoration:

> Our tabernacles will be brought forth as they are laid down, although there will be a restoration effected; every organ, every limb that has been maimed, every deformity caused by accident or in any other way, will be restored and put right. Every limb and joint shall be restored to its proper frame. We will know each other and enjoy each other's society throughout the endless ages of eternity, if we keep the law of God.238

---

233 Revelation 7:17.
234 Isaiah 25:8.
235 D&C 59:2.
236 Moroni 9:25.
237 See Alma 11:43; 40:23.
238 Smith, *Gospel Doctrine*, 447. archive.org/details/gospeldoctrine009956 mbp/page/n465

President Russell M. Nelson said, "The gift of resurrection is the Lord's consummate act of healing. Thanks to Him, each body will be restored to its proper and perfect frame. . . . Thanks to Him, brighter days are ahead, both here and hereafter. Real joy awaits each of us—on the other side of sorrow."[239]

Jesus Christ Conquered Death

The gospel of Jesus Christ teaches that the soul is immortal and that because of Christ's atoning sacrifice, all of us will be resurrected and live again. "And he will take upon him death, that he may loose the bands of death which bind his people."[240]

Jesus Christ was sent by the Father to come to Earth to become our Savior and Redeemer and make the Resurrection of all mankind possible.[241] When Jesus willingly laid down his life on the cross of Calvary, He said, "Father, into thy hands I commend my spirit"[242] and returned to heavenly realms to be with His Father. Christ alone had the power to lay down His life and take it up again and was the first to rise from the dead.[243]

Jesus Christ's Atonement was a selfless act of infinite, eternal consequence, which was arduously earned alone by the Son of God.[244] Through His sacrifice, the Savior broke the bonds of death and opened the gates to exaltation for all who qualify for forgiveness through repentance and obedience. "And since man had fallen he could not merit anything of himself; but the sufferings and death of Christ atone for their sins, through faith and repentance, and so forth; and that he breaketh the bands of death, that the grave shall have no victory, and that the sting of death should be swallowed up in the hopes of glory."[245]

---

239 Russell M. Nelson, "Jesus Christ, the Master Healer," *Ensign*, November 2005, 87–88. media.ldscdn.org/pdf/magazines/ensign-november-2005/2005-11-00-ensign-eng.pdf?lang=eng

240 Alma 7:12.

241 See 3 Nephi 27:13–16; see also D&C 76:40–42.

242 Luke 23:46.

243 See John 10:18.

244 See D&C 133:50.

245 Alma 22:14.

At the conclusion of Christ's atoning sacrifice, Jesus had paid the ransom for all of mankind, allowing us to be freed from the bonds of everlasting death. In addition, Christ acts as our Savior in freeing us from the bonds of sin, which means hell no longer has claim on anyone who chooses to repent. Every soul who ever *has* or ever *will* come to Earth can, if they desire, be redeemed by Christ's infinite sacrifice if they follow the laws and ordinances of the gospel.

President Wilford Woodruff spoke of the comfort that comes from knowing Christ conquered death and that we will be able to return to His presence:

> Without the gospel of Christ the separation by death is one of the most gloomy subjects it is possible to contemplate; but just as soon as we obtain the gospel and learn the principle of the resurrection the gloom, sorrow and suffering occasioned by death are, in a great measure, taken away. I have often thought that, to see a dead body, and to see that body laid in the grave and covered with earth, is one of the most gloomy things on earth; without the gospel it is like taking a leap in the dark. But as quick as we obtain the gospel, as soon as the spirit of man is enlightened by the inspiration of the Almighty, he can exclaim with one of old—"Oh grave, where is thy victory, Oh death, where is thy sting? The sting of death is sin, and the gift of God is eternal life, through our Lord Jesus Christ" (See 1 Corinthians 15:55–57).246

When President Joseph F. Smith's nineteen-year-old daughter, Alice, died on April 29, 1901, he testified of his faith in the Atonement in a letter to his son:

---

246 *Teachings of the Presidents of the Church: Wilford Woodruff,* 82. churchofjesuschrist.org/study/manual/teachings-wilford-woodruff/chapter-8?lang=eng

Our hearts are still bowed down in the earth where the remains of our Sweet girl and those of her little Brothers and Sisters repose in dust. . . . But we will do the best we can, by the help of the Lord, and from our hearts we feel that our Sleeping treasures are all in His holy keeping and will soon awake from the dust to immortality and eternal life. But for the precious assurance and glorious hope in the Gospel of Christ, life would not only *not* be worth the living, but it would be an infamous and damning *farce*! But, "O, what joy this sentence gives, I *know* that *my Redeemer lives*!" Thank God.[247]

Christ Is Our Advocate

In the Doctrine and Covenants, Christ referred to Himself as our "advocate."[248] By definition, an advocate is someone who believes in and rises up to defend us. Jesus stands as our advocate whenever we feel defenseless, abandoned, or bowed down by sorrow and pain. No matter our troubles, we are only a prayer away from accessing our Savior's help. Alma quoted the prophet Zenos, who testified of this, "And thou didst hear me because of mine afflictions and my sincerity; and it is because of thy Son that thou hast been thus merciful unto me, therefore I will cry unto thee in all mine afflictions, for in thee is my joy; for thou hast turned thy judgments away from me, because of thy Son."[249]

The Apostle Paul also said Christ is our advocate and makes divine intercession for us, explaining that Heavenly Father spared not His own Son, but delivered Him up for our sake.[250] Paul added,

---

247 *Teachings of the Presidents of the Church: Joseph F. Smith* (Salt Lake City: The Church of Jesus Christ of Latter-day Saints, 2004, 2011), 86. churchofjesuschrist.org/study/manual/teachings-joseph-f-smith/chapter-10?lang=eng
248 D&C 29:5.
249 Alma 33:11.
250 See Romans 8:32.

> Who shall separate us from the love of Christ?
> shall tribulation, or distress, or persecution, or
> famine, or nakedness, or peril, or sword? Nay,
> in all these things we are more than conquerors
> through him that loved us. For I am persuaded,
> that neither death, nor life, nor angels, nor princi-
> palities, nor powers, nor things present, nor things
> to come, Nor height, nor depth, nor any other
> creature, shall be able to separate us from the love
> of God, which is in Christ Jesus our Lord.[251]

In Psalms, we read, "The Lord is my rock, and my fortress,
and my deliverer; my God, my strength, in whom I will trust;
my buckler."[252]

The Atonement and the Resurrection are clear evidence of
the great love Jesus has for us, and testify of God's wisdom and
goodness. Jesus told us, "In the world ye shall have tribulation:
but be of good cheer; I have overcome the world."[253] Because of
Christ's superlative love, He made it possible for us to conquer
temptation, tribulation, sin, and sorrow, as well as our weaknesses
and mistakes. We can have faith in the future and know that
ultimately, with the power of God on our side, we will prevail.
The Savior is well qualified to be our advocate because no matter
what tribulations we face, how deep our sorrows, or how endless
our pain, Jesus Christ knows how we feel. In Isaiah, we read:

> Surely he hath borne our griefs, and carried our
> sorrows: yet we did esteem him stricken, smitten
> of God, and afflicted. But he was wounded for
> our transgressions, he was bruised for our iniq-
> uities: the chastisement of our peace was upon
> him; and with his stripes we are healed.[254]

---

251 Romans 8:35, 37–39.
252 Psalm 18:2.
253 John 16:33.
254 Isaiah 53:4–5.

A Book of Mormon prophet foretold Christ's suffering, saying, "The world . . . shall judge him to be a thing of naught; wherefore they scourge him, and he suffereth it; and they smite him, and he suffereth it. Yea, they spit upon him, and he suffereth it, because of his loving kindness and his long-suffering towards the children of men."[255]

Jesus fully understands our grief because He suffered every pain that mortals can experience. In the Book of Mormon, we read:

> And he cometh into the world that he may save all men if they will hearken unto his voice; for behold, he suffereth the pains of all men, yea, the pains of every living creature, both men, women, and children, who belong to the family of Adam. And he suffereth this that the resurrection might pass upon all men, that all might stand before him at the great and judgment day.[256]

Christ Has Atoned for Our Mistakes as Well as Our Sins

Christ's infinite atoning sacrifice pays not only for all our sins but also for our shortcomings and mistakes. In Brad Wilcox's book *The Continuous Atonement*, Wilcox talks about a personal experience related by Elder Robert E. Wells of the First Quorum of the Seventy, who spoke to a group of women incarcerated at the Utah State Prison.

Elder Wells told the women about his first wife and their life in South America, where he worked as an international banker. Because they often had to travel great distances, Elder Wells and his wife both had pilot licenses and owned their own planes. On one occasion, they flew from their home in Paraguay to Uruguay with some friends to watch the Saturday sessions of general conference. They had planned to watch the Sunday meetings as

255 1 Nephi 19:9.
256 2 Nephi 9:21–22.

well but decided to leave early because of reports that bad weather was on the way.

The trip began well, but then Elder and Sister Wells flew into thick clouds and lost visual and radio contact with each other. When Elder Wells arrived at the airport where they planned to refuel, he discovered that his wife's plane had crashed. Neither she nor her two passengers had survived. Elder Wells said:

> Words will forever be inadequate in expressing the pain that swelled within me, consuming my emotions and numbing my senses. . . . To make matters worse, as my mind was attempting to deal with the devastating realization of my wife's passing, I found myself experiencing tremendous guilt for having somehow caused the crash.

Elder Wells felt guilty for not having had the plane checked out better before they flew and also berated himself for neglecting to give his wife more adequate instructions on how to fly using instruments only.

After arriving home, Elder Wells told his three children—ages seven, four, and one—about the accident and that their mother would not be coming home. He reassured his children that because of Jesus's Atonement, their mother was still alive but was now living in the spirit world. He assured them that one day they would be together again. Elder Wells said his deep sense of loss and guilt were almost more than he could bear. "Once the tears stopped, I simply lost my desire to continue on." Elder Wells said, "Following my wife's funeral in the United States . . . I became a walking vegetable, able to function only on a minimal level. This I did for the sake of the children and for no other reason. . . . I simply existed—nothing more."

Then Elder Wells had a special spiritual experience where he learned that Christ's Atonement could help him get through his pain and that he didn't have to wait until his life was over to feel the healing power of the Atonement. This experience occurred when

Elder Wells was on his knees in prayer. Suddenly he felt as though the Savior came to his side and said, "Robert, my atoning sacrifice paid for your sins *and your mistakes*. Your wife forgives you. Your friends forgive you. I will lift your burden. Serve me, serve your family and all will go well with you." Elder Wells reported:

> From that moment, the burden of guilt was amazingly lifted from me. I immediately understood the encompassing power of the Savior's Atonement. . . . While I had previously felt like I could have been swallowed up to destruction, I now realized that Christ had comforted me. Just as my mind and emotions had been at the darkest level, I now experienced light and joy like I had never before known. . . . The guilt and despair had disappeared. As my mind assimilated what had transpired, I realized that I had been given an unearned gift—the Lord's unearned gift of grace.[257]

The Assurance of the Resurrection

When faced with the anguish of death, we find comfort in the assurance of the Resurrection. Before coming to Earth, we were taught the gospel plan and understood that if we proved faithful, we could gain eternal life. We knew our spirits would separate from our physical bodies at the time of death, but we trusted our Elder Brother to usher in the Resurrection. "But behold, the resurrection of Christ redeemeth mankind, yea, even all mankind, and bringeth them back into the presence of the Lord."[258]

The Atonement of Jesus Christ ensured the Resurrection; it was the greatest of all events in the history of mankind and is pivotal to the plan of salvation. Knowledge of Christ's sacrifice in bringing about the Resurrection helps us understand essential questions about the nature of God, our relationship to God, and

---

257 Robert E. Wells, as related in Brad Wilcox, *The Continuous Atonement* (Salt Lake City: Deseret Book, 2009), 54–58.
258 Helaman 14:17.

the very purpose of mortality. The Prophet Joseph Smith said: "The fundamental principles of our religion are the testimony of the Apostles and Prophets, concerning Jesus Christ, that He died, was buried, and rose again the third day, and ascended into heaven; and all other things which pertain to our religion are only appendages to it."259

Knowledge of the Resurrection provides us with strength, inspiration, and encouragement that help us live a Christ-centered life. President Dallin H. Oaks said:

> The assurance of resurrection and immortality affects how we look on the physical challenges of mortality, how we live our mortal lives, and how we relate to those around us.
>
> The assurance of resurrection gives us the strength and perspective to endure the mortal challenges faced by each of us and by those we love, such things as the physical, mental, or emotional deficiencies we bring with us at birth or acquire during mortal life. Because of the resurrection, we know that these mortal deficiencies are only temporary!
>
> The assurance of resurrection also gives us a powerful incentive to keep the commandments of God during our mortal lives . . . [and] is a powerful encouragement for us to fulfill our family responsibilities in mortality. . . . Our sure knowledge of a resurrection to immortality also gives us the courage to face our own death. . . . The assurance of immortality also helps us bear the mortal separations involved in the death of our loved ones.260

---

259 *Teachings of the Presidents of the Church: Joseph Smith*, 49. churchofjesuschrist.org/study/manual/teachings-joseph-smith/chapter-3?lang=eng

260 Dallin H. Oaks, "Resurrection," *Ensign*, May 2000, 15. churchofjesuschrist.org/study/ensign/2000/05/resurrection?lang=eng

One of the great blessings that comes from our Savior's Atonement is that a perfected, resurrected body moves us beyond Satan's power. The scriptures state that if Jesus Christ had not completed the Atonement, there would be no resurrection and we would be under Satan's power. In the Book of Mormon, we read:

> O the wisdom of God, his mercy and grace! For behold, if the flesh should rise no more our spirits must become subject to that angel who fell from before the presence of the Eternal God, and became the devil, to rise no more.
>
> And our spirits must have become like unto him, and we become devils, angels to a devil, to be shut out from the presence of our God, and to remain with the father of lies, in misery, like unto himself. . . .
>
> O how great the goodness of our God, who prepareth a way for our escape from the grasp of this awful monster; yea, that monster, death and hell, which I call the death of the body, and also the death of the spirit.[261]

It is only when our spirit and immortal body are inseparably connected in the Resurrection that we can "receive a fulness of joy."[262] Speaking of this glorious doctrine, President Wilford Woodruff stated:

> When the resurrection comes, we shall come forth clothed with immortal bodies; and the persecutions, suffering, sorrow, pain and death, incident to mortality, will be done away forever.
>
> This doctrine of the resurrection of the dead is most glorious. It is comforting, at least to my spirit, to think, that, in the morning of the resurrection,

---

261 2 Nephi 9:8–10.
262 See D&C 93:33; 138:17.

my spirit will have the privilege of dwelling in the very same body that it occupied here.[263]

Come Unto Him

Christ promises that if we come unto Him, He will give us answers to our prayers and rest to our souls. We can always depend on Christ to support and bless us—no matter how pressed down we are under the sorrows of death and other earthly burdens. Our Savior tenderly tells us, "Come unto me, all ye that labour and are heavy laden, and I will give you rest. Take my yoke upon you, and learn of me; for I am meek and lowly in heart: and ye shall find rest unto your souls. For my yoke is easy, and my burden is light."[264]

Through the gospel of Jesus Christ, we learn about the great plan of happiness and how we can be saved and exalted. His gospel offers hope when we experience pain and sorrow. Robert L. Millet, emeritus dean of Religious Education at Brigham Young University, writes, "In a world that offers flimsy and fleeting remedies for mortal despair, Jesus comes to us in our moments of need with a 'more excellent hope' (Ether 12:32). What Jesus Christ *has* done speaks volumes concerning what he *can* do and what he *will* do for us."[265]

We are the reason Jesus Christ laid down His life. *We* are the reason He brought about the Atonement, which saves us and lifts us up, qualifying us to live once more in heavenly realms. The Book of Mormon teaches us, "He doeth not anything save it be for the benefit of the world; for he loveth the world, even that he layeth down his own life that he may draw all men unto him. Wherefore, he commandeth none that they shall not partake of his salvation."[266]

---

263 *Teachings of the Presidents of the Church: Wilford Woodruff*, 81. churchofjesuschrist.org/study/manual/teachings-wilford-woodruff/chapter-8?lang=eng

264 Matthew 11:28–30.

265 Robert L. Millet, *After All We Can Do: Grace Works* (Salt Lake City: Deseret Book, 2003), 62.

266 2 Nephi 26:24.

Christ's love for us is as perfect as it is eternal. His only desire is for us to return to live with Him and Heavenly Father. Prior to His Crucifixion, Jesus urged His disciples to carry on even when they were separated from Him by death. The comforting words He spoke to his disciples also pertain to us: "I go and prepare a place for you, I will come again, and receive you unto myself; that where I am, there ye may be also."[267]

---

267 John 14:3.

CHAPTER 16
WHAT HAPPENS AFTER WE DIE?

Now, concerning the state *of the soul between* death *and the* resurrection—Behold, it has been made known unto me by an angel, that the spirits of all men, as soon as they are departed from this mortal body, yea, the spirits of all men, whether they be good or evil, are taken home *to that God who gave them life.*
And then shall it come to pass, that the spirits of those who are righteous are received into a state of happiness, which is called paradise, a state of rest, a state of peace, where they shall rest from all their troubles and from all care, and sorrow.[268]

TWO THINGS THAT CAN BRING great comfort after losing a loved one are knowing what happens after they pass away and knowing they are happy and well. Knowing of the positive changes to their body, the exceptional beauty of their surroundings, and the feelings of love and peace reported to be felt there, brings us a tremendous sense of solace. It fills our hearts with gladness and brings tranquility to our souls to know they happily reside in a glorious place that is filled with the light of Christ.

God has given all prophets—modern and ancient—some understanding regarding the spirit world. In the Old Testament, we

---

268 Alma 40:11–12; emphases added.

read that after we die, we will "return unto God."[269] After Christ's death, Peter taught that Jesus went to preach the gospel in the spirit world.[270] The prophet Alma in the Book of Mormon taught that as soon as we leave our mortal bodies, we will go home to our God who gave us life.[271]

Alma also said the righteous will be received into a state of happiness, which is called paradise, and that they would rest from all their troubles and from all earthly care and sorrow.[272] When Enos grew old, he testified, "And I soon go to the place of my rest, which is with my Redeemer; for I know that in him I shall rest. And I rejoice in the day when my mortal shall put on immortality, and shall stand before him; then shall I see his face with pleasure, and he will say unto me: Come unto me, ye blessed, there is a place prepared for you in the mansions of my Father. Amen."[273]

Understanding the True Nature of Our Existence and Where We Are Going

The Prophet Joseph Smith felt that all Saints had a right to understand the true nature of our existence on Earth—where we came from and where we are going. He said we should study the purpose of life and death continually, asking Heavenly Father to enlighten our minds, for "If we have any claim on our Heavenly Father for anything, it is for knowledge on this important subject."[274]

What happens after we die is a topic of great interest, not only because all of us have lost dear family members and friends but also because we will die ourselves. When we lose someone we love, we are filled with a deep yearning to know how our loved ones are faring in the spirit world. We also wonder what we will experience when we pass away. It is natural to wonder about the next phase of life, and we need not shy away from thinking about or discussing this sacred subject if it is done in a faithful and devout manner.

269 Ecclesiastes 12:7.
270 See 1 Peter 3:18–20; 4:6.
271 See Alma 40:11.
272 See Alma 40:12.
273 Enos 1:27.
274 Joseph Fielding Smith (ed.), *Scriptural Teachings of the Prophet Joseph Smith*, 324. Used with permission. scriptures.byu.edu/tpjs/STPJS.pdf

The desire to know what comes after this life is a righteous one and can be useful if it prompts us to prepare ourselves to be fit for the kingdom of God. It is necessary to keep in mind that death and what follows is a holy subject and should be discussed with great respect.[275]

Members of The Church of Jesus Christ of Latter-day Saints have been blessed to receive modern revelation regarding the spirit world. The Prophet Joseph Smith taught much about death and the spirit world, and in 1918, Joseph F. Smith received several divine revelations, including a vision of the spirit world, where he saw how the Savior had organized missionary work there. An account of this vision, known as the vision of the redemption of the dead, is found in section 138 of the Doctrine and Covenants. While we don't need to shy away from learning more about the next life, we should resist the urge to speculate unduly. Our main focus should be on living the best we can so that we can be found worthy to return to our Heavenly Father's presence.

The authors wish to explain that when choosing which spiritual experiences to include in this book, and more frequently in this chapter and the next, we have done our best to rely on verified, documented accounts. We wish to stress that these experiences are not to be understood or taught in any way as official doctrine of The Church of Jesus Christ of Latter-day Saints. Although such accounts can be enlightening and informative, it is always best to have faith in and rely on scriptural accounts and Church leaders. Because of the sacred nature of this subject, the authors have chosen to rely heavily on clarification given by Church authorities.

Death Is Not an Ending but a Beginning

As members of The Church of Jesus Christ of Latter-day Saints, we know death is not the end of our existence and take comfort in knowing that our spirits will live on. Death is merely a transition that leads us from mortality to another part of our existence. Immortality is unconditional and universal—a gift

---

275 See Dale C. Mouritsen, "The Spirit World, Our Next Home," *Ensign*, January 1977, 47. churchofjesuschrist.org/study/ensign/1977/01/the-spirit-world-our-next-home?lang=eng

from Jesus Christ through His holy and infinite Atonement. This divine truth has been taught by ancient as well as latter-day prophets and in the holy scriptures. President Spencer W. Kimball spoke of this, saying:

> To friends it [death] brings distress and sorrow, to relatives anguish and grief, to closest dear ones, desolation. . . . To the unbeliever it is the end of all, associations terminated, relationships ended, memories soon to fade into nothingness. But to those who have knowledge and faith in the promise of the gospel of Jesus Christ, death's meaning is . . . a change of condition into a wider, serener sphere of action; it means the beginning of eternal life, a never-ending existence. It means the continuation of family life, the reuniting of family groups, the perpetuation of friendships, relationships, and associations.[276]

The scriptures teach that after our mortal body dies, our spirit will go to the spirit world. The Prophet Joseph Smith confirms that when we die, "The spirits of the just are exalted to a greater and more glorious work; hence they are blessed in their departure to the world of spirits."[277]

Alma taught, "Now, concerning the state of the soul between death and the resurrection—Behold, it has been made known unto me by an angel, that the spirits of all men, as soon as they are departed from this mortal body, yea, the spirits of all men, whether they be good or evil, are taken home to that God who gave them life."[278]

Leaving our physical body and going to the spirit world has been likened to the simple act of stepping through a door into

---

276 Edward L. Kimball, ed., *The Teachings of Spencer W. Kimball* (Salt Lake City: Bookcraft, 1982), 39.
277 Joseph Fielding Smith (ed.), *Scriptural Teachings of the Prophet Joseph Smith*, 326. Used with permission. scriptures.byu.edu/tpjs/STPJS.pdf
278 Alma 40:11.

another phase of our eternal existence. Nobel Prize–winning poet and writer Rabindranath Tagore said, "Death is not extinguishing the light; it is only putting out the lamp because the dawn has come."[279] Death is merely a change in assignment—a transfer to another realm.

Once we arrive in the spirit world, we will abide there until the Resurrection, when our spirit will be reunited with a perfected physical body. There is no need to fear death, for as author Robert L. Millet explains,

> Light has replaced darkness, sound doctrine and pure religion have replaced ignorance and superstition, and men and women may traverse life's paths without the ominous fear of what, if anything, follows death. We know where we came from. We know why we are here. And we know where we are going when death calls each of us. When we pass through the veil that separates time and eternity, we will know the truth of the testimony with which holy writ resounds: in Christ there is peace. In Christ there is hope, hope for deliverance from sin and death. There are no wrongs that shall not be righted in time or in eternity, no burdens that shall not be lifted.[280]

The Postmortal Spirit World, Our Temporary Home

The spirit world is the temporary home of the spirits of all mankind who have died. The Prophet Joseph Smith said, "The righteous and the wicked all go to the same world of spirits until the resurrection."[281] Although the righteous and unrighteous

279 Shuvra Dey, "Death is not extinguishing the light; it is putting out the lamp as dawn has come—Rabindranath Tagore," Get Bengal, 8 August 2020. getbengal.com/details/death-is-not-extinguishing-the-light-it-is-putting-out-the-lamp-as-dawn-has-come-rabindranath-tagore
280 Robert L. Millet, *Life After Death: Insights from Latter-Day Revelation* (Salt Lake City: Deseret Book, 1999), 18–19.
281 Joseph Fielding Smith (ed.), *Scriptural Teachings of the Prophet Joseph Smith*, 310. Used with permission. scriptures.byu.edu/tpjs/STPJS.pdf

will both inhabit the spirit world, each group will dwell apart from one another, being separated by a great gulf.

President Joseph Fielding Smith clarifies this separation: "All spirits of men after death return to the spirit world. There, as I understand it, *the righteous—meaning those who have been baptized and who have been faithful*—are gathered in one part and all the others in another part of the spirit world."[282]

When first arriving in the spirit world, there will be a partial judgment, and people will be directed to one of two areas—either paradise or spirit prison. This partial judgment is not to be confused with the Final Judgment that will occur later, after the Resurrection.[283] Where we go in the spirit world will depend on the decisions we made in mortality. Apostle James E. Talmage explains, "While awaiting resurrection, disembodied spirits exist in an intermediate state, of happiness and rest or of suffering and suspense, according to the course they have elected to follow in mortality."[284]

The spirit world will be our temporary home, and we will dwell there until the Resurrection. It is not the place where Heavenly Father dwells. Parley P. Pratt stated:

> The spirit world is not the heaven where Jesus Christ, his Father, and other beings dwell, who have, by resurrection or translation, ascended to eternal mansions, and been crowned and seated on thrones of power; but it is an intermediate state, a probation, a place of preparation, improvement, instruction, or education, where spirits are chastened and improved, and where, if found worthy, they may be taught a knowledge of the Gospel. In short, it is a place where the Gospel is preached, and where faith, repentance, hope and

---

282 McConkie, *Doctrines of Salvation*, 230.
283 See D&C 138.
284 James E. Talmage, *Jesus the Christ* (Salt Lake City: Deseret Book, 1982), 628. churchofjesuschrist.org/study/manual/jesus-the-christ/chapter-36?lang=eng

charity may be exercised; a place of waiting for the resurrection or redemption of the body.[285]

Joseph F. Smith summed up what we know regarding the period of time between death and the Final Judgment.

The spirits of all men, as soon as they depart from this mortal body, whether they are good or evil, we are told in the Book of Mormon, are taken home to that God who gave them life, where there is a separation, a partial judgment, and the spirits of those who are righteous are received into a state of happiness which is called paradise, a state of rest, a state of peace, where they expand in wisdom, where they have respite from all their troubles, and where care and sorrow do not annoy. The wicked, on the contrary, have no part nor portion in the Spirit of the Lord, and they are cast into outer darkness, being led captive, because of their own iniquity, by the evil one. And in this space between death and the resurrection of the body, the two classes of souls remain, in happiness or in misery, until the time which is appointed of God that the dead shall come forth and be reunited both spirit and body, and be brought to stand before God, and be judged according to their works. This is the final judgment.[286]

Paradise
Paradise is first mentioned in the New Testament. When the Savior was on the cross, He told the thief next to Him, "To day

---

285 Parley P. Pratt, *Key to the Science of Theology* (Liverpool: John Henry Smith, 1883), 132.
286 Smith, *Gospel Doctrine*, 448. archive.org/details/gospeldoctrine009956 mbp/page/n467

shalt thou be with me in paradise."[287] The word occurs subsequently only twice, and we learn that paradise is the abode of the righteous during their period of disembodiment and is in contrast with the "prison" tenanted by disobedient spirits.[288] After inquiring of the Lord regarding the spirit world, the prophet Alma was told, "The spirits of those who are righteous are received into a state of happiness, which is called paradise."[289] Elder Bruce R. McConkie explained that paradise is but a way station where we live temporarily as we continue preparing ourselves for eternal life:

> Paradise—the abode of righteous spirits, as they await the day of their resurrection; paradise—a place of peace and rest where the sorrows and trials of his life have been shuffled off, and where the saints continue to prepare for a celestial heaven; paradise—not the Lord's eternal kingdom, but a way station along the course leading to eternal life, a place where the final preparation is made for that fulness of joy which comes only when body and spirit are inseparably connected in immortal glory![290]

Paradise in the spirit world is not the place of final glory, any more than spirit prison is the final habitation of those who have not yet accepted the gospel of Jesus Christ. The final judgment will not occur until later, after we are resurrected. At that time, we will be judged according to the life we led in mortality. Christ's Judgment will take into consideration our innermost intents and heartfelt desires as well as our actions. We will have a bright recollection of the life we led on Earth, and Christ will use those recollections to provide a just and divine judgment.[291]

---

287 Luke 23:43.
288 See 1 Peter 3:19–20.
289 Alma 40:12.
290 Bruce R. McConkie, *The Mortal Messiah* (Salt Lake City: Deseret Book, 1981), 4:222.
291 See Alma 11:43; 5:18.

Spirit Prison

Some people who go to the spirit world will be directed to live in a place called spirit prison. While the word *prison* may conjure up a picture of a stark existence behind bars, this is not the case at all. Spirit prison is merely a place for people to live while learning the gospel, repenting of their sins, or waiting to have their ordinances done. Spirit prison is chiefly a place of learning, repenting, and waiting—not a place of suffering. It is called a prison only because the spirits there are not allowed to go to paradise until certain conditions have been met.

Spirit prison is inhabited by two major categories of people: those who have transgressed or rejected the gospel and those who died without knowledge of the gospel. Although some people may think of spirit prison as a place where unrighteous spirits live, there are many good people residing there who simply have not yet had a chance to hear and accept the gospel.

The prophet Alma explained why the first category of people are sent to spirit prison: "The spirits of the wicked, yea, who are evil . . . have no part nor portion of the Spirit of the Lord; for behold, they chose evil works rather than good."[292] While these individuals abide there, a just and merciful Heavenly Father will provide them with an opportunity to listen to the gospel message. If they accept the gospel, they can repent of their sins and eventually progress to paradise.

The second category of people includes those who are good and honorable but who either did not have an opportunity during mortality to learn about the gospel or did not have the chance to learn the tenets of the gospel completely and so turned away before fully embracing it. Heavenly Father will not hold anyone accountable if they did not have the chance to hear the complete gospel message while living on Earth.

Missionaries will be sent to spirit prison to teach the same gospel principles that are now being taught by missionaries on Earth: faith, repentance, baptism, receiving the gift of the Holy Ghost by the laying on of hands, and all other principles of the

---

292 Alma 40:13.

gospel one must know in order to qualify for advancement.[293] While in spirit prison, people will have the chance to hear, discuss, understand, and accept the gospel. Then—just as people do here on Earth—they can choose to either accept or reject the gospel.

If a person accepts the gospel in the spirit world and repents, he or she can have necessary saving ordinances performed by mortals who act as proxy for the departed. When the ordinance work is completed, people in spirit prison will be allowed to cross the gulf to paradise and associate with the faithful.[294] On Earth, people must choose the right while facing opposition, and the same will hold true in spirit prison. People in spirit prison will have the same diverse ways of thinking as people have on Earth. If individuals there accept the gospel and prove faithful, they will be given the opportunity of obtaining the highest degree of glory in the celestial kingdom once their temple work is done on Earth.

In the *Encyclopedia of Mormonism*, Robert J. Parsons expands on how individuals can leave spirit prison and go to dwell with the faithful.

> In Latter-day Saint doctrine, the "spirit prison" is both a condition and a place within the post-earthly SPIRIT WORLD. One "imprisons" himself or herself through unbelief or through willful disobedience of God. . . . Those who willfully rebel against the light and truth of the gospel and do not repent remain in this condition of imprisonment. . . . Spirit prison is a temporary abode in the spirit world of those who either were untaught and unrighteous, or were disobedient to the gospel while in mortal life (see Alma 40:11–14; D&C 138:32). . . . Repentance of imprisoned spirits opens the doors of the prison, enabling them to loose themselves from the spiritual darkness of unbelief, ignorance, and

293 See D&C 138:33–34.
294 See *Gospel Principles* (Salt Lake City: The Church of Jesus Christ of Latter-day Saints), 2011, 244.

sin. As they accept the gospel of Jesus Christ and cast off their sins, the repentant are able to break the chains . . . and dwell with the righteous in paradise.[295]

Our Bodies Will Be Made Perfect after the Resurrection

The spirit world will be our temporary abode after we leave mortality. However, at some future point, all who dwell there will be resurrected, meaning our spiritual body will be joined with our perfected physical body. President Ezra Taft Benson said, "Indisputably there is life after death. Mortality is a place of temporary duration—and so is the spirit world. As inevitable as death is to mortals, so also is an eventual resurrection to those in the spirit world."[296]

After the Resurrection, our physical bodies will be restored to a perfect condition, without any physical or mental imperfections. The prophet Alma explained, "The soul shall be restored to the body, and the body to the soul; yea, and every limb and joint shall be restored to its body; yea, even a hair of the head shall not be lost; but all things shall be restored to their proper and perfect frame." [297]

Another Book of Mormon prophet, Amulek, taught:

> The spirit and the body shall be reunited again in its perfect form; both limb and joint shall be restored to its proper frame, even as we now are at this time. . . .
>
> Now, this restoration shall come to all, both old and young, both bond and free, both male and female, both the wicked and the righteous; and even there shall not so much as a hair of their heads be lost; but every thing shall be restored to its perfect frame, as it is now, or in the body.[298]

---

295 Robert J. Parsons, in Daniel H. Ludlow, *Encyclopedia of Mormonism* (New York: Macmillan, 1992), 1406. contentdm.lib.byu.edu/digital/collection/EoM/id/4234

296 Ezra Taft Benson, *The Teachings of Ezra Taft Benson* (Salt Lake City: Bookcraft, 1988), 31.

297 Alma 40:23.

298 Alma 11:43–44.

In modern-day scripture, President Joseph F. Smith wrote that being resurrected would allow "the spirit and the body to be united never again to be divided, that they might receive a fulness of joy."[299] All physical handicaps will be taken away, allowing us and our departed loved ones to enjoy a complete and perfect body. Likewise, all mental disorders, handicaps, and illnesses will also be healed, leaving our brains and minds functioning perfectly.

President Joseph F. Smith explained this more fully while speaking at the funeral of William C. Staines, who had been physically disabled. "Deformity will be removed; defects will be eliminated, and men and women shall attain to the perfection of their spirits, to the perfection that God designed in the beginning." President Smith then spoke about Elder Staines as follows: "He will be restored to his perfect frame—every limb, every joint, every part of his physical being will be restored to its perfect frame. This is the law and the word of God to us, as it is contained in the revelations that have come to us, through the Prophet Joseph Smith."[300]

President Dallin H. Oaks also gives us comfort, affirming that our loved one's bodies, as well as our own, will be made perfect in the next life:

> Many living witnesses can testify to the literal fulfillment of these scriptural assurances of the resurrection. Many, including some in my own extended family, have seen a departed loved one in vision or personal appearance and have witnessed their restoration in "proper and perfect frame" in the prime of life. Whether these were manifestations of persons already resurrected or of righteous spirits awaiting an assured resurrection, the reality and nature of the resurrection of mortals is evident. What a comfort to know that

299 D&C 138:17.

300 Joseph F. Smith, *Gospel Doctrine* (Salt Lake City: Deseret Book Company), 1959. archive.org/details/gospeldoctrine009956mbp/page/n41, 23.

all who have been disadvantaged in life from birth defects, from mortal injuries, from disease, or from the natural deterioration of old age will be resurrected in "proper and perfect frame."[301]

First, a Grand Reunion

Death can be one of the most joyful moments of eternity, when we walk from a darkened room into the light of the spirit world. At the moment of death, it appears that we are not left alone during the transition from the mortal world to the spiritual one. It is a clear indication of God's love that He provides a supportive guide—often a relative or a specially appointed guide. This procedure is reminiscent of the temple, wherein kind guides are provided around every corner, directing those who may be unfamiliar and uncertain about which way to go.

When Mary Hyde Woolf passed away, she saw a person by her side, who told her, "Come with me." An account of another woman, Flora Ann Mayer, who had a near-death experience, states, "A man came from that light and acted as a guide for her." And when Lorenzo Dow Young, brother of Brigham Young, passed away, he "was met immediately. 'In a moment I was out of the body, and fully conscious that I had made the change. At once, a heavenly messenger, or guide, was by me.'"[302]

Author Richard Paul Evans wrote that when his father-in-law, who was an atheist, was on his deathbed from a terminal heart ailment, his eyes suddenly widened. Evans writes,

> Because of the tubes down his throat he was unable to speak but he was clearly attentive, following something across the room with his eyes. My wife, Keri, was at his side. "Dad, do you see someone?"
> He nodded to the affirmative.

301 Dallin H. Oaks, "Resurrection," *Ensign*, May 2000, 15. churchofjesus christ.org/study/ensign/2000/05/resurrection?lang=eng
302 Sullivan, *Gaze into Heaven*, 20.

"Is it Grandma?"

He shook his head.

"Do you know who it is?"

Again he shook his head. Minutes after his passing, his nurse said to me, "I knew he was going to die soon. When they start getting visitations, it's their time." I asked if she'd seen this before. She nodded. "Many times."[303]

After our arrival in the spirit world, we will see our departed friends and family members. After Thomas S. Thomas returned from visiting the spirit world, he said, "The grand greeting you first receive is from your closest of kin—father, mother, brother and sisters—and all that are near and dear to you who passed from earthly life and arrived in the Great Beyond before you. Your nearest and dearest friends and many others come to greet and converse with you."[304]

President Joseph F. Smith talked further on this:

What is more desirable than that we should meet with our fathers and our mothers, with our brethren and our sisters, with our wives and our children, with our beloved associates and kindred in the spirit world, knowing each other . . . by the associations that familiarize each to the other in mortal life? What do you want better than that? What is there for any religion superior to that? I know of nothing. To me it meets my wants, it fulfills my desires, it meets the longing of my heart.[305]

303 Richard Paul Evans, "Are the Dying Visited by the Dead?," Richard Paul Evans. richardpaulevans.com/2015/12/14/are-the-dying-visited-by-the-dead/
304 Sullivan, *Gaze into Heaven*, 35.
305 Joseph F. Smith, "The Resurrection," *Liahona: The Elders' Journal*, vol. 6, no. 8:178. familysearch.org/library/books/records/item/554559-1908-1909-vol-06-no-01-26-liahona-the-elders-journal?viewer=1&offset=1#page=273&viewer=picture&o=&n=0&q=

President Brigham Young also spoke of meeting with friends:

> We have the Father to speak to us, Jesus to speak
> to us, and angels to speak to us, and we shall
> enjoy the society of the just and the pure who are
> in the spirit world until the resurrection. . . . We
> have more friends behind the veil than on this
> side, and they will hail us more joyfully than you
> were ever welcomed by your parents and friends
> in this world; and you will rejoice more when you
> meet them than you ever rejoiced to see a friend
> in this life.306

The Spirit World Is a Place of Beauty

Although we miss our loved ones, we can rejoice to know they
now reside in a magnificently beautiful place. When Marlene was
doing extensive research for her book *Gaze into Heaven: Near-
Death Experiences in Early Church History*, she found that those
who visited the spirit world through visions, dreams, or near-
death experiences often described the spirit world as a place of
unparalleled beauty. A number of people who visited and returned
from the spirit world reported that the flowers, vegetation, trees,
lakes, rivers, buildings, and cities were far more splendid and
lovelier than anything on Earth.

Shortly before President Jedediah M. Grant, who was serving
as second counselor in the First Presidency, passed away, he saw
the spirit world. He described it to President Heber C. Kimball,
who recorded Elder Grant's words: "I have seen good gardens
on this earth, but I never saw any to compare with those that
were there [in the spirit world]. I saw flowers of numerous kinds,
and some with from fifty to a hundred different colored flowers
growing upon one stalk."307

---

306 *Teachings of Presidents of the Church: Brigham Young* (Salt Lake City: The
Church of Jesus Christ of Latter-day Saints, 1997), 282–283. churchofjesuschrist.
org/study/manual/teachings-brigham-young/chapter-38?lang=eng

307 Heber C. Kimball, *Journal of Discourses* (Liverpool: S. W. Richards, 1857), 4:136.
contentdm.lib.byu.edu/digital/collection/JournalOfDiscourses3/id/623/rec/4

Not only will the environment be lush and lovely but there will also be all kinds of animals. For many people, dogs, cats, or other pets are a major part of their family, and it can be devastating when they die. At such times, people may wonder if there will be animals in the next life. We do know a little about the nature of animal life from the scriptures. In Moses we read, "And out of the ground I, the Lord God, formed every beast of the field, and every fowl of the air; and commanded that they should come unto Adam, to see what he would call them; and they were also living souls; for I, God, breathed into them the breath of life."308

Archie J. Graham, who had a near-death experience, stated that he saw pets, fowl, fish, and other animal life in the spirit world. "There were many birds and animals such as deer, sheep, and antelope."309 Modern revelation confirms that every animal has a living spirit and possesses intelligence.

President Joseph Fielding Smith declared, "Animals do have spirits and that through the redemption made by our Savior they will come forth in the resurrection to enjoy the blessing of immortal life."310

President George Albert Smith also visited the spirit world and gave the following description:

> One day . . . I lost consciousness of my surroundings and thought I had passed to the Other Side. I found myself standing with my back to a large and beautiful lake, facing a great forest of trees. There was no one in sight, and there was no boat upon the lake or any other visible means to indicate how I might have arrived there. I realized, or seemed to realize, that I had finished my work in mortality and had gone home. I began

308 Moses 3:19.
309 Sullivan, *Gaze into Heaven*, 83.
310 Joseph Fielding Smith, *Answers to Gospel Questions* (Salt Lake City: Deseret Book, 1958), 2:48.

to look around, to see if I could not find someone. There was no evidence of anyone's living there, just those great, beautiful trees in front of me and the wonderful lake behind me.

I began to explore, and soon I found a trail through the woods which seemed to have been used very little, and which was almost obscured by grass.

After following the trail, President Smith met and talked with his grandfather.[311]

Cities will also be glorious. When Lorenzo Dow Young left mortality for a time, he saw a number of cities in the spirit world and recorded, "In a moment we were at the gate of a beautiful city. A porter opened it and we passed in. The city was grand and beautiful beyond anything that I can describe."[312]

Prevalent Feelings of Peace, Love, and Happiness

Not only will the environment be beautiful, people will experience wonderful feelings of joy, peace, love, and happiness, which come from being in close proximity to Heavenly Father and Jesus Christ. A number of people who visited the spirit world recalled being filled with an overwhelming love and said they were perfectly happy while there. Apostle Francis M. Lyman said this about the blessings of going to the spirit world: "It will be all right when our time comes, when we have finished our work and accomplished what the Lord requires of us. . . . We will be full of joy and happiness, and we will enter into a place of rest, of peace, of joy, rest from every sorrow. What a blessed thing that will be!"[313]

Another aspect of the spirit world is that it will seem natural and familiar. President Brigham Young said,

---

311 George Albert Smith, "Your Good Name," *Improvement Era*, March 1947, 139. archive.org/details/improvementera5003unse/page/n11/mode/2up

312 Sullivan, *Gaze into Heaven*, 28.

313 Francis M. Lyman, *Conference Report*, October 1909, 19. archive.org/details/conferencereport1909sa/page/n19

When you are in the spirit world, everything there will appear as natural as things now do. Spirits will be familiar with spirits in the spirit world—will converse, behold, and exercise every variety of communication with one another as familiarly and naturally as while here in tabernacles. There, as here, all things will be natural, and you will understand them as you now understand natural things.[314]

Going along with this, modern revelation explains that in the next life, we will enjoy the socializing with other people that we have now. "And that same sociality which exists among us here will exist among us there, only it will be coupled with eternal glory, which glory we do not now enjoy."[315] President Young sums up the splendor of the spirit world by saying, "The brightness and glory of the next apartment is inexpressible."[316]

Commenting further on the spirit world, President Young remarked, "And when they get there, they would see that they had formerly lived there for ages, that they had previously been acquainted with every nook and corner, with the palaces, walks, and gardens; and they would embrace their Father, and He would embrace them and say, 'My son, my daughter, I have you again;' and the child would say, 'O my Father, my Father, I am here again.'"[317]

Characteristics of the Spiritual Body

Our spirits will have the same bodily form as we do on Earth, except that it will be perfect.[318] Knowing that our loved ones will no longer suffer from a mortal body ravaged by age, disease, or other physical disabilities can be a great comfort for us. President

---

314 Widtsoe, *Discourses of Brigham Young*, 380. Used with permission.
315 D&C 130:2.
316 *Teachings of the Presidents of the Church: Brigham Young* (Salt Lake City: The Church of Jesus Christ of Latter-day Saints, 1997), 281. churchofjesuschrist. org/study/manual/teachings-brigham-young/chapter-38?lang=eng
317 Young, *Journal of Discourses*, 4:268. contentdm.lib.byu.edu/digital/ collection/JournalOfDiscourses3/id/491/rec/4
318 See Ether 3:16.

Brigham Young said, "Here, we are continually troubled with ills and ailments of various kinds, and our ears are saluted with the expressions, 'My head aches,' 'My shoulders ache,' 'My back aches,' 'I am hungry, dry, or tired;' but in the spirit world we are free from all this and enjoy life, glory, and intelligence."[319]

Although pain may be felt immediately before death, it ceases instantly when the spirit leaves the physical body. In 1923 Walter P. Monson was speaking to a congregation when he was stricken with intense pain from a strangulated hernia. That night, he underwent emergency surgery, but the doctors had little hope that he would recover. The following evening, he temporarily left his body. Standing over his physical body, Monson said, "I was now without pain, and the joy of freedom I felt and the peace of mind that came over me were the sweetest sensations I have ever experienced in all my life."[320]

It also appears that our senses will be heightened—for example, we will see and hear more clearly and have greater mobility. While suffering from typhus fever in 1892, Dr. Wiltse's spirit left his body. One of the first things he noticed was that he could see better than ever before. Dr. Wiltse relates, "I crossed the porch, descended the steps, walked down the path and into the street. There I stopped and looked about me. I never saw that street more distinctly than I saw it then."[321]

The same was true for Lorenzo Dow Young. After his spirit left his body, Lorenzo said, "I gazed on a vast region filled with multitudes of beings. I could see everything with the most minute distinctness."[322]

We will also have the ability to move about freely and without effort. Archie J. Graham reported of his spirit briefly parting from his physical body, "I felt differently than I had ever felt before.

319 Young, *Journal of Discourses*, 14:231. jod.mrm.org/14/227
320 Jeremiah Stokes, *Modern Miracles* (Salt Lake City: Bookcraft, 1945), 78–79.
321 "How One Feels When Dying," *Juvenile Instructor*, vol. 27, September 15, 1892, 571. archive.org/details/juvenileinstruct2718geor/page/570
322 Sullivan, *Gaze into Heaven*, 28.

My body was light in weight. I could move about with the least exertion as though in thought. . . . I felt as though I could fly I was so light."323 President Brigham Young explained:

> When we advance in years we have to be stubbing along and be careful lest we fall down. We see our youth, even, frequently stubbing their toes and falling down. But yonder, how different! They [spirits] move with ease and like lightning. If we want to visit Jerusalem, or this, that, or the other place—and I presume we will be permitted if we desire—there we are, looking at its streets.324

When we progress to the spirit world, our character and personality will remain the same, meaning we will possess the same character, temperament, and disposition we had in mortality. We will have the same appetites and desires that we had while living on Earth. President David O. McKay confirmed this:

> I believe with all my soul in the persistence of personality after death. I cannot believe otherwise. Even reason and observation demonstrate that to me. . . . Personality is persistent and that is the message of comfort. . . . Death cannot touch the spirit of man. . . . Death may have power over the body, for we are, in this life, open to accident and disease; and death may take advantage of these conditions, but there his power ends. Death cannot touch the spirit. . . . If there is any truth that is taught through the gospel of Jesus Christ, it is the truth of the immortality of the soul.325

323 Sullivan, *Gaze into Heaven*, 57.
324 Widtsoe, *Discourses of Brigham Young*, 380. Used with permission.
325 David O. McKay, *Gospel Ideals: Selections from the Discourses of David O. McKay* (Salt Lake City: Improvement Era Publication, 1953), 54–56.

A missionary in the early days of the restored Church, Elder Peter E. Johnson fell ill with malaria, and at one point, his spirit left his body. After perceiving he had died, Peter said:

> I felt perfectly natural, but as this was a new condition I began to make observations. I turned my head, shrugged my shoulders, felt with my hands, and realized that it was I myself. I also knew that my body was lying, lifeless, on the bed. While I was in a new environment, it did not seem strange, for I realized everything that was going on, and perceived that *I was the same in the spirit as I had been in the body.*[326]

Entering into the Lord's Rest

In Doctrine and Covenants, we learn that entering into the Lord's rest can also mean receiving "the fulness of his glory."[327] When we leave mortality, many of the cares and demands we currently face will no longer be part of our lives, enabling us to find peace and rest. In the Book of Mormon, we learn that if we have faith on the Lord and the love of God in our hearts, we can "be lifted up at the last day and enter into his rest."[328]

Blessed are the dead which die in the Lord from henceforth: "Yea, saith the Spirit, that they may rest from their labors; and their works do follow them."[329]

This state of rest is further clarified in the Book of Mormon: "And then shall it come to pass, that the spirits of those who are righteous are received into a state of happiness, which is called paradise, a state of rest, a state of peace, where they shall rest from all their troubles and from all care, and sorrow."[330] From

---

326 Peter E. Johnson, "A Testimony," *The Relief Society Magazine*, August 1920, 451; emphasis added. archive.org/stream/reliefsocietymag07reli#page/451/mode/2up
327 See D&C 84:24.
328 See Alma 13:29.
329 Revelation 14:13.
330 Alma 40:12.

this, we learn that rest is a state of happiness where we will no longer be faced with worldly troubles, care, or sorrow.

Elder Neal A. Maxwell spoke about what is meant by "resting from our labors":

> Some derive from these words that *rest* means no work and merely languid passivity. In fact, the *rest* described is from the troubles, cares, and sorrows of this world.
>
> To begin with, a certain peacefulness and restfulness will occur in paradise, because the faithful will see things with a more complete, restful, and reassuring perspective.[331]

President Rudger Clawson had ideas about what the Lord's rest consists of:

> I rather think it means that they will rest from their worldly anxieties, from pain suffered in this life, from sickness and disease. All those things will pass away. Freed from the anxieties and troubles of mortality I apprehend that they will be very active. I know some people who have claimed that they saw Joseph Smith, the Prophet, in vision or in dreams, but in all such instances he appeared to be exceedingly busy, busier than ever he was in life, in order, apparently, that he might accomplish some important work he had in hand. He seemed to be in a great hurry. I think very likely that is the case with others who die.[332]

---

331 Neal A. Maxwell, *The Promise of Discipleship* (Salt Lake City: Deseret Book, 2001), 106.
332 Rudger Clawson, *Conference Report*, April 1933, 75. archive.org/details/conferencereport1933a/page/n75

When President Clawson said some people had seen Joseph Smith, he was likely referring to an experience that President Wilford Woodruff had. President Woodruff said that during a night vision, he saw the Prophet Joseph Smith at the door of a temple in heaven. Joseph spoke to President Woodruff and said he could not linger because he was in a hurry. President Woodruff then said:

> The next man I met was Father Smith; he could not talk with me because he was in a hurry. I met half a dozen brethren who had held high positions on earth, and none of them could stop to talk with me because they were in a hurry. I was much astonished. By and by I saw the Prophet again and I got the privilege of asking him a question.
>
> "Now," said I, "I want to know why you are in a hurry. I have been in a hurry all my life; but I expected my hurry would be over when I got into the kingdom of heaven, if I ever did."
>
> Joseph said: "I will tell you, Brother Woodruff. Every dispensation that has had the priesthood on the earth and has gone into the celestial kingdom has had a certain amount of work to do to prepare to go to the earth with the Savior when He goes to reign on the earth. Each dispensation has had ample time to do this work. We have not. We are the last dispensation, and so much work has to be done, and we need to be in a hurry in order to accomplish it."
>
> To that, President Woodruff declared, "Of course, that was satisfactory, but it was new doctrine to me."[333]

---

333 G. Homer Durham, ed., *The Discourses of Wilford Woodruff* (Salt Lake City: Bookcraft, 1990), 288–89.

People Will Be Busy and Active

At some time or another, everyone has wondered what their departed loved ones are doing. While we do not know for certain, it appears people there are active and busy. When Peter E. Johnson returned to mortality after a near-death experience, he said,

> While I was in the spirit world I observed that the people there were busy, and that they were perfectly organized for the work they were doing. It seemed to me a continuation of the work we are doing here,—something like going from one stake to another. There was nothing there that seemed particularly strange to me; everything being natural.[334]

"We wonder what our loved ones are doing over there on the other side," President Rudger Clawson said. "If I should make answer I would say that in my opinion they are doing over there just exactly what we are doing here. . . . The work that we are expected to do here, I am sure we will be expected to do over there. . . . There will be no confusion, and the good work will go on."[335]

It was President Brigham Young's belief that people in the spirit world will be doing many of the same things we are now doing:

> You will there see that those spirits we are speaking of [in the spirit world] are active. . . . You will learn that they are striving with all their might— laboring and toiling diligently as any individual would to accomplish an act in this world. . . . They

334 Peter E. Johnson, "A Testimony," *Relief Society Magazine,* August 1920, 455. archive.org/stream/reliefsocietymag07reli#page/455/mode/2up
335 Rudger Clawson, *Conference Report,* April 1933, 75–76. archive.org/details/conferencereport1933a/page/n75

walk, converse, and have their meetings; and the spirits of good men like Joseph and the Elders, who have left this Church on earth for a season to operate in another sphere, are rallying all their powers and going from place to place preaching the Gospel, and Joseph is directing them.[336]

President George Q. Cannon also felt people were busy and happy in the spirit world. "Heaven is a place of activity, a place of progress; that which furnishes man his highest enjoyment on the earth; that which develops and calls out his highest and noblest qualities, we are to have in heaven."[337]

A number of people who visited the spirit world reported that the people they saw were happy, busy, and occupied in various activities and meaningful work. "Some labor this side of the veil, others on the other side of the veil," President Wilford Woodruff said. "If we tarry here we expect to labor in the cause of salvation, and if we go hence we expect to continue our work until the coming of the Son of Man."[338]

Thomas S. Thomas said:

> You will find this a great meeting place of all souls, where information is eagerly sought, concerning earth's conditions, by those who have passed from earthly life and are in this stage of existence. These souls are now busy, in the future existence, working in different habitations. . . . All souls are fully enjoying their positions and surroundings.

---

336 *Teachings of the Presidents of the Church: Brigham Young*, 281. churchofjesuschrist.org/study/manual/teachings-brigham-young/chapter-38?lang=eng

337 George Q. Cannon, *Conference Report*, April 1899, 20. archive.org/details/conferencereport1899a/page/20

338 *Teachings of the Presidents of the Church: Wilford Woodruff*, 81. churchofjesuschrist.org/study/manual/teachings-wilford-woodruff/chapter-8?lang=eng

> You read from their cheerful countenances a con-
> dition of contentment.[339]

When Mary Woolf visited the spirit world briefly, the people there were so busy they hardly noticed her. The account states, "All were busy, but the people in the different places would bow to her as she passed by. Sometimes they were so engaged that they took no notice of her."[340]

Missionary Work Will Continue

Modern revelation reveals that God's work of salvation for His children will go forward in the spirit world. After Jesus rose from the dead, breaking the bands of death, He went to the spirit world and instigated an extensive missionary program to preach the gospel and declare liberty to the captives.[341] We learn more about this from modern revelation:

> But behold, from among the righteous, he orga-
> nized his forces and appointed messengers, clothed
> with power and authority, and commissioned
> them to go forth and carry the light of the gospel
> to them that were in darkness, even to all the
> spirits of men; and thus was the gospel preached
> to the dead.[342]

One of the Lord's most important labors is that of missionary work. There are billions of people on the other side of the veil who died never having heard of Christ and who have never had the opportunity to repent and receive a remission of their sins. To rectify this, many righteous people who depart this Earth will teach the gospel to those on the other side. Although we miss our

---

339 Sullivan, *Gaze into Heaven*, 100.
340 Zina Y. Card, "Manifestation to Mrs. Mary Hyde Woolf," *The Relief Society Magazine*, vol. 8 (August 1921), 492. archive.org/details/reliefsocietymag08reli /page/491/mode/2up
341 See 1 Peter 3:18–19; 4:6; D&C 138.
342 D&C 138:30.

loved ones, we can be happy to know the service they give will bless the lives of many. President Brigham Young said, "Compare those inhabitants on the earth who have heard the Gospel in our day, with the millions who have never heard it, or had the keys of salvation presented to them, and you will conclude at once as I do, that there is an almighty work to perform in the spirit world."[343]

Righteous people in the spirit world are actively engaged in furthering God's work by teaching people and bringing them to a knowledge of the gospel. Speaking of departed members of the Church, President Brigham Young said:

> What are they doing there [in the spirit world]? They are preaching, preaching all the time, and preparing the way for us to hasten our work in building temples here and elsewhere. Every faithful man's labor will continue as long as the labor of Jesus, until all things are redeemed that can be redeemed, and presented to the Father. There is a great work before us.[344]

Heavenly Father's plan of redemption ensures that every person who dies without learning about the gospel will be given that chance in the spirit world. Not one soul shall be overlooked or forgotten. In the spirit world, righteous people who accepted the gospel on Earth will teach those who did not have an opportunity while in mortality to receive it. There, individuals will have the opportunity, if they choose, to listen to the gospel and accept or reject it. If they accept it, they can become heirs of the celestial kingdom of God. President Brigham Young declared:

---

343 Young, *Journal of Discourses*, 4:285. contentdm.lib.byu.edu/digital/collection/JournalOfDiscourses3/id/474/rec/4

344 *Teachings of the Presidents of the Church: Brigham Young*, 280. churchofjesuschrist.org/study/manual/teachings-brigham-young/chapter-38?lang=eng

All that have lived or will live on this earth, will have the privilege of receiving the gospel. They will have apostles, prophets and ministers there, as we have here, to guide them in the ways of truth and righteousness, and lead them back to God. All will have a chance for salvation and eternal life. . . . No one will be denied the privilege of having it.[345]

It is a great consolation to know that departed family members who either did not hear about the gospel or did not accept it will have the opportunity to do so in the spirit world. President Rudger J. Clawson said of this:

Now, there are many of our ancestors who had no opportunity at all in life of hearing the Gospel. That opportunity must come to them. How can it come to them? Only in one way, and that is by the preaching of the Gospel, and the Gospel will be preached to them. . . . The work to be done there is vastly greater than that which is done upon the earth by the Saints of God. There are millions and millions upon millions who have lived and died since the Savior was upon the earth, down to the present time. The work must be done for them. That obligation, brethren and sisters, is resting upon the Church of Jesus Christ of Latter-day Saints. They are looking to us for it.[346]

President Lorenzo Snow believed missionaries would have great success when teaching in the spirit world. During general conference in 1893, he stated:

345 Brigham Young, "Preaching to Spirits in Prison," *The Contributor*, vol. 10, July 1889, 321. archive.org/details/contributor1009eng/page/n9
346 Rudger J. Clawson, *Conference Report*, April 1933, 76. archive.org/details/conferencereport1933a/page/n77

When the gospel is preached to the spirits in prison, the success attending that preaching will be
far greater than that attending the preaching of
our Elders in this life. I believe there will be very
few indeed of those spirits who will not gladly
receive the Gospel when it is carried to them.
The circumstances there will be a thousand times
more favorable.[347]

347 Lorenzo Snow, "Discourse by President Lorenzo Snow," *The Latter-day Saints' Millennial Star*, 56:50. contentdm.lib.byu.edu/digital/collection/MStar/id/19486

CHAPTER 17
WHEN THE VEIL PARTS:
FEELING THE PRESENCE OF YOUR LOVED ONE

He was buried, and that he rose again the
third day according to the scriptures:
And that he was seen of Cephas, then of
the twelve: After that, he was seen of above
five hundred brethren at once. . . .
After that, he was seen of James;
then of all the apostles.[348]

THE GOSPEL TEACHES THAT MARRIAGE and loving family relationships can extend beyond this mortal life. Our loved ones who now reside in the spirit world continue to love us, even as we continue to love them. Although family members may precede us into the next life, familial bonds can remain intact when sealed by the power of the holy priesthood in sacred temple ordinances. With hearts full of gratitude, we look forward to living together in family relationships that extend beyond the powers of death.

There may be times when the veil parts and we are allowed to feel—and in rare cases, even see—our dear departed ones. President Joseph F. Smith said:

---

348 1 Corinthians 15:4–7.

Sometimes the Lord expands our vision from this point of view and this side of the veil, that we feel and seem to realize that we can look beyond the thin veil which separates us from that other sphere. . . . I believe we move and have our being in the presence of heavenly messengers and of heavenly beings. We are not separate from them. . . . We can not forget them; we do not cease to love them; we always hold them in our hearts, in memory, and thus are associated and united to them by ties that we can not break. . . .

And therefore, I claim that we live in their presence, they see us, they are solicitous for our welfare, they love us now more than ever. For now they see the dangers that beset us; they can comprehend better than ever before, the weaknesses that are liable to mislead us into dark and forbidden paths. They see the temptations and evils that beset us in life and the proneness of mortal beings to yield to temptation and to wrong doing; hence their solicitude for us and their love for us and their desire for our well being must be greater than that which we feel for ourselves.[349]

Those Who Die Are Nearby

It can be a great comfort to know that those we love are not far. President Ezra Taft Benson declared:

There is always a great tendency for us to feel when we talk about people who have passed beyond, who have passed through the change called death, that they have gone some great distance away onto another planet or into another world. It is difficult for us to realize that the spirit world is

---

349 Joseph F. Smith, "Opening Address," *Conference Report*, April 1916, 2–3. archive.org/details/conferencereport1916a/page/n3

close by, that it is all part of the operation here on this earth.[350]

President Brigham Young also confirmed that our dear ones are nearby. "Where is the spirit world? It is right here."[351] He went on to clarify that the spirit world "is on this earth that was organized for the people that have lived and that do and will live upon it."[352]

In addition to teaching that the spirit world is very close, the Prophet Joseph Smith offered consolation when he said that the departed are nearby and are aware of what is going on in our lives. Speaking at a funeral service, he declared, "The spirits of the just are exalted to a greater and more glorious work; hence they are blessed in their departure to the world of spirits. Enveloped in flaming fire, *they are not far from us*, and know and understand our thoughts, feelings, and motions."[353]

In ways we do not fully understand, the spirit world appears to be incorporated with this physical world, yet it remains invisible to our mortal eyes because of a veil that has been put over our minds. Elder Parley P. Pratt said:

> As to [the spirit world's] location, it is here on the very planet where we were born; or, in other words, the earth and other planets of a like sphere, have their inward or spiritual spheres, as well as their outward, or temporal. The one is peopled by temporal tabernacles, and the other by spirits. A vail [*sic*] is drawn between the one sphere and the other, whereby all the objects in the spiritual sphere are rendered invisible to those in the temporal.[354]

---

350 Benson, *The Teachings of Ezra Taft Benson*, 30–31.
351 Brigham Young, *Journal of Discourses*, 3:369. contentdm.lib.byu.edu/digital/collection/JournalOfDiscourses3/id/6/rec/3
352 Widtsoe, *Discourses of Brigham Young*, 376. Used with permission.
353 Joseph Fielding Smith, ed., *Scriptural Teachings of the Prophet Joseph Smith* (Salt Lake City: Deseret Book, 1959), 326; emphasis added. Used with permission. scriptures.byu.edu/tpjs/STPJS.pdf
354 Pratt, *Key to the Science of Theology*, 132–33.

At times, our loved ones can visit us, says President Harold B. Lee:

> Where is the spirit world? Is it away up in the heavens? That isn't what the scriptures and our brethren explain. They have told us the spirit world is right here round about us. . . . And if our eyes could be opened we could see those who have departed from us—a father, mother, brother, a sister, a child. We could see them, and sometimes when our physical senses are asleep, sometimes our spiritual self—and we have ears, spiritual ears, and spiritual eyes—sometimes they will be very keen and awake, and a departed one may come while we are lying asleep and come into our consciousness. We'll feel an impression. We'll wake up. Where does it come from? It comes from the spirits of those whom we are sealed to.[355]

The Veil—A Film of Forgetfulness

Everyone on Earth came from a heavenly home, which we cannot now remember because of the veil that was placed over our minds at birth. Before coming to Earth, we were surely informed that this veil—a film of forgetfulness—would temporarily hide our memories of premortal life. When we die and pass into the spirit world, this veil will be stripped away and we will remember all, rather than seeing "through a glass, darkly" as we do now.[356]

There are many wise purposes for the Lord providing us with a veil. One of the reasons behind our sojourn on Earth is to provide us with a time of testing, allowing us to learn how to walk by faith and to see if we will obey God even while out of His presence.

355 Harold B. Lee, "The Veil Is Thin Between this World and the Spirit World." emp.byui.edu/SATTERFIELDB/Quotes/Spirit%20World/Veil%20is%20Thin. html. See also LDS Scripture Teachings, "Angels Are Often Nearby," November 8, 2015. ldsscriptureteachings.org/2015/11/08/angels-are-often-nearby/
356 See 1 Corinthians 13:12.

The veil is vital to this process because if we had a clear memory of premortal life, it would severely curtail our growth and prevent us from learning many valuable lessons.

Another more obscure but possible reason for the veil is that if we had full memory of our previous exalted home, we might suffer from such a longing to return that it would hinder our progress on Earth. Thus, the veil is a protection that allows us to grow and develop without excessive distractions. If we knew the glory and happiness that awaits us upon our return, we would likely find it difficult to continue on and fulfill our earthly missions because we would yearn so intensely to return speedily to our Heavenly Father. President Brigham Young had some experience with this: "I have been near enough to understand eternity so that I have had to exercise a great deal more faith to desire to live than I ever exercised in my whole life to live."357

Despite the veil of forgetfulness covering our minds, there are times when—through the power of the Spirit—the veil becomes thin, allowing us to catch a spark of light that testifies that a dear departed one is near. President Ezra Taft Benson testified:

> I am sure many of you know that the veil can be very thin—that there are people over there who are pulling for us—people who have faith in us and who have great hopes for us, who are hoping and praying that we will measure up—our loved ones (parents, grandparents, brothers, sisters, and friends) who have passed on.358

President Russell M. Nelson said the veil of death is thin and our loved ones can be close:

> As a special witness of Jesus Christ, I testify that He lives! I also testify that the veil of death is very

---

357 Widtsoe, *Discourses of Brigham Young*, 380. Used with permission.
358 Benson, *The Teachings of Ezra Taft Benson*, 31.

thin. I know by experiences too sacred to relate that those who have gone before are not strangers to leaders of this Church. To us and to you, our loved ones may be just as close as the next room—separated only by the doors of death.359

President Ezra T. Benson spoke of that same truth when he said, "Visitors, seen and unseen, from the world beyond, are often close to us. This is part of eternity which we are living today—part of God's plan. There is no veil to the Lord."360

When we depart this life, the veil will be taken from our minds, and we will have perfect recall not only of our premortal life but of our life on Earth. Elder Orson Pratt stated, "Things that may have been erased from your memory for years will be presented before you with all the vividness as if they had just taken place."361

Feeling the Presence of a Loved One

At special times, the veil that covers our mind can part briefly—when God sees fit—and allow us to feel, hear, and occasionally even see the presence of someone we love in order to provide comfort and direction. One of the most notable experiences of this occurs in the New Testament. Three days after Jesus was crucified, the Savior showed Himself to a weeping Mary, who was distraught that His body was no longer lying in the sepulchre. The Savior stood near her and said simply, "Mary." She turned and said to Him joyfully, "Rabboni."362 The Redeemer also appeared to the disciples and stood in the midst of them. Upon seeing that the disciples were afraid, Jesus reassured them, saying, "Behold my hands and my feet, that it is I myself."363

Any parting of the veil will be done only for a wise purpose in the Lord. From the beginning, God has sent angels to convey

359 Russell M. Nelson, "Doors of Death," *Ensign*, May 1992, 74. churchofjesuschrist.org/study/ensign/1992/05/doors-of-death?lang=eng
360 Benson, *The Teachings of Ezra Taft Benson*, 35.
361 Orson Pratt, "The Increased Powers and Faculties of the Mind in a Future State," in Young, *Journal of Discourses*, 2:240. contentdm.lib.byu.edu/digital/collection/JournalOfDiscourses3/id/3975/rec/2
362 See John 20:16.
363 Luke 24:39.

love and concern for His children.364 There are times when ministering angels are allowed to visit and assist us in times of special need. Elder Jeffrey R. Holland said, "In times of special need, He sent angels, divine messengers, to bless His children, reassure them that heaven was always very close and that His help was always very near."365 The Lord has promised to support the faithful, saying, "I will be on your right hand and on your left, and my Spirit shall be in your hearts, and mine angels round about you, to bear you up."366

President Boyd K. Packer declared, "There is no distance in death. The spirit world we know is here around us, but the veil is there, and the curtain is there. On occasions we can see and on more occasions we can feel those who have gone beyond."367

But who are these angels? Gospel doctrine regarding the spirit world and eternal families tells us that many times angels who attend us are our own ancestors. President Joseph F. Smith taught:

> When messengers are sent to minister to the inhabitants of this earth, they are not strangers, but from the ranks of our kindred [and] friends. . . . In like manner our fathers and mothers, brothers, sisters and friends who have passed away from this earth, having been faithful, and worthy to enjoy these rights and privileges, may have a mission given to them to visit their relatives and friends upon the earth again, bringing from the divine Presence messages of love, of warning, or reproof and instruction, to those whom they had learned to love in the flesh.368

---

364 See Moroni 7:22.
365 Jeffrey R. Holland, "Ministry of Angels," *Ensign*, November 2008, 29. churchofjesuschrist.org/study/ensign/2008/11/the-ministry-of-angels?lang=eng
366 D&C 84:88.
367 Boyd K. Packer, *Mine Errand from the Lord: Selections from the Sermons and Writings of Boyd K. Packer* (Salt Lake City: Deseret Book, 2008), 47.
368 Smith, *Gospel Doctrine*, 435–36. archive.org/details/gospel doctrine009956mbp/page/n453/mode/2up

Sometimes individuals are blessed to sense that a departed daughter or son is nearby, full of love for them. Others may feel the presence of their spouse—so close they are tempted to reach out and touch their loved one. Sensing the presence of a loved one can occur because, as President Benson says, "the spirit world is not far away. Sometimes the veil between this life and the life beyond becomes very thin. Our loved ones who have passed on are not far from us."369

The ones you love may be gone from your sight, but their presence can still be felt. Marlene shares the following experience:

On one very special occasion, I was blessed to feel the comforting presence of my departed parents. My father died of a brain tumor in October 1984, and five years later, in August 1989, my mother passed away. A few days after her death, my husband, Kelly, and I drove to visit my sister, Barbara, and her husband, Howard.

A few hours later, we said our goodbyes, and Kelly and I went outside and got into our car. As Kelly began to back out of the driveway, I sensed that my parents were standing on my sister's front lawn, watching us leave. I was hardly able to breathe as Kelly pulled onto the road. I could see them so well in my mind but not with my eyes. I kept wondering if I were imagining things and so said nothing as I stared at where I sensed they were standing side by side. The feeling was so strong that I was a hairbreadth away from seeing them as they held hands and smiled at me. They looked so happy.

A deep feeling of joy and peace fell upon me, and finally—doubting no longer—I asked my husband to stop the car. I told him what I had experienced and asked if we could go back because I had the distinct impression that this experience was meant to bring comfort to my grieving sister. Many years have passed since that night, but the memory of that experience has never faded and has brought me much comfort.

---

369 Ezra Taft Benson, "Life Is Eternal," *Ensign*, June 1971, 33. churchofjesuschrist.org/study/ensign/1971/06/life-is-eternal?lang=eng

Very few people are privileged to actually hear or see someone they love—possibly because those in the spirit world are busy with their own duties and activities or because it could interfere with our personal growth as we try to learn to live by faith. More often people are blessed to sense the presence of dear ones for solace and comfort.

Melvin J. Ballard spoke of why he believed visitations are not a frequent occurrence:

> I am sure that our departed loved ones are near us, and belong to this sphere; yet they have difficulty in talking to us. We sometimes wish we could meet them, shake their hands, and counsel with them, although they operate in another world—but I suppose there is a good reason why we cannot. There must be some law which prevents the law-abiding spirit from talking with man in the flesh. . . . Law-abiding spirits abide the law under which they dwell and do not come [to Earth] unless there is some very good reason, and special permission given; and occasionally that permission is granted.[370]

We do know that visitations from departed ones can occur in the form of dreams. Authors Brook Noel and Pamela D. Blair said, "Many widows and widowers report seeing images of their loved one and feeling their presence. You may have dreams where your partner is still living. According to studies, about one-third to one-half of widows and widowers have these experiences."[371] Singer and songwriter Joan Collins said that after her son's death, she dreamed of him—a dream that was so vivid and real, it seemed more like a visitation. In the dream, her son Clark asked her, "Mother, why are you crying?"[372]

370 Melvin J. Ballard, *Melvin J. Ballard, Crusader for Righteousness* (Salt Lake City: Bookcraft, 1977), 271.
371 Noel and Blair, *I Wasn't Ready to Say Goodbye*, 145.
372 Collins, *The Seven T's*, 145.

During a special event, such as a marriage or the birth or blessing of a baby, family members often hope that departed loved ones might be allowed to attend. President Russell M. Nelson, when celebrating his ninety-fifth birthday at a packed Conference Center, spoke of his departed wife, Dantzel, and two other daughters who had passed away, saying hopefully, "Maybe they got a hall pass to witness this event tonight."373

Inspirational Moments When the Veil Has Parted

Sacred and priceless are the moments when the veil parts. Following are a few special experiences of mourners who were blessed to feel the presence of their deceased loved one.

Lucy Mack Smith

After the death of her two sons at Carthage Jail, Lucy Mack Smith could hardly bear the loss. The bodies of Joseph Smith and his brother Hyrum were taken to Nauvoo to be prepared for burial, and Lucy states:

> I had for a long time braced every nerve, roused every energy of my soul, and called upon God to strengthen me; but when I entered the room, and saw my murdered sons extended both at once before my eyes, and heard the sobs and groans of my family [and] the cries . . . from the lips of their wives, children, brother, and sisters, it was too much—I sank back crying to the Lord in the agony of my soul, "My God! My God! Why has thou forsaken this family?"

It was at that singularly painful moment that Lucy seemed to almost hear them say, "Mother, weep not for us; we have overcome the world by love; we carried to them the gospel, that their souls might be saved—they slew us for our testimony, and thus

---

373 Peggy Fletcher Stack, "Latter-day Saints Celebrate leader's upcoming 95th birthday in song, salute his energy and enthusiasm," *The Salt Lake Tribune*, September 7, 2019, A7.

placed us beyond their power—their ascendancy is for a moment—ours is an eternal triumph."[374]

President Boyd K. Packer

President Boyd K. Packer related a personal visitation that provided him with much comfort:

> I saw my mother once. It was in a vision or a dream, more real than just a dream. She had died in her seventies, died a very painful, long-suffering death. There are two words that I could use to describe my mother when I saw her: the one is beautiful, and the other is glorious. I wondered why it was that I was privileged to see her. Then one day President Spencer W. Kimball in a meeting said that he had seen his father. He described an experience about like I have described it to you. He said, "I wondered for a long time why I was blessed with that experience. I finally came to know that it was his way of saying that he approved of me, that he approved of my life and what I was doing."[375]

A Young Man Returns to Comfort His Mother

President Ezra Taft Benson related the experience of a young man who returned to console his mother. President Benson said:

> A son of Bishop and Sister Wells was killed in a railroad accident on October 15, 1915. He was run over by a freight car. Sister Wells could not be consoled. She received no comfort during the funeral and continued her mourning after her

---

374 Lucy Mack Smith, *History*, 1845, 312–13, josephsmithpapers.org; (spelling and punctuation standardized). josephsmithpapers.org/paper-summary/lucy-mack-smith-history-1845/321. Also found in M. Russell Ballard, "Shall We Not Go On in So Great a Cause?" *Ensign*, May 2020, 10.
375 Packer, *Mine Errand from the Lord*, 47–48.

son was laid to rest. Bishop Wells feared for her health, as she was in a state of deep anguish.

One day, soon after the funeral, Sister Wells was lying on her bed in a state of mourning. The son appeared to her and said, "Mother, do not mourn, do not cry. I am all right."

He then related to her how the accident took place. Apparently there had been some question—even suspicion—about the accident because the young man was an experienced railroad man. But he told his mother that it was clearly an accident. . . .

He also told her that as soon as he realized that he was in another sphere, he had tried to reach his father but could not. His father was so busy with the details of his office and work that he could not respond to the promptings. Therefore, the son had come to his mother.

He then said, "Tell Father that all is well with me, and I want you not to mourn any more."[376]

Edward Hunter

Edward Hunter was baptized a member of The Church of Jesus Christ of Latter-day Saints in its early days. Shortly after, Hyrum Smith, brother of the Prophet, visited him. As they talked, the conversation turned to the state of departed loved ones. Eager for information, Edward asked Hyrum about the condition of children in the next life, as he and his wife had lost a number of children. Edward was especially concerned about a young son, George, who had recently died and to whom he had been especially devoted. After listening to Edward, Hyrum felt inspired to offer Edward some special comfort:

---

376 Ezra Taft Benson, "Seek the Spirit of the Lord," *Ensign*, April 1988, 2. churchofjesuschrist.org/study/ensign/1988/04/seek-the-spirit-of-the-lord ?lang=eng

"It is pretty strong doctrine," said Elder Smith, "but I believe I will tell it. Your son will act as an angel to you; not your guardian angel, but an auxiliary angel, to assist you in extreme trials." The truth of this was manifested to [Edward] about a year and a half later, when, in an hour of deep depression, the little boy appeared to him in vision. Brother Hunter says; "In appearance he was more perfect than in natural life—the same blue eyes, curly hair, fair complexion, and a most beautiful appearance. I felt disposed to keep him, and offered inducements for him to remain." He then said, in his own familiar voice: "George has many friends in heaven."[377]

President Heber J. Grant

Latter-day prophet Heber J. Grant was blessed to receive a comforting manifestation regarding his young son. President Grant wrote:

> I have been blessed with only two sons. One of them died at five years of age and the other at seven. My last son died of a hip disease. I had built great hopes that he would live to spread the Gospel at home and abroad and be an honor to me. About an hour before he died I had a dream that his mother, who was dead, came for him, and that she brought with her a messenger, and she told this messenger to take the boy while I was asleep: and in the dream I thought I awoke and I seized my son and fought for him.

As he struggled, President Grant dreamed he fell on his son, hurting the boy's sore hip. In anguish, President Grant dreamed

---

377 Andrew Jenson, *Latter-day Saint Biographical Encyclopedia*, vol. 1 (Salt Lake City: Deseret News, 1901), 229–30.

he went outside and ran into Brother Joseph E. Taylor. After telling his friend what had happened, Elder Taylor told him:

> Well, Heber, do you know what I would do if my wife came for one of her children—I would not struggle for that child; I would not oppose her taking that child away. If a mother who had been faithful had passed beyond the veil, she would know of the suffering and the anguish her child may have to suffer . . . and whether it would be better or wiser for that child to be relieved from the torture of life.

President Grant replied:

> "I believe you are right, Brother Taylor, and if she comes again, she shall have the boy without any protest on my part."
>
> After coming to that conclusion, I was waked by my brother, B. F. Grant, who was staying that night with us, helping to watch over the sick boy. He called me into the room and told me that my child was dying. I went in the front room and sat down. There was a vacant chair between me and my wife who is now living, and I felt the presence of that boy's deceased mother, sitting in that chair. I did not tell anybody what I felt, but I turned to my living wife and said: "Do you feel anything strange?" She said: "Yes, I feel assured that Heber's mother is sitting between us, waiting to take him away."
>
> I believe that I am naturally affectionate and sympathetic and that I shed tears for my friends. . . . But I sat by the deathbed of my little boy and saw

him die, without shedding a tear. My living wife, my brother, and I, upon that occasion experienced a sweet, peaceful, and heavenly influence in my home, as great as I have ever experienced in my life.[378]

Yvonne Lee

Yvonne Lee was grief-stricken upon finding out that her twenty-eight-year-old son, Sam, had been attacked in the fall of 2011. Two men stabbed Sam, then left him to bleed to death. A little more than a year after his death, Sam appeared to Yvonne, who wasn't sure if he came to her in a dream or a vision. All she knew for certain was that the manifestation was powerful and clear. Yvonne said her son appeared to be a resurrected personage. He told his grieving mother, "Mom, you wanted to touch me and talk to me. I am sent for your assurance." He added, "Don't think I'm a tragic victim. I am beyond your imagination. Think of me as a blessed angel."[379]

Elder Orson F. Whitney

An early leader of the Church, Elder Orson F. Whitney, had a distinguished heritage: one grandfather, Newel K. Whitney, served as a presiding bishop, and another was President Heber C. Kimball. When Orson received a blessing under the hand of Patriarch John Smith, he was promised that if the need arose, he would be able to "commune with the spirits that have gone hence, and they shall visit and revisit thee." Whitney was also told that God "has given thine angel special charge concerning thee." Both of these promises were fulfilled.

Orson Whitney recounted the following experience:

---

378 Heber J. Grant, "In the Hour of Parting," *Improvement Era*, June 1940, 330, 383. archive.org/details/improvementera4306unse/page/n11; archive.org/details/improvementera4306unse/page/n63

379 Stack, "Death's Pain vs. Easter's Promise," *The Salt Lake Tribune*. local.sltrib.com/online/sw/easter/

Early on the morning of April 24, 1918 (Paul and Virginia's [two of his children] birthday) while I lay on my pillow, half asleep, half awake, a pair of hands were laid upon my head. My first thought was that someone was in the house who ought not to be, and that I must lie perfectly still in order to be safe. But the touch was so soft and gentle that all fear soon left me, and with my own hands I took hold of those resting upon my head. They were a woman's hands. Presently I saw my wife Zina, who had been dead for eighteen years. She was hovering over me. I held out my arms to her, and she came into them. It was all so real. I could not doubt that she was actually there, a guardian angel, watching over her children and me.[380]

A Promise Fulfilled

Marlene shares the following experience:

When my husband and I lived in eastern Utah, we became good friends with Bob and Lois Jacobs, who had three young children the same ages as ours. One summer day, Bob's older brother, incensed over a land dispute, went to their house and shot Bob and Lois, leaving their three children orphaned.

At the funeral, a close friend who was a Church leader pointed at the three children and emphatically promised them that their mother would help raise them in this life. It was a marvelous promise, one that touched my heart and gave me goosebumps because I knew how deeply Lois and Bob loved their children and that they would do anything for them—even if it now had to be from the other side of the veil.

I stayed in contact with the children, writing to the oldest son, Robert, whom I had taught in Primary. One day, my

---

380 Orson Whitney, *Through Memory's Halls: The Life Story of Orson F. Whitney* (Independence: Zions Printing and Publishing, 1930), 413. catalog.churchofjesuschrist.org/assets?id=91fed491-d61d-4e01-8010-8ef2b3a1418c&crate=0&index=434

husband and I drove to Salt Lake City to visit the children. After spending time with us, they ran off to play while we talked with their grandmother. With tears in her eyes, she told us that the youngest daughter, approximately two and a half years old, had seen her mother on multiple occasions. She related that at the beginning of each visitation, the little girl would hold out her arms to an unseen being and cry out, "Mama! Mama!"

Hannah Cornaby

Lydia and Hannah Cornaby were not just sisters—they were best friends. They were separated when Lydia, at the age of eleven, passed away in August 1836. Hannah, who was fourteen, grieved so deeply that her health became affected. Then Hannah had a remarkable and comforting experience. She wrote:

> I was praying to God for help to control my grief, desiring again to see my beloved sister and this desire was granted me. One Sunday afternoon, feeling too unwell to go to church, I remained at home, the other members of the family attending. Thus alone, my thoughts reverted to my sister; and lo! She stood before me, as when in perfect health and loveliness. My first impulse was to embrace her, but she moved from me, saying, "No dear, you cannot." . . . I asked her if she lived in Heaven; she replied, "I am where Jesus is." . . . After some further conversation, she disappeared, keeping her face towards me until she vanished from sight. During her stay and after she left I was not in the least alarmed. I knew she had come from the spirit world to gratify my longing desire to see her.[381]

President Wilford Woodruff

President Wilford Woodruff's son, Brigham, was a young man when he passed away. Stricken by his son's death, President

---

381 Marlene Bateman Sullivan, *And There Were Angels Among Them: Spiritual Visitations in Early Church History* (Bountiful: Horizon Publishers, 2001), 64–65.

Woodruff had difficulty understanding why God would take such a fine, upstanding young man and discussed the matter with his friend, President Heber J. Grant. President Grant said of that conversation:

> Brother Woodruff said that all the days of his life he had acknowledged the hand of the Lord in everything which had come to him—life, death, joy, remorse, anything and everything—until he lost this boy. He said when his son Brigham drowned he felt almost rebellious about it. Finally the Lord was good enough to give to him a manifestation to the effect that he had a great work to do here . . . in the temples as soon as they were completed . . . for thousands of his ancestors who had died without a knowledge of the Gospel.
>
> He was told by the Lord . . . that this boy of his was needed on the other side to carry the Gospel to his relatives for whom Brother Woodruff was to do the vicarious labor in the temples when they were completed. This reconciled Brother Woodruff to the inexplicable, though previously he could not feel satisfied regarding the loss of that boy. He said: "I had lived in hopes that this boy would some day follow me. He was more brilliant than I am, and I hoped he might some day be one of the Apostles of the Lord Jesus Christ, and it was a terrible shock to me when he died. But I shall never cease to be grateful to the Lord for giving me a special manifestation to the effect that my boy had gone where he was needed more than he was needed here."[382]

---

382 Sullivan, *And There Were Angels Among Them*, 67–68.

Lydia Knight

In April 1846, Newel Knight left Nauvoo with his wife, Lydia, and their seven children to join the Saints at Winter Quarters. In January 1847, Newel began suffering from an intense pain in his right side. The pain increased over the next few days until Newel realized he was dying. Newel did his best to comfort his wife, telling her that she and the children would be protected as they traveled with the Saints. Newel died January 11, 1847.

Three weeks later, Brigham Young received a revelation about how to organize the Saints to travel to the Salt Lake Valley. However, Lydia felt nothing but despair, wondering how she and her seven children could possibly travel one thousand miles without a husband to help. Fearful and discouraged, Lydia found a secluded spot and cried, "O Newel, why has thou left me?" After Lydia said those words, she experienced the following:

> [Newell] stood by her side, with a lovely smile on his face, and said: "Be calm, let not sorrow overcome you. It was necessary that I should go. . . . The time will come when you shall know why I left you and our little ones. Therefore, dry up your tears. Be patient, I will go before you and protect you in your journeyings."[383]

A Grieving Father

While speaking at a funeral, Apostle Melvin J. Ballard related an incident about a man who felt great despair over the death of his only son. Elder Ballard stated:

> I remember a father being unwilling to reconcile himself to the death of his only son. One day in the mountains he said to me that he had sought the Lord saying, "Why have you taken my boy,

---

383 Sullivan, *And There Were Angels Among Them*, 35.

my son, my hope, my pride from me?" And there came to him the whisperings of the Spirit: "He was my son before he was yours. I loved him more than you will ever know how to love him, but if you are faithful I will give him back to you." And that father was reconciled."384

Marriner W. Merrill

Another Apostle, Marriner W. Merrill, said that when his son died as a young man, he had a hard time dealing with his feelings of sorrow and loss. At the time of his death, Elder Merrill's son had been managing several of his father's farms as well as a mercantile business. President Heber J. Grant relates Elder Merrill's spiritual manifestation:

Brother Merrill said that while sitting in his house upon one occasion, almost rebellious in his feelings because this boy's life was not spared to him and that sufficient faith had not be exercised in administering to him . . . he heard his son's voice as clearly as he had ever heard it while he was alive, and he said, "Father, it is very displeasing to our Heavenly Father for you to be mourning over my death. I am exactly where the Lord wants me to be and doing work that is of far greater importance than the work I would have done had I remained on earth. It is for you to be reconciled to the fact that I am where my Father in Heaven wants me to be." Brother Merrill said of course after that he had no regrets or rebellious feelings in his heart regarding the taking away of his son.385

---

384 Ballard, *Melvin J. Ballard, Crusader for Righteousness*, 274.
385 Heber J. Grant, "Comforting Manifestations," *Improvement Era*, February 1931, 189. archive.org/details/improvementera3404unse/page/n6

CHAPTER 18
HOPE AND HEALING

I love the Lord, because he hath heard
my voice and my supplications.
Because he hath inclined his ear unto me,
therefore will I call upon him as long as I live.
The sorrows of death compassed me. . . .
I found trouble and sorrow.
Then called I upon the name of the Lord;
O Lord, I beseech thee, deliver my soul.
Gracious is the Lord, and righteous; yea, our God is
merciful. . . . I was brought low, and he helped me.
Return unto thy rest, O my soul;
for the Lord hath dealt bountifully with thee.
For thou hast delivered my soul from death,
mine eyes from tears, and my feet from falling.
I will walk before the Lord in the land of the living.[386]

ALTHOUGH DEATH HAS ALWAYS BEEN part of life, it doesn't make losing someone any easier. It may be necessary to dig deep in order to process your grief and heal, but those who have faith in Jesus Christ, the Redeemer of the world, have faith that life will

---

386 Psalm 116:1–9.

continue even when the physical body is laid to rest. President Gordon B. Hinckley declared:

> Death is as much a part of eternal life as is birth. Looked at through mortal eyes, without comprehension of the eternal plan of God, death is a bleak, final, and unrelenting experience. . . .
>
> But our Eternal Father, whose children we are, made possible a far better thing through the sacrifice of His Only Begotten Son, the Lord Jesus Christ. This had to be. Can anyone believe that the Great Creator would provide for life and growth and achievement only to snuff it all into oblivion in the process of death? Reason says no. Justice demands a better answer. The God of heaven has given one. The Lord Jesus Christ provided it.[387]

Death is not something to be dreaded. Instead, it can be thought of as graduating from an earthly existence that can be full of difficulties into a glorious spirit world where you will be free from the trials that so often accompany life on Earth. President Spencer W. Kimball gave us his personal insight regarding death:

> Death is an important part of life. Of course, we are never quite ready for the change. . . . Yet we ought not be afraid of death. We pray for the sick, we administer to the afflicted, we implore the Lord to heal and reduce pain and save life and postpone death, and properly so, but not because eternity is so frightful.[388]

---

387 Gordon B. Hinckley, "The Greatest Miracle in Human History," *Ensign*, May 1994, 72. churchofjesuschrist.org/study/ensign/1994/05/the-greatest-miracle-in-human-history?lang=eng
388 Kimball, *Faith Precedes the Miracle*, 103. Used with permission.

The Healing Process

After losing someone you love, there are two choices: You can start down the road of recovery, or you can live in continual sorrow and misery. Deciding to take the road of recovery may *seem* like an easy choice, yet it can be one of the most difficult journeys you have ever taken. Grief is not an illness but an experience that needs to be worked through. You may never fully get *over* your loss, but you can get *through* it. Having faith in God and in His promises can comfort your heart and help you look forward to the time when His promises to the faithful will be fulfilled. Strive always to stay close to God, for "in the way of righteousness is life; and in the pathway thereof there is no death."389

There may be times when you need to remind yourself that moving forward does not mean you are forgetting your loved one—it means only that you are freeing yourself from unnecessary pain. Sometimes people mistakenly feel that remaining in constant pain is the only way to prove how much they loved the departed, but this is faulty thinking and will result only in pointless pain.

After losing a dear one, life may never be the same, but change is an ever-present and necessary part of life. By going forward and healing, you will discover that life is still worth living and that peace, joy, and happiness can be yours once more.

When pain of loss strikes, people sometimes react with behavior that brings more anguish, such as withdrawing from family and friends, neglecting personal health, putting little effort into their job, or simply losing interest in the world around them. While healing can be arduous, it is preferable to compounding suffering by making unwise and imprudent choices. Your Heavenly Father is waiting anxiously to assist you and lighten your burden. Allow Him to help by praying daily and asking Him to guide, bless, and comfort you.

Although there are dark days that must be survived, the glorious reality of God's divine comfort beckons on the other side of your river of loss. You must pray for enough energy to do what

---

389 Proverbs 12:28.

needs to be done to free yourself from pain's grasp. Plead with God for strength to climb out of your pit of despair. Pray for the patience to wait for the time when you will once again be able to clasp your loved ones in your arms.

As you proceed through the healing process, you may notice that your grief slowly changes. You see more roses and fewer thorns, more sunshine and fewer shadows. Hope blooms in your heart, replacing the despair that held it captive. Focus on the beautiful miracles in life that surround you—colorful flowers in full bloom, lilting songs of birds hiding in leafy treetops, the delicious taste of a crisp apple, the sweet laughter of a child, a tender phone call from a friend. Strive every day to welcome peace and love into your life. Forgive yourself for your weaknesses and forgive those who have injured you.

One day it will no longer break your heart to see the sun, watch children at play, and hear music. You will be able to respond without tears when people ask how you are. As you begin to break out of your cocoon of pain and open yourself up to the world again, you will see light where before there was only darkness. At this point, you may find yourself becoming newly absorbed in things you thought you would never care about again.

Positive factors that indicate the healing process is well underway include taking good care of yourself, being able to continue working, sustaining good friendships, and safeguarding yourself from harm. As you put effort into healing, the physical and emotional pain that have engulfed you will begin to fall away, allowing you to enjoy life once more. You may feel a bit uneasy about following this new road, simply because personal tragedy has taught that there is no way to know what lies ahead. Despite knowing that you have no control over many things, you *do* know you can trust in God to strengthen you as you move forward.

Working through grief allows you to reclaim your life. You will find yourself able to enjoy laughter without feeling it diminishes your loss. You might decide to attend to things around the house that need repair, wear more colorful clothes, or make plans for the future. You may discover yourself having fewer mood swings, becoming more interested in eating, paying more attention to world or local news, and being able to talk about your loss in a normal conversational manner. All these things show that you are successfully moving forward.

Healing Allows Us Opportunities to Grow

While grieving can throw us down a deep well where there is only darkness, every black night is eventually swallowed up in the light of a new day. Despite loss, we can still find meaning in life and strive to accomplish our own personal missions. Heavenly Father prepared this world as a place of growth and testing, and He provides mortal experiences—many of them difficult—to allow us to develop divine characteristics and become more like Him.

Although healing from loss may be one of the hardest things we will do, this experience will provide us with opportunities to grow, learn, and do things we might not have done otherwise. A broken heart is a heart made larger by pain, and it is possible to gain something from our loss if we allow suffering to stretch our soul so we become more loving, empathetic, and compassionate. As we work to develop divine qualities, we can continue to progress until we are glorified in truth and know all things, growing brighter and brighter until the perfect day.[390]

In mortality, earthly challenges often threaten to overwhelm us, but we will be richly blessed if we press forward in faith, continually doing good works and enduring to the end. Always remember that you can receive divine help, which will strengthen you to endure. The Lord told us, "Be of good cheer, for I will lead you along. The kingdom is yours and the blessings thereof are yours, and the riches of eternity are yours."[391]

Paul wrote the following regarding having faith and courage to endure:

---

390 See D&C 93:28.
391 D&C 78:18.

We are troubled on every side, yet not distressed;
we are perplexed, but not in despair;

Persecuted, but not forsaken; cast down, but
not destroyed. . . .

For our light affliction, which is but for
a moment, worketh for us a far more exceeding and eternal weight of glory.[392]

As we strive to increase in light and knowledge, we can perfect
ourselves so that when we lay our physical body down and move
on to the spirit world, we can partake of the glories awaiting
there. "Wherefore, ye must press forward with a steadfastness in
Christ, having a perfect brightness of hope, and a love of God
and of all men. Wherefore, if ye press forward, feasting upon the
word of Christ, and endure to the end, behold, thus saith the
Father: Ye shall have eternal life."[393]

A Place of Rest, Peace, and Joy

Because of our faith in Jesus Christ and in God, the Eternal
Father, we know the glory that awaits us. Shortly before his
death, Moroni remained full of unquestioning faith: "I soon go
to rest in the paradise of God, until my spirit and body shall
again reunite, and I am brought forth triumphant through the
air, to meet you before the pleasing bar of the great Jehovah, the
Eternal Judge of both quick and dead."[394]

The gospel of Christ teaches us where we came from, why we
are here, and where we will go when we leave this life. Leaving
mortality is a transition that plays an essential part in this grand
plan of salvation. Although we sorrow at being separated from
our dear ones, it brings much comfort to know that in the spirit
world, they are physically and mentally rejuvenated and full of joy
and happiness.

Even when death takes away someone close to us, President
Russell M. Nelson assures us that we can still have peace in our
hearts:

392 2 Corinthians 4:8–9, 17.
393 2 Nephi 31:20.
394 Moroni 10:34.

We need not look upon death as an enemy. With full understanding and preparation, faith supplants fear. Hope displaces despair. The Lord said, "Fear not even unto death; for in this world your joy is not full, but in me your joy is full" (D&C 101:36). He bestowed this gift: "Peace I leave with you, my peace I give unto you: not as the world giveth, give I unto you. Let not your heart be troubled, neither let it be afraid" (John 14:27).[395]

President Heber J. Grant said, "I never think of my wives and my dear mother and my two boys, my daughter, and my departed friends, and beloved associates being in the graveyard. I think only of the . . . wonderful joy and satisfaction and happiness that they are having, and it robs the grave of its sting."[396]

We can take solace in and rejoice at the joy our loved ones must surely feel at going to a more glorious sphere. We shall also feel joyous when our time comes to leave this earth and graduate to the next level of our existence. Speaking at the funeral of Thomas Williams, President Brigham Young said we would exult at returning to a more heavenly existence:

> We shall turn round and look upon it [the valley of death] and think, when we have crossed it, why this is the greatest advantage of my whole existence, for I have passed from a state of sorrow, grief, mourning, woe, misery, pain, anguish and disappointment into a state of existence, where I can enjoy life to the fullest extent as far as that can be done without a body. My spirit is set free, I thirst no more, I want to sleep no more, I hunger no more, I tire no more, I run, I walk, I labor, I go, I come, I do this, I do that,

395 Russell M. Nelson, "Doors of Death," *Ensign*, May 1992, 74. churchofjesuschrist.org/study/ensign/1992/05/doors-of-death?lang=eng
396 Heber J. Grant, "In the Hour of Parting," *Improvement Era*, June 1940, 383. archive.org/details/improvementera4306unse/page/n63

whatever is required of me, nothing like pain or weariness, I am full of life, full of vigor, and I enjoy the presence of my heavenly Father, by the power of his Spirit.[397]

Eternal Bonds of Love

During times of parting, it is comforting to remember that the bonds of love you share with your family can be eternal. One day, you will be reunited with your family because of Jesus Christ's great atoning sacrifice. "But behold, the bands of death shall be broken, and the Son reigneth, and hath power over the dead; therefore, he bringeth to pass the resurrection of the dead."[398]

Our Savior made the ultimate sacrifice—doing for us what we could not do for ourselves. Jesus Christ "abolished death, and hath brought life and immortality to light through the gospel."[399] Immortality, which comes to us as a gift from our Savior and a loving Heavenly Father, and eternal life, which comes through our faithfulness, are the greatest of all possible blessings.[400] "For God so loved the world, that he gave his only begotten Son, that whosoever believeth in him should not perish, but have everlasting life."[401]

To all people everywhere, the Savior proclaimed, "I am the resurrection, and the life: he that believeth in me, though he were dead, yet shall he live: And whosoever liveth and believeth in me shall never die."[402] While you mourn the loss of companionship, you know your dear one lives on. "Therefore the grave hath no victory, and the sting of death is swallowed up in Christ."[403]

Although you must remain behind on Earth for a time, the ones you love never truly leave. Their memories stay forever in your heart. You may remember how your mother always greeted others

---

397 Young, *Journal of Discourses*, 17:142. contentdm.lib.byu.edu/digital/collection/JournalOfDiscourses3/id/6617/rec/17
398 Mosiah 15:20.
399 2 Timothy 1:10.
400 See D&C 6:13; 14:7.
401 John 3:16.
402 John 11:25–26.
403 Mosiah 16:8.

with a cheery hello, loved freshly fallen snow, had an affinity for calico cats, and told you to look twice before pulling into traffic because it's better to be safe than sorry. You may recall your father mowing your lawn when you were ill or reminding you on a cold winter's day that as long as your neck is warm, the rest of you will stay warm.

Because of those memories, loved ones are never far away, and now *you* smile brightly when you greet others, mow a neighbor's lawn when they are sick, and look twice before pulling onto a busy road. You may rescue a calico cat from a shelter or wrap a scarf around your neck before taking a walk in the freshly fallen snow.

One of the greatest joys upon entering the spirit world will be seeing our departed loved ones. What a delight it will be to see our dear spouse, mother, father, grandparents, children, and friends! The Prophet Joseph Smith spoke of his own anticipation at seeing family and friends:

> I have a father, brothers, children, and friends who have gone to a world of spirits. They are only absent for a moment. They are in the spirit, and we shall soon meet again. . . . When we depart, we shall hail our mothers, fathers, friends, and all whom we love, who have fallen asleep in Jesus. . . . It will be an eternity of felicity.[404]

Preparing to Be with Our Loved Ones

One glorious day, all of us will be reunited with the loved ones we have lost while on Earth. Until then, hold fast, knowing that your separation is only temporary. The Prophet Joseph Smith gave comforting assurance to those who mourn: "All your losses will be made up to you in the resurrection, provided you continue faithful. By the vision of the Almighty I have seen it."[405]

---

404 Smith, *Scriptural Teachings of the Prophet Joseph Smith*, 359–60. Used with permission. scriptures.byu.edu/tpjs/STPJS.pdf

405 Smith, *Scriptural Teachings of the Prophet Joseph Smith*, 296. Used with permission. scriptures.byu.edu/tpjs/STPJS.pdf

As each of us will eventually pass through the portals of death into the spirit world, we would be wise to prepare now:

> For behold, this life is the time for men to prepare to meet God; yea, behold the day of this life is the day for men to perform their labors.
>
> And now, as I said unto you before, as ye have had so many witnesses, therefore, I beseech of you that ye do not procrastinate the day of your repentance until the end; for after this day of life, which is given us to prepare for eternity, behold, if we do not improve our time while in this life, then cometh the night of darkness wherein there can be no labor performed.
>
> Ye cannot say, when ye are brought to that awful crisis, that I will repent, that I will return to my God. Nay, ye cannot say this; for that same spirit which doth possess your bodies at the time that ye go out of this life, that same spirit will have power to possess your body in that eternal world.
>
> For behold, if ye have procrastinated the day of your repentance even until death, behold, ye have become subjected to the spirit of the devil, and he doth seal you his . . . and the devil hath all power over you; and this is the final state of the wicked.[406]

While our future lies on the other side of the veil, our present dictates that we remain on Earth for an indeterminate time. We would do well, then, to obey God and follow Jesus to the best of our abilities. One of the best gifts we can give our departed loved ones is to live life to the fullest. Falling into a pit of grief and despair is not something they would want. We can honor our

---

406 Alma 34:32–35.

dear one's memory by processing our grief, living a worthy life, and becoming a more noble spirit. While speaking at a funeral, President Howard W. Hunter said:

> In the quiet of this chapel today, our souls have been on their knees. We have contemplated the uncertainties of life and the certainty of death. Each of us in his turn will follow the same course—only the point of time is the difference. Will we be ready? Will the things we intend to accomplish be completed? Will we make right the little wrongs and replace the harsh words with kindness before our call comes? Will we accept the fullness of the gospel of Jesus Christ by following his teachings, keeping his commandments, being of service to our fellowman, ready to enter the tomb, partake of the glorious resurrection, and stand at the judgment as worthy servants?[407]

A Promise of Good Things to Come

If we will strive to do our best to meet the trials of mortality, we will be richly blessed in the next phase of our existence and be joyfully reunited with our loved ones. In the New Testament we read, "Eye hath not seen, nor ear heard, neither have entered into the heart of man, the things which God hath prepared for them that love him."[408]

Elder D. Todd Christofferson offers the following counsel:

> Always remember the promise of good things to come, both now and hereafter, for those who are firm and steadfast in the faith of Christ. Remember "eternal life, and the joy of the saints"

---

407 Clyde J. Williams, ed., *The Teachings of Howard W. Hunter* (Salt Lake City: Bookcraft, 1997), 15–16.
408 1 Corinthians 2:9.

(Enos 1:3), "O all ye that are pure in heart, lift up your heads and receive the pleasing word of God, and feast upon his love; for ye may, if your minds are firm, forever" (Jacob 3:2).[409]

As we heal from our loss, may we see light where before there was darkness; hope when we once felt despair; faith and trust where there was once fear and sorrow; and finally love, joy, and peace in our hearts as we draw closer to God.

By using our time on Earth wisely and serving others, we will be able to say when it is our turn to pass through the doors of death, as did the Apostle Paul, "the time of my departure is at hand. I have fought a good fight, I have finished my course, I have kept the faith: Henceforth there is laid up for me a crown of righteousness, which the Lord, the righteous judge, shall give me at that day."[410]

If we continue faithful and endure our trials well, we can one day stand arrayed in purified white robes before the throne of God. "These are they which came out of great tribulation, and have washed their robes, and made them white in the blood of the Lamb."[411] Those who follow the Savior will be found at the throne of God and be blessed, for "they shall hunger no more, neither thirst any more; neither shall the sun light on them, nor any heat. For the Lamb which is in the midst of the throne shall feed them, and shall lead them unto living fountains of waters."[412]

"And God shall wipe away all tears from their eyes; and there shall be no more death, neither sorrow, nor crying, neither shall there be any more pain: for the former things are passed away."[413]

---

409 D. Todd Christofferson, "Firm and Steadfast in the Faith of Christ," *Ensign*, November 2018, 33. churchofjesuschrist.org/study/ensign/2018/11/saturday-afternoon-session/firm-and-steadfast-in-the-faith-of-christ?lang=eng

410 2 Timothy 4:6–8.

411 Revelation 7:14.

412 Revelation 7:16–17.

413 Revelation 21:4.

ABOUT THE AUTHORS

MARLENE BATEMAN

MARLENE BATEMAN WAS BORN IN Salt Lake City, Utah, and graduated from the University of Utah with a bachelor's degree in English. She is married to Kelly R. Sullivan, and they live in North Salt Lake, Utah.

Marlene has been published extensively in magazines and newspapers and has written a number of nonfiction books for members of The Church of Jesus Christ of Latter-day Saints. She has also written a number of suspense and romance novels. For more information on her books, please visit her website at marlenebateman.info.com.

JOSHUA M. SULLIVAN, LCSW

Joshua M. Sullivan was born in Salt Lake City, Utah. He is a licensed clinical social worker and practices in Utah. He received his MSW from the University of Utah and a master of education from Southern Utah University. Joshua worked for years as a school counselor and currently specializes in childhood and adolescent mental health. Joshua has provided counseling to clients of all ages and works with people seeking help with grief, loss, depression, and trauma. He lives with his wife in Riverton, Utah.

BIBLIOGRAPHY

Church Magazines

Aburto, Reyna I. "Thru Cloud and Sunshine, Lord, Abide with Me!" *Ensign*, November 2019.

Ballard, M. Russell. "The Vision of the Redemption of the Dead." *Ensign*, November 2018.

Benson, Ezra Taft. "He Is Risen!" *Friend*, April 1981.

———. "Life Is Eternal." *Ensign*, June 1971.

———. "Pray Always." *Ensign*, February 1990.

———. "Seek the Spirit of the Lord." *Ensign*, April 1988.

Cannon, George Q. *Conference Report*, April 1899.

Card, Zina Y. "Manifestation to Mrs. Mary Hyde Woolf." *Relief Society Magazine*, August 1921.

Christofferson, D. Todd. "Firm and Steadfast in the Faith of Christ." *Ensign*, November 2018.

Clawson, Rudger. *Conference Report*, April 1933.

Cook, Quentin L. "The Songs They Could Not Sing." *Ensign*, October 2011.

Eyring, Henry B. "The Hope of Eternal Family Love." *Ensign*, August 2016.

———. "Adversity." *Ensign*, May 2009.

Grant, Heber J. "Comforting Manifestations." *Improvement Era*, February 1931.

————. "In the Hour of Parting." *Improvement Era*, June 1940.

Hallstrom, Donald L. "Has the Day of Miracles Ceased?" *Ensign*, November 2017.

Hinckley, Gordon B. "Lord, Increase Our Faith." *Ensign*, November 1987.

————. "The Empty Tomb Bore Testimony." *Ensign*, May 1988.

————. "The Greatest Miracle in Human History." *Ensign*, May 1994.

Holland, Jeffrey R. "Like a Broken Vessel." *Ensign*, November 2013.

————. "Ministry of Angels." *Ensign*, November 2008.

George Q. Cannon, ed. "How One Feels When Dying," in *Juvenile Instructor* 27, September 15, 1892.

Johnson, Peter E. "A Testimony." *Relief Society Magazine*, August 1920.

Lyman, Francis M. *Conference Report*, October 1909.

McConkie, Bruce R. "The Salvation of Little Children." *Ensign*, April 1977.

Monson, Thomas S. "Be Your Best Self." *Ensign*, May 2009.

————. "Come unto Him in Prayer and Faith." *Ensign*, March 2009.

————. "God Be with You Till We Meet Again." *Ensign*, November 2012.

————. "I Will Not Fail Thee, nor Forsake Thee." *Ensign*, November 2013.

————. "What Have I Done for Someone Today?" *Ensign*, November 2009.

Mouritsen, Dale C. "The Spirit World, Our Home." *Ensign*, January 1977.

Nelson, Russell M. "Doors of Death." *Ensign*, May 1992.

————. "Jesus Christ, the Master Healer." *Ensign*, November 2005.

Oaks, Dallin H. "Resurrection." *Ensign*, May 2000.

————. "Strengthened by the Atonement of Jesus Christ." *Ensign*, November 2015.

Packer, Boyd K. "The Balm of Gilead." *Ensign*, November 1977.

Parkin, Bonnie D. "Gratitude: A Path to Happiness." *Ensign*, May 2007.

Schmutz, Evan A. "God Shall Wipe Away All Tears." *Ensign*, November 2016.

Scott, Richard G. "Temple Worship: The Source of Strength and Power in Times of Need." *Ensign*, May 2009.

———. "Trust in the Lord." *Ensign*, November 1995.

———. "Using the Supernal Gift of Prayer." *Ensign*, May 2007.

Smith, Joseph, Jr. "The King Follett Sermon." *Ensign*, May 1971.

Smith, Joseph F. "Opening Address." *Conference Report*, April 1916.

———. "Status of Children in the Resurrection." *Improvement Era*, May 1918.

———. "The Resurrection." *Liahona—The Elders Journal* (August 8, 1908), 6:178.

Smith, George Albert. "Your Good Name." *Improvement Era*, March 1947.

Snow, Lorenzo. "Discourse by President Lorenzo Snow." *Latter-day Saints' Millennial Star*, 56:50.

Thorpe, LeEtta. "Saved After My Daughter's Suicide." *Liahona*, September 2017.

Uchtdorf, Dieter F. "Grateful in Any Circumstances." *Ensign*, April 2014.

———. "Your Great Adventure." *Ensign*, November 2019.

Young, Brigham. "Preaching to Spirits in Prison." *Contributor* 10, July 1889.

Latter-day Saint Historical and Doctrinal Books

Babbel, Frederick W. *On Wings of Faith*. Salt Lake City: Bookcraft, 1972.

Ballard, Melvin J. *Melvin J. Ballard, Crusader for Righteousness*. Salt Lake City: Bookcraft, 1977.

Benson, Ezra Taft. *The Teachings of Ezra Taft Benson*. Salt Lake City: Bookcraft, 1988.

Bytheway, John. *Righteous Warriors: Lessons from the War Chapters in the Book of Mormon*. Salt Lake City: Deseret Book, 2004.

Daughters in My Kingdom: The History and Work of Relief Society. Salt Lake City: The Church of Jesus Christ of Latter-day Saints, 2011.

Durham, G. Homer, ed. *The Discourses of Wilford Woodruff.* Salt Lake City: Bookcraft, 1990.

Gospel Principles. Salt Lake City: The Church of Jesus Christ of Latter-day Saints, 2011.

Heinerman, Joseph. *Spirit World Manifestations.* Salt Lake City: Magazine Printing and Publishing, 1978.

Hinckley, Bryant S. *Heber J. Grant: Highlights in the Life of a Great Leader.* Salt Lake City: Deseret Book, 1951.

———. *Sermons and Missionary Services of Melvin J. Ballard.* Salt Lake City: Deseret Book, 1949.

———. *The Faith of Our Pioneer Fathers.* Salt Lake City: Deseret Book, 1959.

Jenson, Andrew. *Latter-day Saint Biographical Encyclopedia,* vol. 1. Salt Lake City: Deseret News, 1901.

Kimball, Edward, ed. *Teachings of Spencer W. Kimball.* Salt Lake City: Bookcraft, 1982.

Kimball, Heber C. *Journal of Discourse.* Liverpool: S. W. Richards, 1857.

Kimball, Spencer W. *Faith Precedes the Miracle.* Salt Lake City: Deseret Book, 1972.

Maxwell, Neal A. *The Promise of Discipleship.* Salt Lake City: Deseret Book, 2001.

McConkie, Bruce R. *The Mortal Messiah,* vol. 4. Salt Lake City: Deseret Book, 1981.

———, ed. *Doctrines of Salvation, Sermons & Writings of Joseph Fielding Smith, vol. 2.* Salt Lake City: Bookcraft, 1955.

———, ed. *Doctrines of Salvation: Sermons and Writings of Joseph Fielding Smith.* Salt Lake City: Bookcraft, 1955.

McKay, David O. *Gospel Ideals: Selections from the Discourses of David O. McKay.* Salt Lake City: Improvement Era Publication, 1953.

Millet, Robert L. *After All We Can Do: Grace Works.* Salt Lake City: Deseret Book, 2003.

———. *Life After Death: Insights from Latter-Day Revelation.* Salt Lake City: Deseret Book, 1999.

Packer, Boyd K. *Boyd K. Packer, Mine Errand from the Lord: Selections from the Sermons and Writings of Boyd K. Packer.* Salt Lake City: Deseret Book, 2008.

Parsons, Robert J. In Daniel H. Ludlow, *Encyclopedia of Mormonism.* New York: Macmillan, 1992.

Pratt, Orson. "The Increased Powers and Faculties of the Mind in a Future State." In Young, *Journal of Discourses*, 2:240.

Pratt, Parley P. *Key to the Science of Theology*, 5th ed. Liverpool: John Henry Smith, 1833.

Smith, Joseph. *History of the Church,* vol. 6. Salt Lake City: The Church of Jesus Christ of Latter-day Saints, 1951.

———. *History of the Church*, vol. 4. Salt Lake City: The Church of Jesus Christ of Latter-day Saints, 1951.

Smith, Joseph F. *Gospel Doctrine: Sermons and Writings of President Joseph F. Smith.* Salt Lake City: Deseret Book, 1959.

Smith, Joseph Fielding. *Answers to Gospel Questions.* Salt Lake City: Deseret Book, 1958.

———, ed. *Teachings of the Prophet Joseph Smith.* Salt Lake City: Deseret Book, 1939.

———. *Scriptural Teachings of the Prophet Joseph Smith.* Salt Lake City: Deseret Book, 1959.

———, ed. *The Life of Joseph F. Smith.* Salt Lake City: Deseret News Press, 1938.

Smith, Lucy Mack. *History*, 1845, 312–13. josephsmithpapers. org (spelling and punctuation standardized). Also found in M. Russell Ballard, "Shall We Not Go On in So Great a Cause?" *Ensign*, May 2020, 10.

Stokes, Jeremiah. *Modern Miracles.* Salt Lake City: Bookcraft, 1945.

Sullivan, Marlene Bateman. *And There Were Angels Among Them: Spiritual Visitations in Early Church History.* Bountiful: Horizon Publishers, 2001.

———. *Gaze into Heaven: Near-Death Experiences in Early Church History.* Springville: Cedar Fort Inc., 2013.

Talmage, James E. *Jesus the Christ.* Salt Lake City: Deseret Book Company, 1982.

Teachings of the Presidents of the Church: Brigham Young. Salt Lake City: The Church of Jesus Christ of Latter-day Saints, 1997.

Teachings of the Presidents of the Church: Gordon B. Hinckley. Salt Lake City: The Church of Jesus Christ of Latter-day Saints, 2016.

Teachings of the Presidents of the Church: Joseph Smith. Salt Lake City: The Church of Jesus Christ of Latter-day Saints, 2004, 2011.

Teachings of the Presidents of the Church: Joseph F. Smith. Salt Lake City: The Church of Jesus Christ of Latter-day Saints, 2004, 2011.

Teachings of the Presidents of the Church: Joseph Fielding Smith. Salt Lake City: The Church of Jesus Christ of Latter-day Saints, 2013.

Teachings of the Presidents of the Church: Harold B. Lee. Salt Lake City: The Church of Jesus Christ of Latter-day Saints, 2000.

Teachings of the Presidents of the Church: Spencer W. Kimball. Salt Lake City: Deseret Book, 1977.

Teachings of the Presidents of the Church: Wilford Woodruff. Salt Lake City: The Church of Jesus Christ of Latter-day Saints, 2004, 2011.

Whitney, Orson. *Through Memory's Halls: The Life Story of Orson F. Whitney.* Independence: Zions Printing and Publishing, 1930.

Wilcox, Brad. *The Continuous Atonement.* Salt Lake City: Deseret Book, 2009.

Williams, Clyde J., ed. *The Teachings of Howard W. Hunter.* Salt Lake City: Bookcraft, 1997.

Widtsoe, John A., ed. *Discourses of Brigham Young.* Salt Lake City: Deseret Book, 1941.

Young, Brigham. *Journal of Discourses.* Liverpool: S. W. Richards, 1857.

Newspapers

Cabeza, Garrett. "'Let her light shine through you.'" *The Salt Lake Tribune,* November 13, 2018. sltrib.com/news/2018/11/12/let-her-light-shine/

Jacobs, Becky. "This Is Real Life for Us." *The Salt Lake Tribune*, September 15, 2019. sltrib.com/news/2019/09/15 /lehi-mother-shares-impact/

Kamrani, Christopher. "Gifted and intense on the track, U. student and track star Lauren McCluskey is remembered by her community." *The Salt Lake Tribune*, November 5, 2018. sltrib. com/news/2018/11/05/alongside-university/

Kirby, Robert. "Forgiving hearts of a slain cop's parents eased my rage." *The Salt Lake Tribune*, May 6, 2018.

Manson, Pamela. "'A lot of people are protected because of our loss': A Utah woman's death set legal precedent, but her family still feels the pain of her absence." *The Salt Lake Tribune*, January 15, 2018. sltrib.com/news/2018/01/15/ how-a-utah-womans-car-crash-death-led-to-a-precedent- setting-us-supreme-court-decision-on-seat-belts-and- continuing-pain-for-her-family/

Mims, Bob. "New collection of Leonard Arrington's vast journals." *The Salt Lake Tribune*, Wednesday, May 9, 2018.

Noble, Mariah. "Park where 3-Year-old Rachael Runyan was abducted in 1982 serves as her memorial." *The Salt Lake Tribune*, September 25, 2016. archive.sltrib.com/article. php?id=4380727&itype=CMSID.

Richardson, Holly. "There are ways to get through the grief of a miscarriage." *The Salt Lake Tribune*, October 5, 2019.

Stack, Peggy Fletcher. "Death's Pain vs. Easter's Promise." *The Salt Lake Tribune*, April 16, 2017.

———. "Latter-day Saints celebrate leader's upcoming 95th birthday in song, salute his energy and enthusiasm." *The Salt Lake Tribune*, September 7, 2019.

Tanner, Courtney. "After death of U. student, lawmakers OK bill mandating campus safety plans." *The Salt Lake Tribune*, February 26, 2019. sltrib.com/news/education/2019/02/26/ campus-safety-bill/

———. "Utah governor signs campus safety bill that was spurred by U. student's death—and a handful of other education measures." *The Salt Lake Tribune*, March 30, 2019. sltrib.com/news/education/2019/02/26/campus-safety-bill/

Walch, Tad, "LDS Apostle: 'Totally false' that suicide leads to permanent hell," *Deseret News*, July 2, 2018.

Wood, Benjamin. "Suicide rates in Utah outnumber homicides." *The Salt Lake Tribune*, November 15, 2018. deseret.com/2018/7/2/20648210/lds-apostle-totally-false-that-suicide-leads-to-permanent-hell.

"Dad pushes for safety after daughter's death." *The Salt Lake Tribune*, April 2, 2019.

Personal Experience

Haddock, Carroll. Personal experience shared with Marlene Bateman. Used with permission.

Religious Studies Center

McConkie, Bruce R. Quoted by Robert L. Millet. "Alive in Christ: The Salvation of Little Children. In *The Book of Mormon: Fourth Nephi, From Zion to Destruction*. Edited by Monte S. Nyman and Charles D. Tate Jr. Provo, UT: Religious Studies Center, Brigham Young University, 1995, 1–17.

Scriptures

The Book of Mormon, Translated by Joseph Smith, (Salt Lake City: The Church of Jesus Christ of Latter-day Saints, 1949).

The Doctrine and Covenants of The Church of Jesus Christ of Latter-day Saints. (Salt Lake City: The Church of Jesus Christ of Latter-day Saints).

The Holy Bible, King James Version, (Salt Lake City: The Church of Jesus Christ of Latter-day Saints, 1950).

Secular Books

Bozarth, Alla Renee. *A Journey Through Grief—Gentle, Specific Help to Get You Through the Most Difficult Stages of Grieving*. Center City: Hazelden Foundation, 1994.

Coleridge, Samuel Taylor. *Literary Remains*, vol. 1, collected and edited by Henry Nelson Coleridge, Project Gutenberg. gutenberg.org/files/8488/8488-h/8488-h.htm

Collins, Judy. *The Seven T's: Finding Hope and Healing in the Wake of Tragedy*. New York: Penguin Group, 2007.

Lord, Janice Harris. "America's Number One Killer: Vehicular Crashes." In Kenneth J. Doka, (ed.). *Living with Grief After Sudden Loss*. Bristol: Hospice Foundation of America, Taylor & Francis, 1996.

Martha Tarbell quoting Jean Paul Richter, "Sentence Sermons" in *Tarbell's Teachers' Guide to the International Sunday School Lessons for 1907* (Indianapolis: The Bobbs-Merrill Company Publishers), 1906, 221.

Moody, Raymond Jr., and Arcangel, Dianne. *Life After Loss: Conquering Grief and Finding Hope*. San Francisco: Harper Collins, 2001.

Noel, Brook, and Blair, Pamela D. *I Wasn't Ready to Say Goodbye*. Milwaukee: Champion Press, LTD, 2000.

Stearns, Ann Kaiser. *Living Through Personal Crisis*. New York: Ballantine Books, 1985.

Stillion, Judith M. *Living with Grief: After Sudden Loss*. Edited by Kenneth J. Doka. Bristol: Hospice Foundation of America, Taylor & Francis, 1996.

Websites and Online Magazines

"Are People with Pets Happier and Healthier?" *Music City Scale*. scalemusiccity.com/are-people-with-pets-really-healthier-and-happier/#:~:text=Playing%20with%20your%20pet%20increases,of%20Health%20(NIH)%20found

Axelrod, Julie. "The 5 Stages of Grief & Loss." *PsychCentral*, July 8, 2020. psychcentral.com/lib/the-5-stages-of-loss-and-grief/

Boroff, David. "Samantha Josephson's parents urge ride-sharing companies to keep customers safer: 'We trust people and you can't.'" *New York Daily News*, April 15, 2019. nydailynews.com/news/national/ny-samantha-josephson-parents-urge-safety-20190415-oogyi43sdna75ferummhti2bly-story.html

"BYU coach's family to donate 3-year-old daughter's organs after tragic accident." *Fox News*, November 28, 2016. foxnews.com/health/byu-coachs-family-to-donate-3-year-old-daughters-organs-after-tragic-accident

Gilbert K. Chesterton, "The Eternal Revolution" in *Orthodoxy*, Project Gutenberg. gutenberg.org/cache/epub/130/pg130.html

"Daughter of Reno Mahe, BYU running backs coach, dies after accident." ESPN.com, November 30, 2016. www.espn.com/college-football/story/_/id/18170054/daughter-byu-cougars-running-backs-coach-dies-accident

Davis, Jeanie Lerche. "5 Ways Pets Can Improve Your Health." *WebMed*, 2004. webmd.com/hypertension-high-blood-pressure/features/health-benefits-of-pets#1

Donne, John. PoemHunter.com. poemhunter.com/poem/no-man-is-an-island/

Dudley, Graham. "Bodies of 2 Missing Utah County Teens recovered at Utah Lake." KSL.com, May 14, 2020. ksl.com/article/46752932/bodies-of-2-missing-utah-county-teens-recovered-at-utah-lake

Evans, Richard Paul. *Meridian Magazine*, February 6, 2018. richardpaulevans.com/blog/

"Factors that Influence the Ability to Cope with Loss," *Mission Hospice Society*, missionhospice.bc.ca/wp-content/uploads/2018/03/Factors-that-influence-the-ability-to-cope-with-losses.pdf.

"Finding Healing After the Death of a Child, His Grace." *YouTube*; uploaded by The Church of Jesus Christ of Latter-day Saints, July 23, 2020. youtube.com/watch?v=vg8ofUBEQcg

"Finding Hope After Losing a Child." *YouTube*, uploaded by The Church of Jesus Christ of Latter-day Saints; December 21, 2017. youtube.com/watch?time_continue=368&v=gCH_s7BB3fs

Free, Cathy. "Utah Couple Who Lost Five Babies in 11 Months Honor Their Children's Memory: We Wake Up to 'Raw Hearts and Pain.'" *Yahoo! News*, August 7, 2017. yahoo.com/news/utah-couple-lost-five-babies-141048426.html

Gekas, Alexandra. "10 Health Benefits of Owning a Pet." *Women's Day,* February 11, 2011.

Gibran, Kahlil. "Work Is Love Made Visible." *The New York Times on the Web*, Books, July 25, 1948. archive.nytimes.com/nytimes. com/books/98/12/13/specials/gibran-secrets.html

Grenley, Greer. "How Dogs Can Help with Depression." National Alliance on Mental Illness, February 2, 2018.   nami.org/Blogs/NAMI-Blog/February-2018/ How-Dogs-Can-Help-with-Depression

"Grief." *Merriam-Webster.com Dictionary*, Merriam-Webster. merriam-webster.com/dictionary/grief. Accessed April 13, 2021.

Grollman, Earl, as quoted by Noel, Brook, and Blair, Pamela D. *I Wasn't Ready to Say Goodbye.* Milwaukee: Champion Press, LTD, 2000). google.com/books/edition/I_Wasn_t_Ready_to_Say_bye/5R7yqJ UHZ4UC?hl=en&gbpv=1&dq=Earl+Grollman,+It%27s+okay+t o+scream+at+God,+He+can+take+it.%22&pg=PA51&printsec=fr ontcover

Ritchie, Hannah, Max Roser, and Esteban Ortiz-Ospina. "Suicide." OurWorldInData.org. ourworldindata.org/suicide

Hairston, Stephanie. "How Grief Shows Up In Your Body." WebMD, July 11, 2019; News Special Report; Reviewed by Neha Pathak. webmd.com/special-reports/ grief-stages/20190711/how-grief-affects-your-body -and-mind

Hartney, Elizabeth. "How Emotional Pain Affects Your Body." verywell mind. July 7, 2020. Eisenberger NI. The neural bases of social pain: Evidence for shared representations with physical pain. *Psychosom Med.* 2012;74(2):126– 135.   verywellmind.com/physical-pain-and-emotional -pain-22421#citation-9

Lee, Harold B. "The Veil Is Thin Between this World and the Spirit World." See also LDS Scripture Teachings. "Angels Are Often Nearby." November 8, 2015.

Mayer, John. "3 Important Elements of a Good Therapist Relationship."   blog.doctorondemand.com/3-important- elements-of-a-good-therapist-relationship-901bfc7e352c

Mejia, Garna. "Family Hopes to Avoid Future Tragedies with New Initiative at Utah Lake." KSL.com, September 27, 2020. ksl.com/article/50022193/family-hopes-to-avoid-future-tragedies-with-new-initiative-at-utah-lake

The Pain Doctor. March 2, 2018. Accessed April 13, 2021. paindoctor.com/top-10-stressful-life-events-holmes-rahe-stress-scale/

Proctor, Scot and Maurine. "How One Italian Sister Found Solace after her Husband's Murder." *Meridian Magazine*, March 14, 2019. latterdaysaintmag.com/how-one-italian-sister-found-solace-after-her-husbands-murder/

Robinson, Lawrence and Jeanne Segal. "Mood-Boosting Power of Dogs." *HelpGuide.Org*, October 2017. hr.unm.edu/docs/ehp/mood-boosting-power-of-dogs.pdf

Romboy, Dennis. "Utah House Passes 'Hannah's Bill' to Ensure Suicide Crisis Lines Staffed 24/7." KSL.com, January 26, 2018). ksl.com/article/46246751/utah-house-passes-hannahs-bill-to-ensure-suicide-crisis-lines-staffed-247

Scribner, Cari. "Even a Fake Smile Can Boost Your Mood." *ctPost*, August 7, 2013. ctpost.com/healthyyou/home/article/Even-a-Fake-Smile-Can-Boost-Your-Mood-4621347.php

Thomas, Patricia A., Hui Liu, and Debra Umberson. "Family Relationships and Well-Being." *Innovation in Aging*, November 11, 2017; 1(3). ncbi.nlm.nih.gov/pmc/articles/PMC5954612/

Vilvens, Sheila. "Samantha Josephson's father urges USC students be safe using Uber, Lyft. Here are some tips," *Cincinnati Enquirer*, April 1, 2019. greenvilleonline.com/story/news/local/2019/04/01/samantha-josephson-usc-student-killed-uber-father-urges-rideshare-safety/3330536002/

"William James" in Influential Past Teachers, Awaken. awaken.com/2013/07/william-james/

Further Reading

Addresses

Kimball, Spencer W. ". . . the Matter of Marriage." Address delivered at University of Utah Institute of Religion, October 22, 1976.

Church Magazines

Bednar, David A. "Always Retain a Remission of Your Sins." *Ensign*, May 2016.

Caussé, Gérald. "Is It Still Wonderful to You?" *Ensign*, May 2015.

Clayton, Weatherford T. "Our Father's Glorious Plan." *Ensign*, May 2017.

Edwards, David A. "The Resurrection of Jesus Christ and Truths about the Body." *Ensign*, April 2017.

Faust, James E. "Gratitude As a Saving Principle." *Ensign*, May 1990.

Johnson, Paul V. "And There Shall Be No More Death." *Ensign*, May 2016.

Johnson, Peter M. "Power to Overcome the Adversary." *Ensign*, November 2019.

Kimball, Spencer W. "Give Me This Mountain." *Ensign*, November 1979.

Monson, Thomas S. Blessings of the Temple." *Ensign*, May 2015.

———. "Now Is the Time." *Ensign*, October 2001.

———. "The Lighthouse of the Lord." *Ensign*, November 1990.

———. "We Never Walk Alone." *Ensign*, November 2013.

Nelson, Russell M. "The Power and Protection of Worthy Music." *Ensign*, December 2009.

———. "Woman—of Infinite Worth." *Ensign*, November 1989.

Oaks, Dallin H. "Trust in the Lord." *Ensign*, November 2019.

Scott, Richard G. "How to Obtain Revelation and Inspiration for Your Personal Life." *Ensign*, May 2012.

Smith, Hyrum G. *Conference Reports of The Church of Jesus Christ of Latter-day Saints*. April 1917.

Snow, LeRoi C. "Raised from the Dead." *Improvement Era*, October 1929.

Newspapers

"Trayvon's Martin's mom steps onto political stage." *The Salt Lake Tribune*, May 20, 2019.

Religious Books

Dunn, Paul H., and Eyre, Richard. *The Birth That We Call Death*. Salt Lake City: Bookcraft, 1976.

Kimball, Camilla E., and others. *Joy*. Salt Lake City: Deseret Book, 1980.

Madsen, Truman. *Eternal Man*. Salt Lake City: Deseret Book, 1966.

Maxwell, Neal A. *All These Things Shall Give Thee Experience*. Salt Lake City: Deseret Book, 1980.

———. *But for a Small Moment*. Salt Lake City: Deseret Book, 1986.

———. *If Thou Endure It Well*. Salt Lake City: Bookcraft: 1996.

———. *Lord, Increase Our Faith*. Salt Lake City: Bookcraft, 1994.

———. *One More Strain of Praise*. Salt Lake City: Deseret Book, 1981.

———. *Notwithstanding My Weakness*. Salt Lake City: Deseret Book, 1981.

———. *We Will Prove Them Herewith*. Salt Lake City: Deseret Book, 1982.

Packer, Boyd K. *Let Not Your Heart Be Troubled*. Salt Lake City: Bookcraft, 1991.

———. *That All May Be Edified*. Salt Lake City: Bookcraft, 1982.

Ridges, David. Doctrine and Covenant's Study Guide: Part 1, 2 & 3. Springville: Cedar Fort, 2005.

Talmage, James E. *A Study of the Articles of Faith*. Salt Lake City: The Church of Jesus Christ of Latter-day Saints, 1924.

Top, Brent L. *What's on the Other Side? What the Gospel Teaches Us about the Spirit World.* Salt Lake City: Deseret Book, 2012.

———. *When You Can't Do It Alone, Take the Savior's Hand.* Salt Lake City: Deseret Book, 2008.

Secular Books

Bonanno, George A. *The Other Side of Sadness.* New York: Basic Books, 2009.

Cornils, Stanley. *Your Healing Journey Through Grief—A Practical Approach to Grief Management.* San Francisco: Robert D. Reed Publishers, 2002.

Dresser, Norine, and Fredda Wasserman. *Saying Goodbye to Someone you Love.* New York: DemosHealth, 2010.

Lewis, C. S. *A Grief Observed.* London: Farber, 1961.

———. *The Problem of Pain.* New York: Simon & Schuster, 1996.

Mitchell, Ellen, and others. *Beyond Tears: Living After Losing a Child.* New York: St. Martin's Griffin, 2004.

Praagh, James Van. *Healing Grief: Reclaiming Life After Any Loss.* New York: American Library/Penguin Putnam, 2001.

Websites and Online Magazines

Berk, Lee Berk, Dr., Assoc Res Pro Loma Linda School of Medicine, as quoted by Sebastian Gendry, "Why Laughter Is Good for The Immune System, Opens Inner Cellular Pharmacy," LOU; Laughter Online University.

Borchard, Therese J. "9 Ways That Humor Heals." *Psychcentral.*

———. "Good-for-You Guffaws: 5 Health Benefits of Laughter." *Everyday Health.* August 11, 2017.

Cherry, Kendra. "How to Think Like an Optimist and Stay Positive." *verywell mind.* December 9, 2019.

Eaton, Nate. "Young mom of 3 pushing for changes after husband dies in Idaho avalanche." EastIdahoNews.com, February 22, 2018.

Isackson, Darla. "Though Grief Is Inevitable, Misery Is Not." *Meridian Magazine*, November 1, 2017.

Thompson, Dennis. "With Depression, Helping Others May in Turn Help You." *MedicineNet.*

Van Edwards, Vanessa. "The Benefits of Music: How the Science of Music Can Help You." *Science of People.*